PROPERTY
PRACTICE

Benjamin Jones

Series editors: Amy Sixsmith and David Sixsmith

First published in 2023 by Fink Publishing Ltd

British Library Cataloguing in Publication Data
A catalogue record for this book is available from the British Library
ISBN: 9781914213175

This book is also available in various ebook formats.
Ebook ISBN: 9781914213243

Multiple-choice questions advisor: Mark Thomas
Cover and text design by BMLD (bmld.uk)
Production by River Editorial
Typeset by Westchester Publishing Services
Commissioning by R Taylor Publishing Services
Development Editing by Sonya Barker
Indexing by Terence Halliday

Revise SQE
Fink Publishing Ltd
E-mail: hello@revise4law.co.uk
www.revise4law.co.uk

Contents

About the author

Benjamin Jones is a senior lecturer in law and legal practice, and a course leader at the University of South Wales. He has taught and led on a range of undergraduate, postgraduate, and professional law courses for over nine years and is a fellow of the Higher Education Academy. He has extensive experience as a solicitor in private practice, where he specialised in Commercial Property work in corporate/commercial firms. He was winner of the Lawcareers.Net 'Law Lecturer of the Year Award' in 2016, and he has taught Property Law (including Commercial Property) throughout his teaching career. He is also the author of *Revise SQE: Business Law and Practice* and a contributor to *Revise SQE: Ethics and Professional Conduct.*

Series editors

Amy Sixsmith is a senior lecturer in law and programme leader for LLB at the University of Sunderland, and a senior fellow of the Higher Education Academy.

David Sixsmith is assistant professor in law at Northumbria University, and a senior fellow of the Higher Education Academy.

Introduction to Revise SQE

Welcome to *Revise SQE*, a new series of revision guides designed to help you in your preparation for, and achievement in, the Solicitors Qualifying Examination 1 (SQE1) assessment. SQE1 is designed to assess what the Solicitors Regulation Authority (SRA) refer to as 'functioning legal knowledge' (FLK); this is the legal knowledge and competencies required of a newly qualified solicitor in England and Wales. The SRA has chosen single best answer multiple-choice questions (MCQs) to test this knowledge, and *Revise SQE* is here to help.

PREPARING YOURSELF FOR SQE

The SQE is the new route to qualification for aspiring solicitors introduced in September 2021 as one of the final stages towards qualification as a solicitor. The SQE consists of two parts:

SQE1
- **Functioning legal knowledge (FLK)**
- two x 180 MCQs
- closed book; assessed by two sittings, over 10 hours in total.

SQE2
- **Practical legal skills**
- 16 written and oral assessments
- assesses six practical legal skills, over 14 hours in total.

In addition to the above, any candidate will have to undertake two years' qualifying work experience. More information on the SQE assessments can be found on the SRA website; this revision guide series will focus on FLK and preparation for SQE1.

It is important to note that the SQE can be perceived to be a 'harder' set of assessments than the Legal Practice Course (LPC). The reason for this, explained by the SRA, is that the LPC is designed to prepare candidates for 'day one' of their training contract; the SQE, on the other hand, is designed to prepare candidates for 'day one' of being a newly qualified solicitor. Indeed, the SRA has chosen the SQE1 assessment to be 'closed book' (ie without permitting use of any materials) on the basis that a newly qualified solicitor would know all of the information tested, without having to refer to books or other sources.

With that in mind, and a different style of assessments in place, it is understandable that many readers may feel nervous or wary of the SQE. This is especially so given that this style of assessment is likely to be different from what readers will have experienced before. In this *Introduction* and revision guide series, we hope to alleviate some of those concerns with guidance on preparing for the SQE assessment, tips on how to approach single best answer MCQs and expertly written guides to aid in your revision.

What does SQE1 entail?

SQE1 consists of two assessments, containing 180 single best answer MCQs each (360 MCQs in total). The table below breaks down what is featured in each of these assessments.

Assessment	Contents of assessment ('functioning legal knowledge')
FLK assessment 1	• Business law and practice • Dispute resolution • Contract • Tort • The legal system (the legal system of England and Wales and sources of law, constitutional and administrative law and European Union law and legal services)
FLK assessment 2	• Property practice • Wills and the administration of estates • Solicitors' accounts • Land law • Trusts • Criminal law and practice

Please be aware that in addition to the above, ethics and professional conduct will be examined pervasively across the two assessments (ie it could crop up anywhere).

Each substantive topic is allocated a percentage of the assessment paper (eg 'legal services' will form 12–16% of the FLK1 assessment) and is broken down further into 'core principles'. Candidates are advised to read the SQE1 Assessment Specification in full (available on the SRA website). We have also provided a *Revise SQE checklist* to help you in your preparation and revision for SQE1 (see below).

HOW DO I PREPARE FOR SQE1?

Given the vastly different nature of SQE1 compared to anything you may have done previously, it can be quite daunting to consider how you could possibly prepare for 360 single best answer MCQs, spanning 11 different substantive topics (especially given that it is 'closed book'). The *Revise SQE FAQ* below, however, will set you off on the right path to success.

Revise SQE FAQ

Question	Answer
1. Where do I start?	We would advise that you begin by reviewing the assessment specification for SQE1. You need to identify what subject matter can be assessed under each substantive topic. For each topic, you should honestly ask yourself whether you would be prepared to answer an MCQ on that topic in SQE1.
	We have helped you in this process by providing a *Revise SQE checklist* on our website (revise4law.co.uk) that allows you to read the subject matter of each topic and identify where you consider your knowledge to be at any given time. We have also helpfully cross-referenced each topic to a chapter and page of our *Revise SQE* revision guides.
2. Do I need to know legal authorities, such as case law?	In the majority of circumstances, candidates are not required to know or use legal authorities. This includes statutory provisions, case law or procedural rules. Of course, candidates will need to be aware of legal principles deriving from common law and statute.
	There may be occasions, however, where the assessment specification does identify a legal authority (such as *Rylands v Fletcher* in tort law). In this case, candidates will be required to know the name of that case, the principles of that case and how to apply that case to the facts of an MCQ. These circumstances are clearly highlighted in the assessment specification and candidates are advised to ensure they engage with those legal authorities in full.

Revise SQE FAQ (continued)

Question	Answer
3. Do I need to know the history behind a certain area of law?	While understanding the history and development of a certain area of law is beneficial, there is no requirement for you to know or prepare for any questions relating to the development of the law (eg in criminal law, candidates will not need to be aware of the development from objective to subjective recklessness). SQE1 will be testing a candidate's knowledge of the law as it stands four calendar months prior to the date of the first assessment in an assessment window.
4. Do I need to be aware of academic opinion or proposed reforms to the law?	Candidates preparing for SQE1 do not need to focus on critical evaluation of the law, or proposed reforms to the law either.
5. How do I prepare for single best answer MCQs?	See our separate *Revise SQE* guide on preparing for single best answer MCQs below.

Where does *Revise SQE* come into it?

The *Revise SQE* series of revision guides is designed to aid your revision and consolidate your understanding; the series is not designed to replace your substantive learning of the SQE1 topics. We hope that this series will provide clarity as to assessment focus, useful tips for sitting SQE1 and act as a general revision aid.

There are also materials on our website to help you prepare and revise for the SQE1, such as a *Revise SQE checklist*. This *checklist* is designed to help you identify which substantive topics you feel confident about heading into the exam – see below for an example.

Revise SQE checklist

Property Practice

SQE content	Corresponding chapter	Revise SQE checklist		
Investigation of a registered and unregistered freehold title	Chapter 1, Pages 2–7 Chapter 2, Pages 18–21, 21–28, and 28–42 Chapter 4, Page 102	I do not know this subject and I am not ready for SQE1 □	I partially know this subject, but I am not ready for SQE1 □	I know this subject and I am ready for SQE1 □

Property Practice (continued)

SQE content	Corresponding chapter	Revise SQE checklist		
Pre-contract searches and enquiries	Chapter 3, Pages 50–63 and 64–66	I do not know this subject and I am not ready for SQE1 ☐	I partially know this subject, but I am not ready for SQE1 ☐	I know this subject and I am ready for SQE1 ☐
Law Society Conveyancing Protocol	Chapter 1, Pages 12–13	I do not know this subject and I am not ready for SQE1 ☐	I partially know this subject, but I am not ready for SQE1 ☐	I know this subject and I am ready for SQE1 ☐

PREPARING FOR SINGLE BEST ANSWER MCQS

As discussed above, SQE1 will be a challenging assessment for all candidates. This is partly due to the quantity of information a candidate must be aware of in two separate sittings. In addition, however, an extra complexity is added due to the nature of the assessment itself: MCQs.

The SRA has identified that MCQs are the most appropriate way to test a candidate's knowledge and understanding of fundamental legal principles. While this may be the case, it is likely that many candidates have little, if any, experience of MCQs as part of their previous study. Even if a candidate does have experience of MCQs, SQE1 will feature a special form of MCQs known as 'single best answer' questions.

What are single best answer MCQs and what do they look like?

Single best answer MCQs are a specialised form of question, used extensively in other fields such as in training medical professionals. The idea behind single best answer MCQs is that the multitude of options available to a candidate may each bear merit, sharing commonalities and correct statements of law or principle, but only one option is absolutely correct (in the sense that it is the 'best' answer). In this regard, single best answer MCQs are different from traditional MCQs. A traditional MCQ will feature answers that are implausible in the sense that the distractors are 'obviously wrong'. Indeed, distractors in a traditional MCQ are often very dissimilar, resulting in a candidate being able to spot answers that are clearly wrong with greater ease.

In a well-constructed single best answer MCQ, on the other hand, each option should look equally attractive given their similarities and subtle differences. The skill of the candidate will be identifying which, out of the options provided, is the single best answer. This requires a much greater level of engagement with the question than a traditional MCQ would require; candidates must take the time to read the questions carefully in the exam.

For SQE1, single best answer MCQs will be structured as follows:

A woman is charged with battery, having thrown a rock towards another person intending to scare them. The rock hits the person in the head, causing no injury. The woman claims that she never intended that the rock hit the person, but the prosecution allege that the woman was reckless as to whether the rock would hit the other person.

The factual scenario. First, the candidate will be provided with a factual scenario that sets the scene for the question to be asked.

Which of the following is the most accurate statement regarding the test for recklessness in relation to a battery?

The question. Next, the candidate will be provided with the question (known as the 'stem') that they must find the single best answer to.

A. There must have been a risk that force would be applied by the rock, and that the reasonable person would have foreseen that risk and unjustifiably taken it.

B. There must have been a risk that force would be applied by the rock, and that the woman should have foreseen that risk and unjustifiably taken it.

The possible answers. Finally, the candidate will be provided with **five** possible answers. There is only one single best answer that must be chosen. The other answers, known as 'distractors', are not the 'best' answer available.

C. There must have been a risk that force would be applied by the rock, and that the woman must have foreseen that risk and unjustifiably taken it.

D. There must have been a risk that force would be applied by the rock, and that both the woman and the reasonable person should have foreseen that risk and unjustifiably taken it.

E. There must have been a risk that force would be applied by the rock, but there is no requirement that the risk be foreseen.

Now that you know what the MCQs will look like on SQE1, let us talk about how you may go about tackling an MCQ.

How do I tackle single best answer MCQs?

No exact art exists in terms of answering single best answer MCQs; your success depends on your subject knowledge and understanding of how that subject knowledge can be applied. Despite this, there are tips and tricks that may be helpful for you to consider when confronted with a single best answer MCQ.

1. Read the question twice	2. Understand the question being asked	3. If you know the answer outright	4. If not, employ a process of elimination	5. Take an educated and reasoned guess	6. Skip and come back to it later

1. Read the entire question at least twice

This sounds obvious but is so often overlooked. You are advised to read the entire question once, taking in all relevant pieces of information, understanding what the question is asking you and being aware of the options available. Once you have done that, read the entire question again and this time pay careful attention to the wording that is used.

- **In the factual scenario:** Does it use any words that stand out? Do any words used have legal bearing? What are you told and what are you not told?
- **In the stem:** What are you being asked? Are there certain words to look out for (eg 'should', 'must', 'will', 'shall')?
- **In the answers:** What are the differences between each option? Are they substantial differences or subtle differences? Do any differences turn on a word or a phrase?

You should be prepared to give each question at least two viewings to mitigate any misunderstandings or oversights.

2. Understand the question being asked

It is important first that you understand what the question is asking of you. The SRA has identified that the FLK assessments may consist of single best answer MCQs that, for example,

- require the candidate to simply identify a correct legal principle or rule
- require the candidate to not only identify the correct legal principle or rule, but also apply that principle or rule to the factual scenario
- provide the candidate with the correct legal principle or rule, but require the candidate to identify how it should be properly applied and/or the outcome of that proper application.

By first identifying what the question is seeking you to do, you can then understand what the creators of that question are seeking to test and how to approach the answers available.

3. If you know the answer outright

You may feel as though a particular answer 'jumps out' at you, and that you are certain it is correct. It is very likely that the answer is correct. While you should be confident in your answers, do not allow your confidence (and perhaps overconfidence) to rush you into making a decision. Review all of your options one final time before you move on to the next question.

4. If you do not know the answer outright, employ a process of elimination

There may be situations in which the answer is not obvious from the outset. This may be due to the close similarities between different answers. Remember, it is the 'single best answer' that you are looking for. If you keep this in your mind, it will thereafter be easier to employ a process of elimination. Identify which answers you are sure are not correct (or not the 'best') and whittle down your options. Once you have only two options remaining, carefully scrutinise the wording used in both answers and look back to the question being asked. Identify what you consider to be the best answer, in light of that question. Review your answer and move on to the next question.

5. Take an educated and reasoned guess

There may be circumstances, quite commonly, in which you do not know the answer to the question. In this circumstance, you should try as hard as possible to eliminate any distractors that you are positive are incorrect and then take an educated and reasoned guess based on the options available.

6. Skip and come back to it later

If time permits, you may think it appropriate to skip a question that you are unsure of and return to it before the end of the assessment. If you do so, we would advise

- that you make a note of what question you have skipped (for ease of navigation later on), and
- ensure you leave sufficient time for you to go back to that question before the end of the assessment.

The same advice is applicable to any question that you have answered but for which you remain unsure.

We hope that this brief guide will assist you in your preparation towards, and engagement with, single best answer MCQs.

GUIDED TOUR

Each chapter contains a number of features to help you revise, apply and test your knowledge.

Make sure you know Each chapter begins with an overview of the main topics covered and why you need to understand them for the purpose of the SQE1 assessments.

SQE assessment advice This identifies what you need to pay particular attention to in your revision as you work through the chapter.

What do you know already? These questions help you to assess which topics you feel confident with and which topics you may need to spend more time on (and where to find them in the chapter).

Key term Key terms are highlighted in bold where they first appear and defined in a separate box.

Exam warning This feature offers advice on where it is possible to go wrong in the assessments.

Revision tip Throughout the chapters are ideas to help you revise effectively and be best prepared for the assessment.

Summary This handy box brings together key information in an easy to revise and remember form.

Practice example These examples take a similar format to SQE-type questions and provide an opportunity to see how content might be applied to a scenario.

Procedural link Where relevant, this element shows how a concept might apply to another procedural topic in the series.

Key point checklist At the end of each chapter, there is a bullet-point summary of its most important content.

Key terms and concepts These are listed at the end of each chapter to help ensure you know, or can revise, terms and concepts you will need to be familiar with for the assessments.

SQE-style questions Five SQE-style questions on the chapter topic give you an opportunity to test your knowledge.

Answers to questions Check how you did with answers to both the quick knowledge test from the start of the chapter and the SQE questions at the end of the chapter.

Key cases, rules, statutes, and instruments These list the key sources candidates need to be familiar with for the SQE assessment.

SQE1 TABLE OF LEGAL AUTHORITIES

The SQE1 Assessment Specification states the following in respect of legal authorities and their relevance to SQE1:

> On occasion in legal practice a case name or statutory provision, for example, is the term normally used to describe a legal principle or an area of law, or a rule or procedural step (eg *Rylands v Fletcher*, CPR Part 36, Section 25 notice). In such circumstances, candidates are required to know and be able to use such case names, statutory provisions etc. In all other circumstances candidates are not required to recall specific case names, or cite statutory or regulatory authorities.

This *SQE1 table of legal authorities* identifies the legal authorities you are required to know for the purpose of the SQE1 Functioning Legal Knowledge assessments for *Property Practice*.

Legal authority	Corresponding *Revise SQE* chapter/pages
Law Society Conveyancing Protocol	**Chapter 1: Key elements and structure of freehold property transactions: an overview, page 12**
Code for Leasing Business Premises	**Chapter 6: Structure and content of a lease, page 169**
Jervis v Harris [1996] Ch 195	**Chapter 8: Commercial leasehold remedies, page 223**
Landlord and Tenant Act 1954 (Part II)	**Chapter 9: Termination of leases and security of tenure under Part II of the Landlord and Tenant Act 1954, page 235**

TABLE OF CASES

TABLE OF STATUTES AND STATUTORY INSTRUMENTS

Key elements and structure of freehold property transactions: an overview

■ MAKE SURE YOU KNOW

This chapter provides an overview of the key elements and structure of freehold property transactions, as well as the requirements of the Law Society Conveyancing Protocol, and an introduction to finance for property transactions (sources of finance/types of mortgage). It outlines the conveyancing process, from taking instructions and pre-contract matters, through to exchange of contracts, completion and post-completion. The purpose of this chapter is to allow you to see the bigger picture of the process as a whole, before breaking it down into the individual stages, in **Chapters 2–5**. Candidates usually have a better understanding of the conveyancing process when they appreciate how these stages link together. For the SQE1 assessments, you will need to understand the detail of each stage, as well as how it fits into the bigger process.

■ SQE ASSESSMENT ADVICE

For SQE1, you are required to understand the structure of the conveyancing process, as well as the detail behind each step. Therefore, this is an important foundational chapter.

As you work through this chapter, remember to pay particular attention in your revision to:
* The concept of conveyancing and what it entails.
* The structure of a conveyancing transaction and the key stages of pre-contract, exchange of contracts, pre-completion, completion, and post-completion.
* Some of the key terms involved in the stages of a conveyancing transaction.
* The main points on which you would need to take instructions for a freehold property transaction and initial areas of concern that might arise.
* The requirements of the Law Society Conveyancing Protocol.
* Sources of finance for a property transaction and types of mortgage.

■ WHAT DO YOU KNOW ALREADY?

Attempt these questions before reading this chapter. If you find some difficult or cannot remember the answers, remember to look more closely at that topic during your revision.

1) What is conveyancing?

   [Key elements and structure of freehold property transactions, page 2]

2) True or false? The parties are usually free to withdraw from a conveyancing transaction before exchange of contracts.

   [Key elements and structure of freehold property transactions, page 2]

3) True or false? Completion is when the parties become committed to enter into a property transaction.

   [Key elements and structure of freehold property transactions, page 2]

4) True or false? Exchange of contracts is when the purchase monies are paid over, and the buyer receives the keys to the property.

   [Key elements and structure of freehold property transactions, page 2]

KEY ELEMENTS AND STRUCTURE OF FREEHOLD PROPERTY TRANSACTIONS

Chapters 1–5 of this volume deal with the **conveyancing** process in typical freehold property transactions. **Chapters 6–7** outline additional considerations concerning leasehold transactions. (Remember that freehold ownership of land is capable of lasting indefinitely and is the closest thing to absolute ownership of land in England and Wales; whereas leasehold ownership of land is granted for a specific period of time, by a landlord to a tenant (see also *Revise SQE: Land Law*).)

Key term: conveyancing

Conveyancing is the process of transfer of title (ownership) to property between the seller (transferor) and the buyer (transferee).

The two key stages (sometimes referred to as 'milestones') in a typical property transaction are **exchange of contracts** and **completion**.

Key term: exchange of contracts

This is when a deposit is paid (typically 10% of the purchase price) and, through the exchange of contracts, both parties become bound to complete the transaction on the agreed completion date (see **Chapter 4**). The buyer gains an equitable interest in the property under a constructive trust (see *Revise SQE: Trusts Law*). Until exchange of contracts, the parties are usually free to withdraw from the transaction, as it remains 'subject to contract' (see **Practice example 1.1**).

Key term: completion

This is when the balance purchase price is paid, the keys are handed over and the Transfer deed is completed (see **Chapter 5**). The buyer becomes entitled to apply to become registered as the proprietor and gains legal ownership (subject to registration at HM Land Registry). More specifically, in the case of land with *registered title* (see **Chapter 2**), the legal transfer *does not* technically take place until it is registered at HM Land Registry. Whereas, in the case of land with *unregistered title* (see **Chapter 2**), the legal transfer *does* take place on completion but will become void if the title is not registered within two months of completion.

Practice example 1.1

Jesper has agreed to sell a property to Laurits. Contracts have not yet been exchanged, but Laurits has decided to withdraw from the transaction.

How would you advise Jesper?

Laurits should be free to withdraw from the transaction, without penalty before contracts are exchanged. Laurits will not be liable to Jesper for wasted time and costs in the conveyancing process. Once contracts are exchanged, the parties will be committed to complete, the transaction will no longer be merely 'subject to contract,' and there will be remedies in the event of a delay or failure to complete (see **Chapter 5**).

Prior to exchange of contracts, a great deal of work will have been carried out following taking instructions and giving initial advice (see **Taking instructions**, below), as part of the **pre-contract stage**.

Key term: pre-contract stage

The *seller's solicitor* carries out an **investigation of title** and then undertakes a **deduction of title** for the buyer's solicitor. They provide a draft contract and supporting documentation, as well as replies to standard pre-contract enquiries, and they respond to any additional pre-contract enquiries and **requisitions on title** raised by the buyer's solicitor. They also deal with any proposals to amend the draft contract, produce clean copies for signature, and request a redemption statement from any mortgagee(s).

The *buyer's solicitor* carries out an investigation of title under the principle of **caveat emptor**. They check, approve, and may amend the draft contract, and carry out and review the results of standard

pre-contract searches and enquiries of both the seller and third parties (see **Chapter 3**). They also raise any additional enquiries and requisitions on title.

Both solicitors arrange for the contract to be signed and the buyer's solicitor reports to their client (and possibly their mortgagee) and obtains the deposit in readiness for exchange of contracts. The buyer is usually advised to insure the property from exchange of contracts.

The pre-contract stage is summarised in **Table 1.1** and is dealt with in full in **Chapters 2–4**.

Table 1.1: Summary of the pre-contract stage

Seller's solicitor	Buyer's solicitor
Investigation and deduction of title.	Investigation of title and raises pre-contract searches and enquiries.
Provides draft contract, supporting documentation, and replies to pre-contract enquiries.	Reviews draft contract, supporting documentation, and replies to pre-contract searches and enquiries.
Responds to additional pre-contract enquiries and requisitions on title.	Raises additional pre-contract enquiries and requisitions on title.
Responds to proposals to amend the contract and produces clean copies for signature.	Amends draft contract.
Arranges for contract to be signed by the seller. Requests redemption statement from mortgagee(s).	Reports to buyer (and possibly their mortgagee) and arranges for contract to be signed by the buyer. Obtains deposit in readiness for exchange of contracts.

Key term: investigation of title

The process whereby title to the property is checked/examined to ensure that the seller is entitled to sell and that the title is good and marketable, with all necessary rights and with no materially adverse incumbrances (eg easements/covenants burdening the property – see **Chapters 2 and 4**). These could have an impact on use, value, enjoyment, marketability, and the security of the property for lending purposes. The seller's solicitor will complete this process in order to deduce title and pre-empt requisitions on title that may be raised by the buyer's solicitor. The buyer's solicitor will also undertake the process as part of the principle of caveat emptor.

Key term: deduction of title

The process whereby the seller's solicitor provides to the buyer's solicitor proof/evidence of the seller's title/ownership. This consists of either copy title deeds (in the case of unregistered land), or official copies of the registers of title (in the case of registered land) (see **Chapter 2**).

Key term: pre-contract searches and enquiries

Standard pre-contract *enquiries* are made of the seller's solicitor to ascertain further information about the property that should be known by the seller. Pre-contract *searches* are made of third parties (eg the local authority and local water authority), to ascertain important information about the property that is held by third parties (see **Chapter 3**).

Key term: requisitions on title

These are additional enquiries of the seller's solicitor as part of investigation of title and the results of pre-contract searches and enquiries. They are specific questions about an issue that require a solution. The buyer is generally not entitled to raise further requisitions on title after contracts have been exchanged (see **Chapters 2 and 4**).

Exam warning

Pre-contract requisitions on title must be distinguished from *Completion information and undertakings*, which form part of pre-completion, rather than pre-contract procedure (see **Chapter 5**). Candidates often confuse or conflate the two, probably because the former used to be known as *Completion information and requisitions on title*.

Key term: caveat emptor

This means 'let the buyer beware' and means that the onus is on the buyer to investigate the title fully and find out as much as possible about the property, so they are aware of any problems and issues. The seller only has a limited duty of disclosure as part of the conveyancing process (see **Chapter 2**).

Following exchange of contracts, the next main stage is **pre-completion**.

Key term: pre-completion stage

The *buyer's solicitor* prepares the draft transfer deed for approval by the seller's solicitor and the mortgage deed for execution by the buyer. They carry out pre-completion searches and enquiries of the seller's solicitor and third parties, submit their certificate of title/report on title to the lender and request the mortgage advance. They also request from their client the balance due in order to complete, and deal with any amendments to the transfer deed requested by the seller's solicitor, producing a clean copy for execution (see **Chapter 5**).

The *seller's solicitor* approves the transfer deed and arranges for it to be executed by the seller. They also respond to the buyer's completion information and undertakings form (which includes an undertaking to discharge any pre-existing mortgage(s)).

The pre-completion stage is summarised in **Table 1.2** and is dealt with in full in **Chapter 5**.

Table 1.2: Summary of the pre-completion stage

Seller's solicitor	Buyer's solicitor
Approves draft transfer deed and requests clean copy incorporating any proposed amendments.	Prepares draft transfer deed for approval by seller's solicitor.
	Prepares mortgage deed for execution by buyer.
Responds to completion information and undertakings form from the buyer's solicitor.	Carries out pre-completion searches and enquiries of the seller's solicitor and third parties.
	Submits certificate of title/report on title to the lender and requests the mortgage advance.
	Requests from the buyer balance due in order to complete.
Arranges for clean copy transfer deed to be executed by the seller.	Deals with any amendments to the transfer deed requested by the seller's solicitor, producing a clean copy for execution.

Following completion, the next main stage is **post-completion**.

Key term: post-completion stage

The *seller's solicitor* discharges any existing mortgage(s) and provides the buyer's solicitor with proof of discharge. They also pay any estate agent's costs (if authorised to do so by the seller) and account to their client.

The *buyer's solicitor* deals with the submission of the Stamp Duty Land Tax (SDLT) or Land Transaction Tax (LTT) return and payment of the tax (see **Chapters 5 and 10**). They then deal with registration at HM Land Registry and sometimes Companies House.

The post-completion stage is summarised in **Table 1.3** and is dealt with in full in **Chapter 5**.

Table 1.3: Summary of the post-completion stage

Seller's solicitor	Buyer's solicitor
Discharges existing mortgage(s) and provides buyer's solicitor with proof of discharge.	Submits SDLT or LTT return with payment of relevant tax.
Pays estate agent's costs.	Deals with registration at HM Land Registry.
Accounts to client.	Deals with registration at Companies House (if applicable).

TAKING INSTRUCTIONS

For SQE1, it is important to appreciate the need to take detailed instructions and anticipate any potential issues at the beginning of a transaction.

Revision tip

The matters on which instructions are required flow from the conveyancing process, and candidates usually have a better appreciation of them when they understand each stage within a typical transaction. You should therefore revisit this section as your revision progresses.

Some of the basic transactional information below will be provided by the estate agent, as part of a memorandum of the sale. However, instructions should be confirmed with the client in all cases. Most firms will provide a standard checklist, but the key issues of concern are summarised in **Table 1.4**.

Table 1.4: Taking instructions

In all cases
Full details of buyer and seller.
Estate agent's details.
Details of solicitors acting for the other side.
Property address and tenure (eg freehold or leasehold (see *Revise SQE: Land Law*)).
Agreed purchase price and deposit.
Details of any fixtures to be removed, or fittings to be included. Remember that *fixtures* pass on completion, whereas *fittings* do not (see *Revise SQE: Land Law*). Therefore, it is important to contract out of the general rules by specifying any *fixtures that are to be removed* (with damage being made good) and any *fittings that are to remain* (see **Chapter 4**).
Anticipated/proposed completion date.
Details of any related sale/purchase, where **synchronisation** will be required.

Table 1.4: (Continued)

Position as regards the **Energy Performance Certificate.**
Details of who is in occupation (this will be relevant for the purposes of the contract, see **Chapters 3 and 4**).
Details of the existing use and past alterations and additions. These will be relevant when considering planning matters (see **Chapter 3**).
Consider conduct issues (see *Revise SQE: Ethics and Professional Conduct* for a full consideration of key conduct and ethical issues in Property Practice).
Verify client's identity.
Advise on costs, funds required on account, and anticipated disbursements (including bank transfer fees, search fees, SDLT/LTT (see **Chapter 10**), HM Land Registry fees, and other disbursements, as appropriate).
Produce formal engagement letter.
For non-residential properties: Ascertain the VAT position (see **Chapters 4 and 10**).
Details of any other terms agreed between the parties.
For the seller
Details of the agreed estate agent's commission/costs.
Details of any existing mortgage(s), including the approximate balance(s) due, account number(s), and, for unregistered land (see **Chapter 2**), the location of any title deeds.
Ask client to complete standard property information forms (see **Chapter 3**).
In the case of co-owned property, ascertain whether the equitable interest is held as joint tenants or tenants in common (see **Chapter 2**).
Advise on liability for Capital Gains Tax (CGT) (or Corporation Tax on capital gains for companies) (see **Chapter 10**).
For the buyer
Details of any proposed mortgage and, if required, generic advice on the option(s) (see **Sources of finance/types of mortgage**, below).
Position concerning the age of the property, property survey, and advice on types of survey (see **Advice on survey**, below, and **Chapter 3**).
Details of the proposed use and proposed alterations and additions. These will be relevant when considering planning matters (see **Chapter 3**).
Situation of the property – eg is it near to industrial premises, open land, or a watercourse? This will be relevant when considering which optional searches and enquiries to undertake (see **Chapter 3**).
Advise on co-ownership and the holding of the equitable interest (see **Chapters 2 and 5**). Depending on the circumstances, an express declaration of trust (see **Chapter 5**) and the making of wills (see *Revise SQE: Wills and the Administration of Estates*) should be advised.
Advise on potential future liability for CGT (or Corporation Tax on capital gains for companies) (see **Chapter 10**).

Key term: synchronisation

Synchronisation is imperative where a client has a related sale and purchase. It involves making sure that contracts on the sale are exchanged at the same time as contracts on the purchase, with the same completion date. In the residential context, it ensures that the client does not end up without somewhere to live, or being committed to buy another property without someone being committed to purchase their existing property. Synchronisation can be more difficult for newbuild properties (see **Chapter 4**).

Key term: Energy Performance Certificate (EPC)

A certificate, produced by an accredited energy assessor, which details the property's energy use, costs and efficiency, based on an official rating from A (most efficient) to G (least efficient). It provides recommendations to improve the energy efficiency rating and is valid for a period of ten years. It must usually be made available by the seller, without charge, before or within 7 days of marketing and in any event, within 28 days. Listed properties are excepted from the requirement. For newbuild properties, a Predicted Energy Assessment must usually be produced, with a full EPC, following construction.

Sources of finance/types of mortgage

Most clients will need to rely on borrowing to finance a purchase, usually from a high street bank or building society. The lender will usually require the loan to be secured by a first legal mortgage over the property (see *Revise SQE: Land Law*) and in most straightforward residential property transactions you may act for both buyer/borrower and lender (see *Revise SQE: Ethics and Professional Conduct*).

It is important to appreciate that when acting for both parties, a solicitor will have *two clients* and the needs of both of them will need to be satisfied. For example, both parties will be keen to ensure that adverse matters do not affect the value of the property, its use, enjoyment, marketability, and value for secured lending purposes. Acting for a lender, including compliance with their specific requirements and the terms of the *UK Finance Mortgage Lenders' Handbook* are dealt with more comprehensively in **Chapters 4 and 5**.

At this stage, a client may require advice concerning a mortgage and it is important to realise that, under the Financial Services and Markets Act 2000, you may only give generic advice concerning the main types of mortgage (see *Revise SQE: The Legal Systems and Services of England and Wales*). The two main types of mortgage are a **repayment mortgage** and an **interest-only mortgage**.

Key term: repayment mortgage

Under a repayment mortgage:
- There are usually monthly payments of *both* interest and capital.
- The interest rate may be variable, fixed or tracked (ie it follows/tracks a nominated base rate).
- As *both* interest and capital are repaid, *the full amount will be repaid* by the end of the mortgage term.
- The key advantage of a repayment mortgage is that, although monthly repayments will be higher, the buyer will be mortgage free at the end of the term.

Key term: interest-only mortgage

Under an interest-only mortgage:
- There are usually monthly payments of interest *only*.
- Again, the interest rate may be variable, fixed or tracked.
- However, as *only* interest is repaid, *the full amount will not be repaid* by the end of the mortgage term. The capital will remain outstanding.
- The key advantage of an interest-only mortgage is that monthly repayments will be lower; however, if the buyer wishes to keep the property, they will need to find another way to repay the capital (eg from savings or an investment).

Advice on survey

A buyer should also be advised on whether to commission a **survey** of the property before exchange of contracts (see also **Chapter 3**).

Key term: survey

A survey is a professionally produced report following an inspection of the property. There are three main types – a **basic valuation**, a **full structural survey** and a **homebuyer's valuation and report/survey**.

For SQE1, you should be able to advise on which type of survey would be most/more appropriate in given circumstances (see **Practice example 1.2**).

The need for a survey of the property by a qualified surveyor will depend on a number of factors, including:
- Its age (eg the property is more than 100 years old).
- Its value.
- Whether it has been extended/altered in the past.
- Whether the buyer has plans for extension(s)/structural alteration(s).
- Whether it is of non-standard construction.
- Whether it is in a former mining area or one that is affected by subsidence (see **Chapter 3**).

The structural condition of the property can have an impact on its stability, value, use, enjoyment, marketability, and its value for secured lending purposes. If defects are discovered, a buyer may choose to withdraw from the transaction, require completion of works, or seek a reduction in the purchase price. In all circumstances, adverse matters and any reduction in the purchase price must be reported to the buyer's mortgagee, who may withdraw, be willing to offer less, or make a retention from the advance (ie retain part of the money until works are carried out).

Key term: basic valuation

This is the most basic form of 'survey' in that it does not assess the physical state and condition of the property in any detail. It is commissioned by a lender as a minimum requirement to ascertain the market value of the property and its value for secured lending purposes. Its basic purpose is to assure the lender that the property will be worth sufficiently more than its security so that the lender will get its money back in the event of the exercise of its power of sale (see *Revise SQE: Land Law*). It is simple and cheap, but of limited value to a buyer.

Key term: full structural survey

This is the most comprehensive form of survey and contains a detailed assessment of the physical state and condition of the property. It is also the most expensive type of survey, although it is important to be aware of any limitations within the report. The reassurance of a full structural survey may be worth the expense, especially if the property is old, particularly valuable, or there have been past or proposed alterations. It may be used to re-negotiate the purchase price if adverse matters are revealed and the results and any reduction in purchase price must also be reported to the lender.

Key term: homebuyer's valuation and report/survey

The detail of a homebuyer's valuation and report/survey lies somewhere between a basic valuation and a full structural survey. Although it will refer to the need for repairs/maintenance, it is important to appreciate the very real limitations attached to this type of survey. For example, physical inspection may have been limited to exposed and accessible areas. Although it is a compromise, its value to a buyer may be affected depending on these limitations.

Practice example 1.2

Lill is buying a Victorian terraced house with the aid of a mortgage.

Which type of survey would you recommend in these circumstances?

The mortgagee will probably insist on a basic valuation. However, Lill should be informed of the limitations of this and that its general purpose will be to give the mortgagee assurance as to the value of the property as security. Lill should be advised to commission a more comprehensive survey and, given the age of the property (it is more than 100 years old), a full structural survey should be recommended. Lill should also be warned of the limitations of a homebuyer's valuation and report.

Revision tip

For newbuild or newly converted properties, a lender will usually undertake a basic valuation and a further survey will not usually be appropriate (particularly when the property has yet to be constructed). Instead, the developer should provide a **structural defects insurance policy**.

Key term: structural defects insurance policy

A structural defects insurance policy typically covers defects in design and construction for a period of ten years. The National House Building Council (NHBC), through its 'Buildmark' scheme, provides the most common type of policy, although other products are available. For the first two years from construction (the initial liability period) the builder is responsible for remedying defects, and for the final eight years (the structural liability period) the NHBC is responsible for structural defects. The cover includes resolution processes as well as protection in the event of the developer's insolvency and for environmental liability (see **Chapter 3**). The full detail of the cover is beyond the scope of this book, but further information can be found at www.nhbc.co.uk. For the purposes of SQE1, you need to be aware of the basic nature of the cover and that having it in place, for properties under ten years old, is a requirement of most lenders (see **Chapter 4**).

THE LAW SOCIETY CONVEYANCING PROTOCOL

For SQE1, it is important to be aware of the **Law Society Conveyancing Protocol**, when it should be used and its basic implications for property transactions.

Key term: Law Society Conveyancing Protocol

The Protocol sets out to standardise the residential conveyancing process, making it more transparent and efficient and improving the experience for all involved. It provides a standard set of steps/instructions to follow when acting in the sale and/or purchase of a freehold or leasehold residential property as a home for an owner-occupier. It also provides standard forms to be used as part of the conveyancing process (eg the *Property Information Form* (see **Chapter 3**) and the *Completion Information and Undertakings form* (see **Chapter 5**)).

The Protocol is usually adopted as a matter of course in relevant transactions, and the forms are often used, even if the Protocol is not expressly adopted. It does not usually apply on the sale of newbuild properties. The most recent version of the Protocol is 2019 and you can access it at www.lawsociety.org.uk.

Although it is recommended, it is only compulsory to adopt the Protocol for firms that are part of the **Law Society's Conveyancing Quality Scheme**.

Key term: Law Society's Conveyancing Quality Scheme

The Law Society's Conveyancing Quality Scheme provides, for members that are accredited as part of the scheme, a recognised quality standard for residential conveyancing practices. It aims to improve consumer confidence by including a client service charter and mandatory training and enforcement procedures. Membership is often a prerequisite to act for major lenders (see **Chapter 4**).

◼ KEY POINT CHECKLIST

This chapter has covered the following key knowledge points. You can use these to structure your revision, ensuring you recall the key details from each point. Remember to refer to this chapter throughout your revision, so that you appreciate each stage in context:

- Conveyancing is the process of transfer of title (ownership) to property between the seller (transferor) and the buyer (transferee).
- The key stages of a conveyancing transaction, following taking instructions, are pre-contract, exchange of contracts, pre-completion, completion, and post-completion.
- The pre-contract stage involves investigation and deduction of title, agreement of the contract, and carrying out pre-contract searches and enquiries.
- At exchange of contracts, a deposit is usually paid and both parties become bound to complete the transaction on the agreed completion date.
- The pre-completion stage involves a number of practical matters including preparation and execution of the transfer and mortgage deed, pre-completion searches and enquiries, and the buyer's solicitor reporting to the lender.
- Completion involves the balance purchase price being paid and the keys and transfer being handed over. The buyer gains legal ownership (subject to registration at HM Land Registry).
- Post-completion involves the discharge of any existing mortgage as well as completion of the SDLT/LTT and HM Land Registry formalities.
- It is important to take comprehensive instructions at the beginning of a conveyancing transaction in order to comply with obligations on costs information and client care, pre-empt any issues, provide an efficient and effective service, and manage client expectations.

- You may give a buyer generic advice on types of mortgage, and the two main ones are a repayment mortgage and an interest-only mortgage.
- You should give advice to a buyer on which type of survey would be most appropriate in the circumstances.
- Most firms adopt the Law Society Conveyancing Protocol, which provides standard documentation and forms for typical residential property transactions. It is compulsory for firms that are part of the Conveyancing Quality Scheme.

■ KEY TERMS AND CONCEPTS

- conveyancing (**page 2**)
- exchange of contracts (**page 2**)
- completion (**page 3**)
- pre-contract stage (**page 3**)
- investigation of title (**page 4**)
- deduction of title (**page 5**)
- pre-contract searches and enquiries (**page 5**)
- requisitions on title (**page 5**)
- caveat emptor (**page 5**)
- pre-completion stage (**page 5**)
- post-completion stage (**page 6**)
- synchronisation (**page 9**)
- Energy Performance Certificate (**page 9**)
- repayment mortgage (**page 10**)
- interest-only mortgage (**page 10**)
- survey (**page 10**)
- basic valuation (**page 11**)
- full structural survey (**page 11**)
- homebuyer's valuation and report/survey (**page 11**)
- structural defects insurance policy (**page 12**)
- Law Society Conveyancing Protocol (**page 12**)
- Law Society's Conveyancing Quality Scheme (**page 13**)

■ SQE1-STYLE QUESTIONS

The other chapters in this book include five SQE1-style questions per chapter. However, as this chapter provides foundational information only, it is not appropriate to include SQE1-style questions here.

■ ANSWERS TO QUESTIONS

Answers to 'What do you know already?' questions at the start of the chapter

1) Conveyancing is the process of transfer of title (ownership) to property between the seller (transferor) and the buyer (transferee).

2) True. Until exchange of contracts, the parties are usually free to withdraw from a conveyancing transaction. They will not usually be liable for wasted time and costs.

3) False. Exchange of contracts is when the parties become committed to enter into a property transaction and complete on the agreed completion date. Completion is when the actual legal transfer takes place (subject to registration).

4) False. Exchange of contracts is when the deposit monies are usually paid, with the balance purchase monies and keys being handed over on completion.

Answers to end-of-chapter SQE1-style questions
Not applicable.

■ KEY CASES, RULES, STATUTES, AND INSTRUMENTS

The SQE1 Assessment Specification does not require you to know any statutory authorities or specific case names for this topic. Specific sections of statutes (if any) are set out for ease of reference. Although neither a statute nor a statutory instrument, you should be aware of the Law Society Conveyancing Protocol, as specific reference is made to it in the SQE1 Assessment Specification.

Pre-contract (1): deduction and investigation of title

■ MAKE SURE YOU KNOW

This chapter provides an overview of the deduction and investigation of registered and unregistered freehold titles. It will focus on the process of analysing HM Land Registry official copy entries (in registered land) and the process of analysing an epitome of title and deducing ownership (in unregistered land). It will go on to consider issues that could arise from an investigation of title and the further action/practical solutions required. For the SQE1 assessments, you will need to understand the detail of each of these elements, as well as how they fit into the bigger picture (see **Chapter 1**).

■ SQE ASSESSMENT ADVICE

For SQE1, you are required to understand what deduction and investigation of title involve, as well as how title issues may be dealt with.

As you work through this chapter, remember to pay particular attention in your revision to:
- The differences between registered and unregistered title.
- The meaning of deduction of title and how it is achieved with registered and unregistered freehold titles.
- The meaning of investigation of title and the different processes involved for registered and unregistered freehold titles.
- Understanding title documents, identifying problems, and finding solutions to title issues.

■ WHAT DO YOU KNOW ALREADY?

Attempt these questions before reading this chapter. If you find some difficult or cannot remember the answers, remember to look more closely at that topic during your revision.

1) Explain what is meant by a good root of title in the context of unregistered freehold titles.

   [Deduction and investigation of title – unregistered freehold titles, page 21]

2) Where will ancillary rights and restrictive covenants usually appear in a registered title?
    [Deduction and investigation of title – registered freehold titles, page 18]

3) Explain the necessary Land charges searches on the acquisition of an unregistered freehold title.
    [Deduction and investigation of title – unregistered freehold titles, page 22]

4) True or false? On a sale by the last surviving beneficial joint tenant, where title is registered, it will be necessary to appoint an additional trustee to receive the capital monies.
    [Co-ownership, page 30]

DEDUCTION AND INVESTIGATION OF TITLE

For SQE1, it is important to be able to distinguish between *deduction of title* and *investigation of title* (see **Chapter 1**). The requirements differ according to whether there is **registered title** or **unregistered title** to the property.

Key term: registered title

Registered title is where the seller's title is registered at HM Land Registry. Title is deduced by the seller's solicitor providing to the buyer's solicitor official copies of the registers of title, as well as a copy of the title plan and official copies of any documents referred to and filed under the title (see **Deduction and investigation of title – registered freehold titles**).

Key term: unregistered title

Unregistered title is where the seller's title is not registered at HM Land Registry. Title is deduced by the seller's solicitor providing to the buyer's solicitor an epitome of title, which is comprised of copy paper title deeds and documents (see **Deduction and investigation of title – unregistered freehold titles**).

Investigation of title is an important first step by the seller's solicitor as a precursor to *deduction of title*. It allows them to pre-empt any potential issues that are likely to be raised by the buyer's solicitor, specify the relevant incumbrances in the contract (see **Chapter 4**), and consider possible solutions to problems at an early stage. The buyer's solicitor will then carry out their own investigation of title, raise requisitions on title (see **Chapter 1**), and will need to make sure that the seller's solicitor resolves any issues. The buyer's lender will also need to be satisfied that title is good and marketable and in accordance with its requirements (see **Chapter 4**) so that they may be able to sell the property in the event of default by the buyer/borrower, to cover the outstanding debt.

From December 1990, it became compulsory throughout all of England and Wales to register title to land on sale or change of ownership. Following the Land Registration Act 1925, registration was introduced on a piecemeal basis, starting with the main metropolitan areas and cities. Therefore, unregistered titles may still be encountered, particularly where land has not changed hands for well over thirty years.

Revision tip

HM Land Registry Practice Guide 1: First Registrations confirms when first registration became compulsory in areas throughout England and Wales. This should always be consulted when dealing with unregistered land in practice to ascertain whether the title should have been registered previously (because registration was compulsory in the relevant area at the time of an earlier disposition, eg transfer of ownership). If so, the seller's solicitor should be asked to do everything necessary to procure registration before the transaction proceeds.

DEDUCTION AND INVESTIGATION OF TITLE – REGISTERED FREEHOLD TITLES

In land with registered title, title is deduced (ownership proved) by the seller's solicitor providing official copies of the registers of title (**official copies**) and a copy of the title plan filed at HM Land Registry (sometimes referred to as the 'filed plan'). They must also provide official copies of any documents referred to in the registers and filed at HM Land Registry, where the full detail is not set out in the register (see **Practice example 2.1**). It is a requirement of the Law Society Conveyancing Protocol (see **Chapter 1**) that the documents must be official copies (not photocopies) and must be no more than six months old when issued.

Official copies and filed plan are applied for using HM Land Registry form OC1, with form OC2 being used for official copies of documents referred to in the title. Applications may be submitted online for firms with access to HM Land Registry online services (the HM Land Registry portal).

Practice example 2.1

You act on the sale of a freehold property, title to which is registered at HM Land Registry. An entry in the *property register* (see **Key term** below) states that *'the property has the benefit of the rights granted by but is subject to the rights reserved in a Conveyance of the land in the title dated 14 November 1990 (copy filed)'*. The title is also subject to the restrictive covenants in a Conveyance of the land in the title dated 26 September 1928, and these are set out in full in the *charges register* (see **Key term**).

What action must you take to deduce title?

You must deduce title by providing official copies and a copy of the title plan. You must also produce an official copy of the Conveyance dated 14 November 1990, so that the buyer has full information about the rights (HM Land Registry has a copy filed). You do not need to provide an official copy of the Conveyance dated 26 September 1928, as the covenants are set out in full in the charges register.

Key term: official copies

Official copies of the registers of title carry a title number, which is unique to the title and is comprised of two or three letters relating to the administrative area (eg 'WM' for parts of the West Midlands), followed by a number, an edition date (when the title was last updated, eg following the last sale) and a precise **search from date**. There are three separate registers comprising the registers of title: the **property register**, the **proprietorship register**, and the **charges register**.

Once received, the buyer's solicitor must review the official copies as part of the process of investigation of title (see **Chapter 1**). The key elements are referred to below, but as an initial step, the buyer's solicitor must check that they are official copies and are less than six months old (see above).

Key term: search from date

The specific date and time on which the official copies were issued by HM Land Registry (eg *'28 December 2022 at 14:30:25'*). The buyer is usually not permitted, under the contract, to raise requisitions on title after exchange of contracts, other than in respect of matters appearing on the title after this date (see **Chapter 4**). The date is also crucial to the buyer's pre-completion HM Land Registry search (see **Chapter 5**). The *search from date* should not be confused with the *edition date* (see above).

Key term: property register

The property register describes the property, its extent, and rights benefiting the property. It includes the following information:

- Whether it is a freehold or leasehold title (ie tenure – see **Chapter 1** and *Revise SQE: Land Law*).
- A description, with reference to the title plan. In the case of a residential property, this will usually be the full postal address.
- Any exclusions or limitations on the title (eg in former mining areas it is common for mines and minerals and associated rights of working to be excluded from the title – see **Title problems and solutions**, below).
- Rights benefiting the property (eg easements that the property has the *benefit* of – see *Revise SQE: Land Law*). It is also possible that rights

burdening the property could be included here (eg an entry might state that the property has the benefit of the rights granted by, but is subject to the rights reserved in, a specific conveyance, a copy of which is filed at HM Land Registry (see **Practice example 2.1**)).
• Declarations as to light and air (see **Title problems and solutions**, below).

When reviewing the property register, it is important to verify the tenure and the extent of the property and check that they are consistent with the memorandum (written note) of sale and the buyer's and lender's expectations. Any exclusions should be pointed out and the client should be asked to confirm their understanding as to the boundaries. It should also be checked whether the property has all the necessary rights benefiting it, and additional enquiries concerning them should be raised (see **Title problems and solutions** and **Chapter 3**).

The buyer's solicitor will also need to check that the property description within the contract is consistent with that in the official copies (see **Chapter 4**).

Key term: proprietorship register

The proprietorship register contains details as to the ownership of the property, the **class of title**, and any **restrictions** on dealings. It includes the following information:
• Name(s) and address(es) of the registered proprietor(s). See **Title problems and solutions**, for what to do if the registered proprietor(s) is/are not the same as the seller(s).
• For dispositions registered after 1 April 2000, the price paid by the current owner.
• Whether an indemnity covenant was given by the owner on the purchase (see **Title problems and solutions**).

Key term: class of title

The class (or quality) of title is state guaranteed. There are three options that apply for both freehold and leasehold titles, and one that applies to leasehold titles only:
• *Absolute title* is the best and most widespread class. The state guarantees the title, generally subject only to entries appearing on the registers of title and **overriding interests**. In the case of absolute leasehold title, HM Land Registry will also have approved the landlord's title.
• *Possessory title* is usually given where title deeds were lost prior to first registration, or the owner's title is based on adverse possession (see **Revise SQE: Land Law**). It is also subject to any adverse matters at the date of first registration.

- *Qualified title* is given where there is a specific defect in title referred to in the registers of title (eg a missing title document containing unknown covenants), such that absolute title cannot be given.
- *Good leasehold title* (leasehold only) is given where HM Land Registry approves the leasehold title but not the landlord's title (see **Chapter 7**).

See **Title problems and solutions** for how to deal with problems arising from the class of title and unknown covenants.

Key term: restrictions

Restrictions restrict or prevent dealings with the title. The two most common ones likely to be encountered in practice are the Form A restriction (sometimes arising in the context of co-ownership – see **Co-ownership**) and a restriction to protect a mortgagee's interest (see **Title problems and solutions**).

Key term: overriding interests

These are interests that, although not substantively registrable, can bind a purchaser (see *Revise SQE: Land Law* for more detailed information). They include interests of persons in actual occupation, local land charges (see **Chapter 3**), legal easements arising by virtue of long user (prescription) and legal leases of seven years or less. The existence of overriding interests is usually ascertained through pre-contract searches and enquiries (see **Chapter 3**).

Key term: charges register

The charges register contains adverse matters affecting the property (ie incumbrances or things that *burden* it). It includes the following information:

- Mortgages and charges.
- Covenants burdening the property.
- Easements over the property.
- Leases.
- Notices.

See **Title problems and solutions**, for how to deal with all of these entries when acting for a buyer.

DEDUCTION AND INVESTIGATION OF TITLE – UNREGISTERED FREEHOLD TITLES

In land with unregistered title, title is deduced (ownership proved) by the seller's solicitor providing to the buyer's solicitor an **epitome of title**, which is comprised of copy paper title deeds and documents, and which must evidence a **good root of title**. The seller's solicitor must investigate title (see **Chapter 1**) to ascertain the root of title, so the *first step* will always be to obtain the original **title deeds** and documents and then to confirm that the property has not previously been registered. It would be best practice for the seller's solicitor to conduct an index map search at this stage (see **Chapter 3**).

Key term: title deeds

These are usually comprised of conveyances, deeds of gift, assents (see **Personal representatives**), mortgages, Land charges searches (see **Land charges searches**) and sometimes, ancillary documents, such as old pre-contract searches and copy planning documents.

Normally, the owner, a solicitor/firm of solicitors, or the seller's mortgagee (if the land is subject to a mortgage) may hold the title deeds. A mortgagee will usually provide them to the seller's solicitor subject to an *undertaking* to hold them to their order and not deal with the property without their consent or discharge of the sums secured by the mortgage (see *Revise SQE: Ethics and Professional Conduct*).

Key term: epitome of title

An epitome of title is simply a list of material title deeds and documents, set out in date order, starting with the root of title, and including other documents cross-referred to in it.

For example, the root of title may say that the property has the benefit of easements or is subject to the easements or covenants set out in an earlier conveyance (which are not set out again in the root of title), or it may even define the property by reference to a plan annexed to an earlier conveyance. In these circumstances, these documents would need to be included in the epitome of title so that the buyer has full information about the title to the property. It is also good practice to include old Land charges searches that are available (see **Land charges searches**).

Copies of the documents (not the originals) are attached to the epitome of title at this stage. On a typical *sale of the whole* of the land comprised within the title, the original documents are handed over on completion. On a typical *sale of part* of the land comprised within the title, certified copies of the original documents are handed over on completion (see **Chapter 5**).

Key term: good root of title

The seller's solicitor must find a good root of title when investigating the title deeds and documents. A good root of title is defined in s 44 Law of Property Act 1925 as a document that:
- Is at least 15 years old.
- Deals with the whole of the legal and equitable/beneficial interest in the property (ie it refers to the transfer of the *fee simple* (freehold) by the

transferor(s) *as beneficial owner(s)* – see **Revise SQE: Land Law** and **Co-ownership**).
- Provides an adequate and identifiable description of the property.
- Does not cast doubt on the title.

Once the root of title has been ascertained for the purposes of the epitome of title, other documents may be set aside unless they are cross-referred to in the root of title (see **Practice example 2.2**).

Set out below are some key things to consider when selecting the root of title:
- The *best document* for a root of title is a *conveyance* (ie a transfer of land). This is because the property will usually have been transferred for value, often between unconnected parties. There will therefore be the so-called 'double guarantee' that the title will have been investigated before on the previous purchase.
- A *mortgage* may also be used, but it is less satisfactory as it does not usually contain all title information (eg details of incumbrances).
- A *deed of gift* or *an assent* (ie a transfer of property by personal representatives (PRs), see **Personal representatives**) may also be used as a good root of title, although they do not usually have the added benefit of the 'double guarantee' of a conveyance, so they will not be the best root of title.

For SQE1, you should be able to identify the best and most appropriate root of title in given circumstances. **Practice example 2.2** provides an example of deduction of title in practice.

Practice example 2.2

A solicitor acts on the sale of a freehold property, title to which is unregistered at HM Land Registry. The title deeds and documents are comprised of the following:
- Land charges searches.
- An assent to the current seller, dated 15 March 1972, which provides that the property is defined in the conveyance dated 12 February 1967.
- A mortgage dated 30 January 1975.
- A conveyance dated 12 February 1967, which provides that the property: (a) is defined on the plan annexed to the conveyance dated 15 March 1952 (the 'Conveyance'), (b) has the benefit of the rights referred to and fully set out in the Conveyance, and (c) is subject to the restrictive covenants referred to and fully set out in the Conveyance.
- The Conveyance.
- A conveyance dated 28 December 1942.

Which document provides the *best and most appropriate* root of title and which documents should be included within the epitome of title?

> **The assent should be a good root of title, but the 1967 conveyance will probably be the best and most appropriate, as it will provide the usual 'double guarantee'. In any event, a copy of the assent (to evidence devolution to the seller) and the Conveyance (to give full information as to the property description, ancillary rights, and restrictive covenants affecting the property) should be provided. The mortgage should also be included as it affects the seller's interest in the property. It is also best practice to provide the copy Land charges searches. The 1942 conveyance does not need to be provided as it is not cross-referred to in the root of title or other relevant documents.**

Once received, the buyer's solicitor must review the documents in the epitome of title as part of the process of investigation of title (see **Chapter 1**). The key elements are elaborated upon below and summarised in **Figure 2.1**, but as an initial step, the buyer's solicitor must check there is a *good root of title*.

The buyer's solicitor will also want to check that the property is *not already registered* and that there are no cautions against first registration. This can be ascertained by carrying out an index map search (now known by the acronym 'SIM' – 'search of the index map') (see **Chapter 3**).

It is also important to check whether the property *should have been registered* before (see above).

The buyer's solicitor must now examine the title deeds and documents, adopting the approach set out in **Figure 2.1** and elaborated upon below.

Check that there is a *clear and unbroken chain of ownership* to the current seller

↓

Make sure the *property description* is clear and consistent

↓

Check that all documents have been *properly stamped*

↓

Make sure all documents have been *properly executed*

↓

Check for *incumbrances* (eg easements and covenants burdening the property) and *ancillary rights* (eg easements benefiting the property) (see **Title problems and solutions**)

↓

Check *Land charges searches* (see **Title problems and solutions**)

Figure 2.1: Investigation of title – unregistered freehold titles

Clear and unbroken chain of ownership

The chain of ownership must lead to the current owner(s):

- Spellings should be double-checked, and the seller's solicitor should be asked to account for any missing links from the root of title.
- Evidence of any deaths (certified copy death certificate) or changes of name (eg certified copy marriage certificate) will need to be provided.
- For a disposition by PRs (see **Personal representatives**), a certified copy of the grant of representation must be obtained (see **Revise SQE: Wills and Administration of Estates**).

Property description

This must be clear and consistent throughout the title documents and should also be reflected in the contract (see **Chapter 4**).

Proper stamping of documents

Prior to the introduction of *Stamp Duty Land Tax* in December 2003 (a tax on land transactions – see **Chapter 10**) there was a system of *Stamp Duty* in place (a tax on documents). The regime involved sending certain conveyancing documents to the stamping authorities, where they would receive physical stamping.

There were two types of Stamp Duty:

- The first was '*ad valorem*' Stamp Duty which was payable on the value of a conveyance on sale. Lower value transactions were exempt or subject to a reduced rate, if there was a 'certificate of value' in the document, confirming that the value did not exceed the relevant threshold. Ad valorem Stamp Duty was not payable on mortgages after 1971 and deeds of gift or assents after the end of April 1987 (provided there was a 'certificate of exemption' in the document).
- The other type of Stamp Duty was the Inland Revenue *Particulars Delivered* (or PD) stamp, which required conveyances on sale (and some other documents) to be stamped from 1931.

Revision tip

For the purposes of SQE1, it is not necessary to know the exact rules for stamping particular documents at particular times. In practice, this is something that can be ascertained using tables within practitioner texts. However, you should be aware of the need for conveyances on sale to be properly stamped for both ad valorem Stamp Duty and Particulars Delivered, depending on the rules that were in operation at the time of the previous land transaction. If any documents are not stamped or properly stamped, the seller should remedy this at their expense, dealing with the payment of any interest or penalties.

Proper execution of documents

Generally, all conveyances of land must be made by deed (s 52 Law of Property Act 1925) otherwise they are void for the purpose of conveying a legal estate. The requirements vary for deeds before 31 July 1990 and after this date:

- *For deeds after 31 July 1990*, the requirements of a deed are set out in s 1(2) of the Law of Property (Miscellaneous Provisions) Act 1989. This provides that the document must be:
  - *In writing* and *clear on the face of it that it is intended to be a deed* (eg it is expressed to be executed as a deed, or otherwise clearly stated to be a deed).
  - *Signed in the presence of a witness who attests (witnesses) the signature.*
  - *Delivered as a deed* (ie the executing party intends to be bound by the deed – this is presumed following execution).
- *For deeds before 31 July 1990*, the requirements of a deed were that it had to be signed, *sealed*, and delivered. Sealing (usually affixing a red circle to the execution clause) was a strict requirement for the proper execution of a deed.

The execution of deeds by companies is considered in **Chapter 5**.

The seller(s)/transferor(s) must *always* execute transfers of land. The buyer(s)/transferee(s) only need to execute transfers of land when they are making a new declaration (eg a declaration of trust as to co-ownership of the equitable interest or a declaration as to light and air) or entering into a fresh covenant (eg an indemnity covenant) (see **Chapter 5**).

Ancillary rights and incumbrances

The buyer's solicitor must check that the property has the *benefit* of all necessary *ancillary rights* for the reasonable and proper use of the property. This includes easements benefiting the property (usually found after the words '*together with*' in a conveyance).

They must also check that the property is not subject to materially adverse rights or restrictions (incumbrances). This includes easements burdening the property (usually found after the words '*excepting and reserving*' in a conveyance) or onerous/burdensome covenants (usually found after the words '*subject to*' in a conveyance) (see **Title problems and solutions**).

Land charges searches

The Land Charges Act 1925 introduced a partial system of registration for certain commercial rights in unregistered land created after 1 January 1926 (see *Revise SQE: Land Law*). Registration of a land charge in the name of the estate owner of the burdened land when it was granted is necessary to protect the holder of the right and bind subsequent owners. The most common rights likely to be encountered in practice are the following:

- C(iv) Estate contract.
- D(ii) Restrictive covenant.
- D(iii) Equitable easement.
- F Home rights.

Land charges searches (using form K15) must therefore be made against all estate owners mentioned in the documents within the epitome of title for their years of ownership (unless search results have already been provided as part of the epitome of title) (see **Chapter 3**). If the precise dates of ownership are unclear, then the buyer's solicitor should search back to the earliest date the relevant estate owner could have owned the property, or 1926 (the year the system was introduced – see **Practice example 2.3**). All versions of names within the deeds and the correct counties must be searched against (see the **Revision tip** set out below **Practice example 2.3**).

Revision tip

The system of *land charges* under what is now the Land Charges Act 1972, administered by the Land Charges Registry in Plymouth, must not be confused with the system of *local land charges*, administered by either local authorities or HM Land Registry (see **Chapter 3**). *Quite understandably, candidates frequently conflate the two systems, but they do deal with separate issues.*

Practice example 2.3

You act on the purchase of a freehold property with unregistered title. The seller is Joy Fleming, and the root of title is a conveyance dated 03 January 1980 and made between (1) Kikki Danielsson and (2) Joy Fleming (the 'Conveyance'). The Conveyance is expressed to be subject to the covenants contained within an earlier conveyance of the land in the title dated 28 December 1974 and made between (1) Lill Lindfors and Birthe Kjaer and (2) Kikki Danielsson. The covenants are set out in full in the Conveyance.

Which Land charges searches would you need to make?

Joy Fleming – 1980 (date of purchase) to present year.

Kikki Danielsson – 1974 (date of purchase) to 1980 (date of sale).

Lill Lindfors and Birthe Kjaer – 1926 (we cannot tell from the documents provided when they purchased, so it is safest to go back to this date) to 1974 (date of sale). We need to search against Lill and Birthe, as their names are available from the title documents within the epitome of title, even though the document does not form the root itself.

Revision tip

The history of local government boundaries and county names in England and Wales is complicated, particularly in metropolitan areas, and there were many changes in 1974. Luckily, HM Land Registry sets out former counties in its *Practice Guide 63*, which is invaluable for these purposes. Although it is not necessary to know the full detail for the purposes of SQE1, it is crucial to be aware of the need to search against all relevant (including historic) counties in practice.

TITLE PROBLEMS AND SOLUTIONS

Once the solicitor acting for the buyer has interpreted the official copies (for registered title) or checked/interpreted the documents within the epitome of title (for unregistered title), it is necessary to adopt a systematic approach to problem solving and raise any necessary requisitions on title. Set out below are the key title problems and possible solutions that you should be aware of for the purposes of SQE1.

It is important to consider and seek to resolve title problems as they could have an impact on the ability to register the property or disposition at HM Land Registry. They could also have financial implications such as liability for costs, or an impact on the value of the property, its use, enjoyment, marketability, and its value as security for lending purposes (referred to below as *'the usual concerns'*). Therefore, any title problems should be reported to the buyer, their mortgagee and in some circumstances, their surveyor.

Mines and minerals are excluded from the title

The exclusion of mines and minerals from the title (in either the property register for registered land, or the title documents in unregistered land) is very common in former mining areas. It is usually accompanied by ancillary rights to enter the property to access the mines/minerals, and it may also refer to an associated right for compensation.

In such circumstances, the buyer's solicitor should conduct a coal mining search (see **Chapter 3**). Strictly speaking, it is also advisable to conduct an index map search (SIM) to ascertain whether the mining rights are comprised in a registered title and, if so, who owns them (see **Chapter 3**). The rights are usually vested in the Coal Authority.

The presence of past mining may give rise to the usual concerns (see above), and the impact on stability of the property would compound these concerns.

Therefore, the following specific enquiries should be raised of the seller's solicitor:
- If known, who has the benefit of the rights?
- Have the rights been exercised in the past and has any compensation been payable?
- Is the seller aware of any proposal(s) to exercise such rights?
- Has the property suffered from structural problems such as subsidence, landslip, or heave (where the ground pushes up from the surface)? If so, these should be reported.

Although the return of active mining in former mining areas would be subject to feasibility, licences, and planning consents, making it unlikely (particularly in built-up areas), these questions should still be raised as a matter of good practice.

Rights benefiting the property

The rights benefiting the property should be checked to make sure that the property has the benefit of all necessary ancillary rights and that they are sufficient, suitable, and adequate. For example, there should be an expressly granted right of way referred to in the property register, or within the epitome of title documents, if the property does not immediately abut a highway maintainable at public expense (see **Chapter 3**).

The most common rights/easements benefiting a property are rights of way, rights of support, and rights to services/utilities and drainage running over private land.

The *benefit of legal easements will run with the land*, but the terms should be checked carefully to make sure they are suitable. For example, a right of way should be at all times and for all purposes connected with the reasonable use and enjoyment of the land and (depending on the nature of the right) may need to be with or without vehicles. It is common for such rights to be subject to the payment of a reasonable sum towards the maintenance of the right of way, and the buyer will usually be bound by such an obligation if they take the benefit of the right.

The following specific enquiries should be raised of the seller's solicitor about ancillary rights:
- Have there been any problems or disputes with regard to the exercise of the rights or the payment towards them?
- Have there been any notices with regard to the rights?
- Have any contributions towards maintenance been paid or requested and are any costs anticipated? If so, further details will be required.

The buyer's surveyor should be informed of any significant potential maintenance liability, so that this can be assessed as part of the survey.

The seller(s) is/are not the same as the registered proprietor(s)

The seller(s) may not be the same as the registered proprietor(s) for a number of reasons. The most important ones for the purposes of SQE1 are the death of a co-owner (see **Co-ownership**) or a sale by PRs (see **Personal representatives**). It could be as simple as a marriage or civil partnership; in which case a certified copy of the relevant certificate (marriage certificate or civil partnership certificate) will need to be provided.

Co-ownership

Co-ownership concerns the situation where there is concurrent ownership of the same property by more than one person, and it always gives rise to a trust of land (the separation of the legal and equitable interests – see *Revise SQE: Land Law*). The legal interest will *always* be owned as joint tenants and the equitable interest may be held as a **joint tenancy** or by way of a **tenancy in common** (see also *Revise SQE: Land Law*). The legal interest concerns who may convey the legal estate (essentially who signs/executes the transfer) and the equitable (or beneficial) interest concerns who is entitled to the proceeds of sale.

Key term: joint tenancy

- Joint tenants own the whole of the interest together.
- It is *incorrect* to talk of joint tenants holding separate undivided shares. Together they own everything, but individually they hold nothing.
- Ownership of a joint tenancy may be seen to be like a solid *golf ball* – it cannot easily be seen to be divided up into separate shares.
- The right of survivorship applies, and it is not possible to leave a beneficial share under a normal will or on intestacy (see *Revise SQE: Wills and Administration of Estates*). This means that the joint tenancy usually 'trumps' a will, and the deceased joint tenant's interest in the whole of the property will pass automatically to the survivor(s) on death.

Key term: tenancy in common

- Tenants in common own separate undivided shares of the equitable interest (which may be equal or unequal).
- It is therefore *correct* to talk of tenants in common holding separate undivided shares. Individually, they hold a separate share.
- Ownership of a tenancy in common could be seen to be like a segmented *orange* – it can easily be seen to be divided up into separate shares.
- The right of survivorship does not apply to a tenancy in common. The deceased's beneficial share will pass in accordance with their will or under the intestacy rules.

If all the co-owners are alive, then there are no conveyancing problems provided that all co-owners are party to the contract and the transfer. If one or more co-owners have died, then it is necessary to ascertain whether the equitable interest was held as joint tenants or tenants in common.

In registered land, the position is that 'equity follows the law' and co-owners will hold the equitable interest as joint tenants, *unless* there is a **Form A restriction** in the *proprietorship register* (see **Key term**). In unregistered land, express words in the conveyance to the owners will state whether they hold the beneficial interest as joint tenants or tenants in common.

Key term: Form A restriction

A Form A restriction in the proprietorship register will read as follows:

RESTRICTION: No disposition by a sole proprietor of the registered estate (except a trust corporation) under which capital money arises is to be registered unless authorised by an order of the court.

The Form A restriction serves as a reminder to comply with the overreaching procedure (ie the appointment of an additional trustee – see **Beneficial tenants in common**, and *Revise SQE: Land Law*) in the event of a disposition by a sole proprietor.

Once beneficial ownership of the co-owners has been ascertained, the following action should be taken by the buyer's solicitor if there has been a death of a co-owner.

Beneficial joint tenants

With regard to beneficial joint tenants:
- *In all cases*: Obtain a certified copy of the death certificate from the seller's solicitor.
- *In registered land*: The surviving co-owner(s) can convey the property. It can be assumed that there has been no severance of the equitable joint tenancy (converting the status of the severing co-owner to a tenant in common – see *Revise SQE: Land Law*) unless there is a Form A restriction entered in the proprietorship register.
- *In unregistered land*: The surviving co-owner(s) can convey the property provided that the following three conditions are satisfied (from the Law of Property (Joint Tenants) Act 1964):
  (i)   There is no memorandum of severance endorsed on the conveyance to the joint tenants.
  (ii) There are no bankruptcy proceedings registered against any of the joint tenants at the Land Charges Registry.
  (iii) The transfer by the surviving joint owner states that the survivor is solely and beneficially entitled to the land.
  All three conditions must be met, and if this is not possible, an additional trustee must be appointed if acquiring from the sole surviving co-owner (see **Beneficial tenants in common**).

Therefore, in *unregistered land*:
- A Land charges search should be made against all the joint tenants.
- The conveyance to the joint tenants should be inspected to see whether a memorandum (written note) of severance has been entered on it. For added security it is advisable to raise a requisition for *confirmation that there is no memorandum of severance endorsed on the conveyance* (the copy could be incomplete/that part may not have been copied).
- Finally, it should be confirmed that the conveyance by the survivor will contain the necessary statement that they are solely and beneficially entitled to the property.

Beneficial tenants in common

With regard to beneficial tenants in common:
- *In all cases*: Obtain a certified copy of the death certificate from the seller's solicitor.
- *In all cases*: If acquiring from a sole surviving co-owner, a second trustee (legal owner) needs to be appointed to overreach the equitable interest of the deceased co-owner. This can be done either in a separate deed, or by a simple provision in the transfer, but it must be provided for in the contract as an obligation on the seller.

Figures 2.2 and 2.3 provide suggested approaches to dealing with issues of co-ownership.

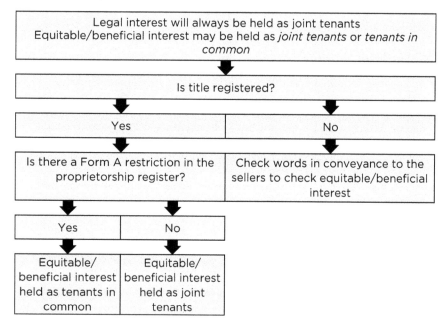

Figure 2.2: Co-ownership – Ascertaining how the equitable/beneficial interest is held

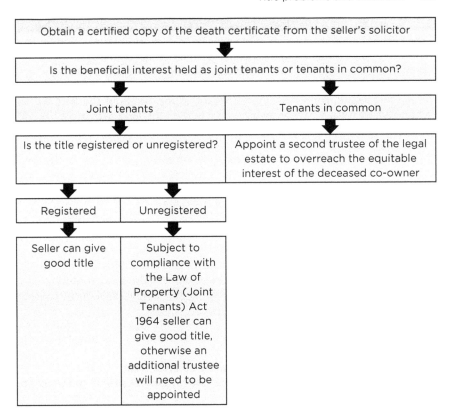

Figure 2.3: Disposition by last surviving co-owner

Personal representatives

The situation on a disposition by PRs will depend on whether title is registered or unregistered.

Although a sole PR can give a valid receipt for the capital monies, in any event *all PRs must be joined into the transfer/conveyance*. Therefore, if any have died, evidence of death should be provided by obtaining a certified copy of the death certificate.

Registered title

PRs may apply to be *registered as proprietors*. In these circumstances, there will be no conveyancing problems, provided that any restriction on the register is complied with.

Otherwise, PRs may sell the property or pass the legal estate to beneficiaries under an **assent**.

Key term: assent

The vesting of the legal estate in the beneficiary/beneficiaries, rather than the sale or transfer of it to a third party. An assent must be made to vest the property in the assentee, even if they are the sole PR and sole beneficiary.

In registered land, form AS1 (for an assent of the whole of the land within the title(s)) or form AS3 (for an assent of part of the land within the title(s)) must be used.

On a *sale* by PRs *who are not registered as proprietors*, a buyer should not complete the purchase until the seller's solicitor has provided a certified copy of the court-issued grant of representation. Without it, the PRs will not have authority to deal with the estate of the deceased.

Unregistered title

The risks in land with unregistered title are that the property may, inadvertently, be disposed of more than once and, as the buyer is not entitled to see the will, they may not be sure that the person who the property was assented to (the assentee) was the properly entitled person. The Administration of Estates Act 1925 (AEA) deals with both concerns.

Section 36(6) AEA provides that a buyer will take good title from PRs provided that:
• The conveyance to the buyer contains a **s 36 statement**,
• There is no memorandum of a previous conveyance or assent endorsed on the grant of representation, and
• Any prior disposition is not for valuable consideration.

Section 36(7) AEA provides that an assent or conveyance is sufficient evidence that the assentee or buyer is the person properly entitled in the absence of a prior memorandum endorsed on the grant.

Key term: s 36 statement

A statement in the conveyance to the buyer under s 36 Administration of Estates Act 1925, confirming that there have been no previous dispositions (assents or conveyances) of the same land made by the PRs.

On a *sale by PRs* of land with *unregistered title* the following should be checked:
• The certified copy grant of representation to check the PR's/PRs' authority.
• That all PRs are joined in.
• That there is no memorandum of a previous disposition endorsed on the grant of representation.
• That a memorandum of the conveyance is endorsed on the grant of representation.
• That the conveyance to the buyer contains a s 36 statement and an acknowledgment for production of the original grant.

Revision tip

It is good practice to raise a specific requisition regarding endorsements on the grant of representation, as an incomplete copy may have been provided in error (eg with endorsements on the back page).

If there has been *a disposition by a beneficiary as beneficial owner*, you must ensure that the property has been properly vested by way of an assent.

In unregistered land, any *assent by PRs* must be in writing and made by deed if the assentee gives new covenants.

On an *assent by PRs* of land with *unregistered title* the following must also be checked:
- The certified copy grant of representation to check the PR's/PRs' authority.
- That all PRs are joined in.
- That there is no memorandum of a previous disposition endorsed on the grant of representation.
- That a memorandum of the assent is endorsed on the grant of representation.
- That the assent contains an acknowledgement for production of the original grant.

Class of title

If the property is registered with less than absolute title (eg possessory or qualified title) then the usual concerns would apply (see above). As a preliminary step, the lender's requirements should be checked and complied with (see **Chapter 4** – eg the lender may require indemnity insurance to be put in place).

The seller should be asked to remedy the problem at their own expense (see *HM Land Registry Practice Guide 42: Upgrading the class of title*). If the property has been registered with possessory title for at least 12 years, it may be possible to make an application to HM Land Registry to upgrade to absolute title. If qualified title has been given (eg because of a missing conveyance containing covenants) the buyer should ask whether the document can be located and sent to HM Land Registry, whereupon the class of title may be upgraded to absolute title.

If it is not possible to upgrade the class of title, an **indemnity insurance** policy must be provided at the seller's expense to protect the buyer, the buyer's mortgagee, and their respective successors in title in respect of the defect in title.

Key term: indemnity insurance

An insurance policy, usually provided at the seller's expense, to cover the risk of enforcement/legal action in respect of a defect in title. It is important to ensure that the policy has a suitable limit of indemnity (often the market value) and provides for increases in line with inflation. It must also cover mortgagees and successors in title and comply with the relevant lender's requirements in the *UK Finance Mortgage Lenders' Handbook* (see **Chapter 4**).

Similar problems arise if the property is registered with qualified, possessory, or good *leasehold* title (see **Chapter 7**).

Exam warning

Indemnity insurance must not be confused with *indemnity covenants* (see **Positive covenants** and **Chapter 4**). Candidates often conflate the two concepts.

Restrictions

The terms of any restrictions in the proprietorship register of a registered title must be checked carefully as a disposition cannot usually be registered without compliance with its terms. As indicated above, the two most common ones likely to be encountered in practice are the Form A restriction (see **Co-ownership**) and a restriction to protect a mortgagee (see **Mortgages**). These will usually be removed on registration of the disposition to the buyer, but they will need to be complied with to enable the buyer to be registered as proprietor and any new mortgage to be registered.

An indemnity covenant was given by the seller(s) on their acquisition

See **Positive covenants** and **Chapter 4**.

Declarations of light and air

On sale of part of land within a title, it is common for the seller to keep, for the benefit of the retained land, the right freely to build/rebuild on it by providing that the buyer and its successors in title will not be entitled to any rights of light or air over the retained land. Such a declaration will appear in the property register (for registered land) or title documents within the epitome of title (for unregistered land).

If there is such a provision, a specific enquiry should be raised of the seller's solicitor as to the extent of the land benefiting/the retained land if this is not apparent from the title documents.

The impact of any such declaration should be pointed out to the buyer, but it is not typically of significant concern.

Mortgages

Existing undischarged mortgages entered in the charges register or referred to in the epitome of title will not usually be a problem and the buyer will not take subject to them, provided that:

- An undertaking will be in place to discharge them on completion, as part of Completion Information and Undertakings (see **Chapter 5**).
- They are *not* included in the list of specified incumbrances within the contract (see **Chapter 4**).

At this stage, it is worth raising a requisition of the seller's solicitor that a suitable undertaking will be provided before completion, to discharge the charge(s) on or before completion and provide evidence of discharge, so that the buyer may be registered as proprietor, with any restriction being removed.

In *registered land*, a mortgage will usually be protected as follows:

- Two entries in the charges register – one referring to the date of the charge and the other giving details of the proprietor of the charge (typically a building society or high street bank).
- These entries are usually supported by a restriction in the proprietorship register providing that no disposition of the property may be made without the consent of the lender. Although this is usually provided for within the charge itself, the restriction provides the lender with an additional safeguard that its interests will not be overlooked.

In *unregistered land*, a copy of any mortgage itself will be provided as one of the documents within the epitome of title. If the mortgage has a receipt/acknowledgement of receipt of all monies due under the mortgage written/endorsed onto it (known as a vacating receipt), then it has already been discharged and will not be a problem for the buyer.

Restrictive covenants

Restrictive covenants restrict the use of land (they are subtractive in that they take rights away from the owner of land). The question of whether a covenant is restrictive in nature is one of substance, rather than form (see **Revise SQE: Land Law**).

The burden of restrictive covenants usually runs with the land and so they are normally binding on a buyer following completion. Covenants in registered land will be set out or referred to in the charges register, and restrictive covenants in unregistered land dated after 1 January 1926 will need to be registered as a Class D (ii) Land Charge to be binding on a buyer.

The usual concerns (see above) apply to onerous restrictive covenants, so it is important to check them carefully and report about them to the buyer and their mortgagee.

If there are restrictive covenants affecting the title, the following enquiries should be raised of the seller's solicitor:
• Has the covenant been complied with and can evidence of compliance be provided?
• Has/have there been any breach(es) of covenant? If so, details should be provided.
• Have there been any notices served, any action taken, or is any action anticipated in respect of the covenants?

Any breaches should be rectified at the seller's expense, or indemnity insurance should be considered as the main option (see **Revision tip**, below).

If a restrictive covenant is likely to be problematic for a buyer (eg it restricts development (see **Chapter 3**) when development is proposed, restricts use to residential use when business use is proposed, or the seller has failed to comply with it) there are three available options (see **Table 2.1**).

Table 2.1: Restrictive covenants – solutions for problems

Ascertain from the seller who has the benefit of the covenant so that they can be approached with a request to release or vary the covenant or provide a one-off deed of consent
The disadvantage of this is that it is not always easy to ascertain the person with the benefit of a covenant, particularly for older covenants. If they are known, they may not be aware of the covenant, so approaching them may be counterproductive. Although it may be easier to find the person with the benefit of a newer covenant, they may be less willing to release it.
Make an application to the Upper Tribunal (Lands Chamber) for modification or discharge under s 84 Law of Property Act 1925
The detail of this provision is beyond the scope of this book, but the disadvantage of this is that it would involve cost, uncertainty, and time.
Ask the seller to provide a restrictive covenant indemnity policy for the benefit of the buyer, the buyer's mortgagee, and their respective successors in title
This is a quick and easy solution, but the disadvantage is that if the covenant is recent and the person with the benefit is known, they are likely to take action in the event of egregious breaches.

Revision tip

For the purposes of SQE1, it is important to be able to balance the options available should a problematic or onerous restrictive covenant arise in the context of a question. The age of the covenant and whereabouts of the person(s) with benefit are key points. *It will usually be a condition of an indemnity insurance policy that approaches have not been made of the person with the benefit, so approaching them or applying to modify/discharge the covenant should be approached with great caution.* In any event, the requirements of the mortgagee should be ascertained.

Revision tip

It is important to appreciate that although restrictive covenants may seek *privately* to restrict development of land, planning matters are a separate and distinct *public* requirement that need to be complied with (see **Chapter 3**).

Positive covenants

Positive covenants require the owner of land positively to do something, which typically involves the expenditure of money. The question of whether a covenant is positive in nature is one of substance, rather than form (see *Revise SQE: Land Law*).

The usual concerns (see above) apply to onerous positive covenants, so it is important to check them carefully and report about them to the buyer and their mortgagee.

The burden of positive covenants does not usually run with the land. However, they may indirectly be binding through a chain of indemnity covenants (see **Chapters 4 and 5** and *Revise SQE: Land Law*).

The first step is therefore to ascertain whether the current seller gave an indemnity covenant to the transferor when they acquired the property. In unregistered land, the covenant will appear in the conveyance itself. In registered land, the following provision will appear in the proprietorship register:

> '*The transfer to the proprietor contains a covenant to observe and perform the covenants referred to in the Charges Register and an indemnity in respect thereof.*'

If the current seller gave an indemnity covenant to the transferor when they purchased the property, the seller will usually insist that the buyer gives a corresponding indemnity covenant on their acquisition. This is usually provided for in the contract (see **Chapter 4**) and the covenant itself will appear in the Transfer (see **Chapter 5**). If there is no evidence of such a covenant, then the buyer should refuse to give an indemnity since the burden will not usually pass to them.

If the buyer will be liable for positive covenants because of an indemnity covenant, the following additional enquiries must be raised of the seller's solicitor:

- Have the covenants been complied with, and have they been enforced? If so, details should be provided.
- What costs have been involved in complying with the covenants and are any costs anticipated?
- Have there been any problems or disputes with regard to the covenants or any payments made under them?
- Have there been any notices served, any action taken, or is any action anticipated in respect of the covenants or any payments made under them?
- Have any contributions been paid or requested and are any costs anticipated? If so, further details will be required.

The buyer's surveyor should be informed of any significant potential liability, or particularly/unusually onerous positive covenants, so that they can be assessed as part of the survey.

Any breaches should be rectified at the seller's expense, or indemnity insurance should be considered as the main option.

Missing covenants

Sometimes land is known to be subject to covenants, but the nature and substance of the covenants are unknown. This is often because of a lost or missing deed.

The seller will usually refer to the missing covenants as a specified incumbrance within the contract (see **Chapter 4**) so that requisitions may not be made about them after exchange of contracts. The buyer should insist on the provision of an indemnity insurance policy to cover the risk and should raise additional enquiries referring to restrictive and positive covenants in general terms (see above).

Adverse rights/easements

Adverse easements (easements burdening the property) must be checked carefully to make sure they are not onerous. The *burden of legal easements will run with the land*.

The usual concerns (see above) apply to onerous rights, and these could be compounded if the development potential is materially adversely affected.

In all circumstances, they should be reported upon to the buyer and their mortgagee.

The following specific enquiries should be raised of the seller's solicitor about adverse easements:
- Have the rights been exercised?
- Have there been any problems or disputes with regard to the exercise of the adverse rights or any payment towards them?
- Have there been any notices with regard to the rights?
- Have any contributions towards maintenance been paid or requested and are any costs anticipated? If so, further details will be required.

The buyer's surveyor should be informed of any particularly/unusually onerous adverse rights so that they can be assessed as part of the survey.

Indemnity insurance could be considered as an option, particularly if the rights are old and have not been exercised.

Leases
If the property is subject to a legal lease of more than seven years, this should be noted against the landlord's title in the charges register. Legal leases of seven years or less may be overriding interests, and equitable leases (see *Revise SQE: Land Law*) may also be overriding interests if the tenant is in actual occupation. In any event, it should be ascertained whether there are any tenants or other third-party occupants, so that additional enquiries can be made (see **Chapter 3**).

Notices and home rights
Notices may be registered in the charges register of a registered title to protect third party interests. They may be entered either with the consent of the owner (agreed notice) or without their consent (unilateral notice).

Notices are frequently used in registered land to protect third party interests such as estate contracts or the rights of a non-owning spouse or civil partner to occupy the property under the Family Law Act 1996 (home rights) (see *Revise SQE: Land Law*). If home rights are revealed as either a notice, or a Class F Land Charge in unregistered land, in addition to seeking removal of the notice/land charge on or before completion, the interested party should also waive their rights in the property in the contract (see **Chapter 4**).

If any other notice is revealed, the seller must be asked to confirm the interest to which it relates. If it is obsolete or if the buyer does not wish to take subject to it, the seller should be asked to remove it on or before completion (preferably before exchange of contracts). This can be dealt with by a contractual agreement and/or an undertaking from the seller's solicitor.

■ KEY POINT CHECKLIST

This chapter has covered the following key knowledge points. You can use these to structure your revision, ensuring you recall the key details from each point:

- The seller's solicitor investigates title to deduce title to the buyer's solicitor.
- For land with registered title, deduction of title involves providing official copies of the HM Land Registry register entries and the filed plan, together with official copies of any documents referred to by reference in the title and filed at HM Land Registry.
- The registers of title are comprised of the property register, the proprietorship register, and the charges register, and different classes of title are available.
- For land with unregistered title, deduction of title involves providing an epitome of title, comprising copy title deeds and documents, and commencing with a good root of title.
- The buyer's solicitor then investigates title. In land with registered title, this involves detailed consideration of the official copies. In land with unregistered title, this involves: (a) checking for a clear and unbroken chain of ownership, (b) verifying that the property description is clear and consistent, (c) checking that all documents have been properly stamped and executed, (d) investigating the incumbrances and ancillary rights, and (e) undertaking Land charges searches.
- Title issues and problems must be dealt with methodically and systematically as they could have legal and financial implications such as liability for costs, or an impact on the value of the property, its use, enjoyment, marketability, and its value as security for lending purposes. Any title problems should be reported to the buyer, their mortgagee and, where appropriate, the surveyor, and suitable solutions should be sought.

■ KEY TERMS AND CONCEPTS

- registered title (**page 17**)
- unregistered title (**page 17**)
- official copies (**page 19**)
- search from date (**page 19**)
- property register (**page 19**)
- proprietorship register (**page 20**)
- class of title (**page 20**)
- restrictions (**page 21**)
- overriding interests (**page 21**)
- charges register (**page 21**)
- title deeds (**page 22**)

- epitome of title (**page 22**)
- good root of title (**page 22**)
- joint tenancy (**page 30**)
- tenancy in common (**page 30**)
- Form A restriction (**page 31**)
- assent (**page 34**)
- s 36 statement (**page 34**)
- indemnity insurance (**page 36**)

■ SQE1-STYLE QUESTIONS

QUESTION 1

A solicitor acts on the sale of a freehold property with unregistered title and is in the process of examining the title deeds and documents, to deduce title to the buyer's solicitor.

Which of the following would most likely provide the best and most appropriate root of title?

A   A conveyance of the property dated 28 December 1985.

B   An assent of the property dated 16 June 1989.

C   A mortgage of the property dated 28 December 1985.

D   A deed of gift of the property dated 10 January 2020.

E   A conveyance of the property dated 29 June 1972.

QUESTION 2

A solicitor acts on the purchase of a freehold property with unregistered title and is in the process of investigating title. The epitome of title includes the root of title, which is a conveyance dated 23 March 1972 made between (1) a man, and (2) the vendor (the 'Conveyance'). The Conveyance states that the property is subject to an easement granted in an earlier conveyance of the same property dated 15 September 1964 (the 'Second Conveyance') and made between (1) a woman, and (2) the man referred to in the Conveyance. A copy of the Second Conveyance has been provided, and no other parties are referred to in it. No Land charges search results have been provided with the epitome of title, and the names referred to are consistent throughout the documents.

Which of the following best describes the Land charges searches that the solicitor should undertake?

A   Searches against the woman from 1925 until 1964, the man from 1964 until 1972, and the vendor from 1972 until the current year.

B   Searches against the woman from 1926 until 1964, the man from 1964 until 1972, and the vendor from 1972 until the current year.

C   Searches against the man from 1964 until 1972, and the vendor from 1972 until the current year as these are the names referred to in the root of title.

D   Searches against the man from 1964 until 1972, and the vendor from 1972 until the current year. The solicitor will also need to see all other title deeds and documents covering the period from 1926 so that all other estate owners may be searched against.

E   Searches against the woman from 1926 until 1964 and the man from 1964 until 1972. The search against the vendor will be undertaken as a pre-completion search.

QUESTION 3

A solicitor acts on the purchase of a freehold residential property, title to which is registered at HM Land Registry. The solicitor, who has dealt with several properties on the same development, expects that the property will have the benefit of a legal right of way over a private shared driveway and other ancillary rights over the neighbouring land. They also expect that rights will have been reserved over the property for the benefit of neighbouring properties and that the property will be subject to restrictions on use and further development, originally imposed by the developer.

Which of the following best describes where information regarding these matters may be found in the official copy entries of title?

A   The rights granted will be referred to in the property register, and the rights reserved and the covenants will be referred to in the charges register.

B   The rights granted will be referred to in the proprietorship register, and the easements reserved and covenants will be referred to in the charges register.

C   The easements and covenants will be referred to in the charges register.

D   The rights granted will be referred to in the property register. The rights reserved should be referred to in the charges register, but they may also be referred to in the property register. The covenants will be referred to in the charges register.

E   The rights granted will be referred to in the property register, and the rights reserved and the covenants will be entered as a restriction in the proprietorship register or a notice in the charges register.

QUESTION 4

A solicitor acts on the purchase of a freehold commercial property (a convenience store), which is subject to a valid historic covenant dated 1932, preventing the sale of alcohol on the premises. The buyer is borrowing to fund the purchase, and a mortgage will be granted in favour of a high street lender. The current seller and former owners have been in breach of the covenant for over thirty years, and it would continue to be breached by the buyer if the purchase were to go ahead. However, replies to pre-contract enquiries of the seller have revealed that they do not know who has the benefit of the covenant, no notices have been served and no action has been taken or is anticipated in respect of the breach.

Which of the following best describes the most appropriate and cost-effective form of action?

A   The seller should be asked to approach the person with the benefit of the covenant to obtain consent or release of the covenant.

B   A suitable restrictive covenant indemnity insurance policy should be provided at the seller's expense.

C   The buyer should be advised to withdraw from the transaction.

D   The seller should be asked to deal with an application to the Upper Tribunal (Lands Chamber) for modification or discharge of the covenant.

E   The buyer should take a commercial view and continue with the transaction on the basis that the risk of enforcement action is not great.

QUESTION 5

A solicitor acts on the sale of a freehold property and the registered proprietors are a husband and wife. The wife has recently died, and the husband has decided to sell the property. There are no relevant restrictions in the proprietorship register.

Which of the following best describes the position as regards the sale?

A   The husband and wife held the beneficial interest in the property as tenants in common. Provided that a certified copy of the death certificate is provided, the husband may convey the property and the buyer will obtain good title.

B   The husband and wife held the beneficial interest in the property as tenants in common. Provided that a certified copy of the death certificate is provided, and an additional trustee is appointed to receive the sale proceeds, the husband may convey the property and the buyer will obtain good title.

C   The husband and wife held the beneficial interest in the property as joint tenants. Provided that a certified copy of the death certificate is provided, and an additional trustee is appointed to receive the sale proceeds, the husband may convey the property and the buyer will obtain good title.

D   The husband and wife held the beneficial interest in the property as joint tenants. Provided that a certified copy of the death certificate is provided, the husband may convey the property and the buyer will obtain good title.

E   The husband and wife held the beneficial interest in the property as tenants in common. Provided that a certified copy of the grant of representation, together with a certified copy of the death certificate are provided, the husband may convey the property and the buyer will obtain good title.

■ ANSWERS TO QUESTIONS

Answers to 'What do you know already?' questions at the start of the chapter

1) A good root of title is defined in s 44 Law of Property Act 1925 as a document that (a) is at least 15 years old; (b) deals with the whole of the legal and equitable/beneficial interest in the property; (c) provides an adequate and identifiable description of the property; and (d) does not cast doubt on the title.

2) Ancillary rights will usually appear in the property register, whereas adverse rights usually appear in the charges register, but may also be mixed in with ancillary rights in the property register. Restrictive covenants appear in the charges register.

3) Where land has unregistered title, Land charges searches (using form K15) must be made against all estate owners mentioned in the documents within the epitome of title for their years of ownership (unless search results have already been provided as part of the epitome of title). If the precise dates of ownership are unclear, then the buyer's solicitor should search back to the earliest date from which the relevant estate owner could have owned the property, or 1926 (the date the system was introduced). All versions of names within the deeds and the correct counties must be searched against.

4) False. In land with registered title, on a sale by the last surviving beneficial joint tenant, it will not be necessary to appoint an additional trustee to receive the capital monies and good title may be given, if evidence of death (a certified copy of the death certificate) is provided.

Answers to end-of-chapter SQE1-style questions

Question 1

The correct answer was A, if it satisfies all the requirements of a good root of title under s 44 of the Law of Property Act 1925 (LPA). The assent could also be used but it would be preferable to use the conveyance as it was a transaction for value and should therefore provide the 'double guarantee' that title will have been investigated twice. Therefore, option B is incorrect. It would be preferable to use the conveyance rather than the mortgage of the same date, as mortgages do not usually contain all necessary and relevant information in respect of the title. Therefore, option C is incorrect. Option D is incorrect as the document is too recent and would also not carry the 'double guarantee'. The 1972 conveyance could also be used (option E), but the 1985 conveyance would be the most appropriate document as it is the most recent document to potentially satisfy the requirements of s 44 of the LPA.

Question 2

The correct answer was B. All estate owners referred to in the epitome of title should be searched against for the relevant years, going back to 1926 (when the land charges system was introduced). As we do not know who owned the property before the woman, we need to use her name going back to this date. Option A is incorrect as although the first Land Charges Act was dated 1925, the system was not introduced until 1926. Option C is incorrect, as it does not refer to the earlier known estate owner from the epitome of title documents. Option D is incorrect, as this would go beyond the requirements of a good root of title in s 44 of the Law of Property Act 1925, although it would be the most cautious approach. There is a system of compensation in place for land charges that were not discoverable because the relevant names were not provided on deduction of title, but this is beyond the scope of this book. Option E is incorrect, as a search will usually be undertaken at both the pre-contract and pre-completion stages.

Question 3

The correct answer was D. The rights granted will always be referred to in the property register, as also suggested in options A and E (not the proprietorship register as suggested in option B). Option A is also partially correct as although rights *reserved* and covenants are usually referred to in the charges register (making options B and C partially correct), it is possible that rights reserved may be mixed in with rights granted in the property register, which makes option D the best answer. Option C is incorrect as it fails to distinguish between rights granted (ancillary rights, benefiting the property) and rights reserved (rights that benefit other land, but burden the property). Option E is also incorrect as the rights reserved and covenants will not be referred to as a restriction in the proprietorship register, and although a notice may be used to protect third party rights, covenants usually simply appear in the charges register.

Question 4

The correct answer was B. Option A is incorrect, as due to the age of the covenant it may be difficult to find who currently has the benefit of it. Furthermore, any approaches could put them on notice of a covenant about which they were not aware and could be counterproductive as it may mean that indemnity insurance would not be available at all or at a reasonable cost. This option would therefore be costly and time consuming, as would option D. Although the age of the covenant would work in favour of a successful application for modification or discharge, such an outcome cannot be guaranteed. If the value of the property were particularly high, this may have been worth pursuing. In the circumstances, option C would be quite drastic, particularly as indemnity insurance may be available at reasonable cost. Option E is also incorrect as in the circumstances this is not just the buyer's decision to make. The covenant could have an impact on use, enjoyment, marketability, and value for secured lending purposes, so the lender's requirements would need to be consulted and a report/disclosure made to them.

Question 5

The correct answer was D. In the case of co-ownership, the legal title will always be held as joint tenants and the equitable/beneficial interest may be held as either joint tenants or tenants in common. As there is no Form A restriction in the proprietorship register, they held the equitable interest as joint tenants (therefore options A, B and E are incorrect in this respect, although option C is correct). Provided that a certified copy of the death certificate is produced, the husband may convey good title and a second trustee would not need to be appointed (as suggested in option C). In the case of a sale by the sole surviving *tenant in common*, an additional trustee would need to be appointed to effect overreaching (reference to this is omitted in option A), and a certified copy of the death certificate would also need to be provided (as set out in all options). Option B would have been correct had the beneficial interest been owned as tenants in common. Option E would have been incorrect had the beneficial interest been held as tenants in common, as the appointment of an additional trustee would satisfy the requirements of the Form A restriction.

■ KEY CASES, RULES, STATUTES, AND INSTRUMENTS

The SQE1 Assessment Specification does not require you to know any statutory authorities or specific case names for this topic. Specific sections of statutes are set out for ease of reference.

3

Pre-contract (2): searches and enquiries and planning matters

■ MAKE SURE YOU KNOW

This chapter provides an overview of the range and purpose of making pre-contract searches and raising pre-contract enquiries. It covers who makes the searches and raises the enquiries and how to deal with issues surrounding the results (problems and solutions). The chapter then goes on to deal with core principles of planning law, including what does and does not fall within the statutory definition of 'development', when planning permission and/or building regulations approval are/are not required, and enforcement of planning and building control law (including the time limits and the range of the local authority's enforcement powers). For the SQE1 assessments, you will need to understand the detail of each of these elements as well as how they fit into the bigger process (see **Chapter 1**).

■ SQE ASSESSMENT ADVICE

For SQE1, you are required to understand the need for pre-contract searches and enquiries, what they reveal, and how to deal with the results. You also need to have a sound understanding of core principles of planning and building control law, so you can advise on the requirements relating to past or proposed works.

As you work through this chapter, remember to pay particular attention in your revision to:
- The pre-contract searches and enquiries that are generally required for all conveyancing transactions.
- The additional/optional pre-contract searches and enquiries that are applicable, relevant or advisable for different types of conveyancing transactions.
- Interpreting the results of searches and enquiries and finding solutions for problems.
- The definition of 'development' under planning legislation, and when planning permission and/or building regulations approval are required.
- Enforcement powers and time limits under planning and building control legislation.
- Finding solutions for planning problems.

■ WHAT DO YOU KNOW ALREADY?

Attempt these questions before reading this chapter. If you find some difficult or cannot remember the answers, remember to look more closely at that topic during your revision.

1) Which pre-contract searches and enquiries are relevant to all conveyancing transactions?

   [Pre-contract searches and enquiries, page 50]

2) Which search(es) will reveal whether the roads abutting the property are adopted and maintainable at public expense and whether the property is connected to the mains water supply, with both foul and surface water draining to public sewers?

   [Pre-contract searches and enquiries, page 50]

3) True or false? Planning permission will always be required for building work on a property.

   [Definition of development – when planning permission is required, page 67]

4) True or false? The erection of a small rear extension or conservatory will not usually require planning permission.

   [Matters that do not require express planning permission, page 69]

PRE-CONTRACT SEARCHES AND ENQUIRIES

For the purposes of SQE1, you need to know why pre-contract searches and enquiries are carried out/raised. They are usually undertaken by the buyer's solicitor, to ascertain as much information as possible about the property from the seller (pre-contract enquiries) and third parties (pre-contract searches). The buyer's solicitor needs to carry them out due to the principle of caveat emptor (see **Chapter 1**). Although a seller may be liable in misrepresentation for misleading replies to enquiries, they are generally under no duty positively to disclose adverse matters, save for specified incumbrances affecting the title (see **Chapter 4**).

There are some searches and enquiries that are undertaken for all transactions and some that apply in certain circumstances only (see summary in **Table 3.1**). For SQE1, you need to be able to understand which searches and enquiries would be appropriate in given circumstances. You also need to be aware of how to deal with typical search results, so that problems/issues may be dealt with, and the buyer may make an informed decision as to purchase. Adverse search results may have ongoing financial and practical implications, including an impact on the value of the property, its use, enjoyment, and marketability, as well as its value as security for lending purposes (the 'usual concerns'). They should therefore also be reported to any lender and, in some circumstances, the surveyor. If problems cannot be resolved to the buyer's satisfaction, they may withdraw from the transaction prior to exchange of contracts taking place and them becoming committed to the purchase (see **Chapter 4**).

Table 3.1: Summary of pre-contract searches and enquiries

Search	Applicable in all situations?
Enquiries before contract	Yes – Also consider additional property/ transaction-specific enquiries.
Personal inspection/survey	Yes
Local search (in two parts)	Yes – Also consider optional enquiries.
Water/drainage search	Yes
Environmental search	Yes
Flood search	Yes
Chancel repair liability search	Often routine but particularly important where no prior disposal for value since 13 October 2013. Insurance may be more cost effective.
Mining search(es)	In mining areas or where mines and minerals are excepted and reserved from the title.
Canal and River Trust/ Environment Agency/ Natural Resources Wales search	Where property is near/adjacent to a river or canal.
Commons registration search	Where open land is nearby, or property constructed on a greenfield site.
Highways search	Where there is a potential gap between the property and the highway.
Railways search	Where the property is near/adjacent to a railway line and development works are proposed.
Index map search	Where the title is apparently unregistered or where mines and minerals are excepted and reserved from the title.
Land charges searches	Where the title is unregistered.
Company search	Where the seller is a company, or title is unregistered and the epitome of title reveals company estate owners. Also, where the buyer is a company, and a lender is involved.
Bankruptcy/insolvency search	Where a lender is involved.

Enquiries before contract

Enquiries before contract are raised routinely in all transactions.

Key term: enquiries before contract

These are enquiries raised by the buyer's solicitor of the seller's solicitor and concern information that should be known to the seller. They will vary according to the nature of the property (eg whether it is residential or commercial, freehold or leasehold, or subject to tenancies). They provide useful information that may not usually be available from third parties, or the title documents.

Residential property

For solicitors using the Law Society Conveyancing Protocol (see **Chapter 1**), standard protocol forms (property information forms) will be used. They are also widely used even where the Protocol is not adopted, and they are summarised in **Table 3.2**.

Table 3.2: Pre-contract Protocol forms

TA6 – *Property information form*
This is routinely used in most conveyancing transactions. It contains questions on boundaries and fences, disputes and complaints, notices and proposals, alterations, planning, building control and use, guarantees and warranties, insurance, environmental matters and flooding, rights and informal arrangements, parking, other charges, occupiers, services and facilities, and transaction information.
TA10 – *Fittings and contents form*
This is routinely used in most conveyancing transactions. It details fixtures that are to be removed and fittings that are to be included in the sale.
TA7 – *Leasehold information form*
This raises additional enquiries applicable to leasehold property.
TA8 – *New home information form*
This form is for new/recently built properties.

The Law Society also produces form LPE1 (leasehold property enquiries form) and LPE2 (buyer's leasehold information summary form). The former serves a similar purpose to form TA7 and the latter is designed to help report leasehold information to the buyer.

It is important to be familiar with these forms, and copies can be viewed at www.lawsociety.org.uk.

Some solicitors may have more detailed, standard enquiries, which supplement the protocol forms or are used instead.

Aside from standard pre-contract enquiries, the buyer's solicitor will also raise any *additional enquiries* that may result from the replies to enquiries and the results of pre-contract searches (see **Results of searches and enquiries**).

Commercial property

For commercial properties, more detailed enquiries may be used, and it is common to use the Commercial Property Standard Enquiries (CPSEs), which are approved by the British Property Federation. The main CPSEs to be aware of are summarised in **Table 3.3**.

Table 3.3: CPSE enquiries

CPSE1
General enquiries for all commercial property transactions. (Note that CPSE7 provides a shorter form for more straightforward transactions).
CPSE2
Additional enquiries for property subject to commercial tenancies.
CPSE3
Additional enquiries on the grant of a new lease (see **Chapter 7**).
CPSE4
Additional enquiries on the assignment of a lease (see **Chapter 7**).

CPSE1 or CPSE7 enquiries are raised in most transactions, with the additional enquiries raised where applicable. They are more detailed than standard residential enquiries before contract and include questions on VAT (see **Chapter 10**).

Personal inspection and survey

A buyer should always be advised to carry out a **personal inspection** of the property before exchange of contracts.

Key term: personal inspection

A personal inspection should be used to ascertain the physical state and condition of the property as well as to check its extent/boundaries, confirm its contents, and check for third-party occupiers as well as both adverse and ancillary rights (see **Chapter 2**) (eg is there any evidence of third-party rights being exercised and are ancillary easements freely exercisable?).

It is only on very rare occasions that a solicitor will make a personal inspection of the property. However, this can be invaluable, and the costs justified, in some commercial transactions (eg where a site is being acquired for development).

A buyer should also be advised on whether to commission a survey of the property before exchange of contracts (see **Chapter 1**).

Local search

A local search is made routinely in all transactions. It is submitted to the local authority, together with a plan of the property and the associated fee. It is comprised of two parts – a **local land charges search** and **enquiries of the local authority**.

Key term: local land charges search (form LLC1)

The local land charges search provides details of financial charges or restrictions on the use of the land imposed by public authorities under statute and known to the local authority. There are twelve parts to the register of local land charges and they include general and specific financial charges, planning charges, miscellaneous charges, land compensation charges, listed buildings charges, and drainage scheme charges.

The most common things likely to be revealed by the search are planning consents with conditions attached to them, financial charges, enforcement notices, tree preservation orders, compulsory purchase orders, the designation of listed buildings and conservation areas, and whether a smoke control order is in place (see **Results of searches and enquiries**).

Key term: enquiries of the local authority (form CON29)

There are two parts to the enquiries of the local authority:
- The first part is standard enquiries of the local authority (form CON29). These are routinely raised in all transactions. CON29 provides information in relation to planning and building regulations decisions and pending applications and restrictions on development, listed building and conservation area consents, planning designations and proposals for the area, the adoption of roads and footpaths, public rights of way, whether the land is required for public purposes or road works, drainage matters, nearby road, railway and traffic schemes, outstanding notices, contraventions of building regulations, planning notices, orders, directions and proceedings, conservation areas, compulsory purchase orders, and contaminated land notices.
- The second part is comprised of optional enquiries of the local authority (form CON29O) which a solicitor may choose to raise based

on the property/transaction/circumstances. CON29O provides several property-specific enquiries, including environmental and pollution notices, food safety notices, and commons registration (see **Commons registration search**, below). The need for these should be considered on a case-by-case basis.

The most common things likely to be revealed by the search are planning and building regulations approvals, Article 4 Directions (see **Matters that do not require express planning permission**), listed building and conservation area consents, and the adoption of roads and footpaths (see **Results of searches and enquiries**).

Revision tip

It should be pointed out to the buyer that the results of the local search do not extend to adjoining and/or neighbouring properties; so for example, they will not reveal proposals for a change of use of, and/or construction works on, such properties, which may affect the use and enjoyment of the property.

Revision tip

Under the Infrastructure Act 2015, HM Land Registry is set to become the sole authority for keeping and maintaining the register of local land charges, taking the responsibility away from local authorities and centralising the register and searches of it. The process is not yet complete and details of progress to date can be found by searching for 'local land charges programme' at www.gov.uk. At the time of writing, several local authorities have completed the migration process.

Water/drainage search

A **water/drainage search** is made routinely in all transactions. It is submitted to the local water authority/company, together with a plan of the property and the associated fee.

Key term: water/drainage search (form CON29DW)

A water/drainage search confirms whether foul and surface water drain to public sewers (ie whether the drains and sewers have been adopted), whether the property is connected to the mains water supply and what charges are payable (eg whether the supply is metered). It will also reveal details of any assets owned by the local water authority and which are within the boundaries (eg sewers). The local water authority will have statutory rights of access to these, and they may restrict the development potential of the property.

If the drains and sewers serving the property are not adopted, the buyer will be responsible for their maintenance. They may also be liable for bringing them up to an adoptable standard should the water authority elect to adopt them (see **Results of searches and enquiries**).

If there have been any building works over local water authority assets (these are shown on the plan(s) annexed to the report), a copy of the consent to build over should be obtained. If not obtained, retrospective consent or a suitable indemnity insurance policy (see **Chapter 2**) would be recommended.

Environmental search

An **environmental search** is made routinely in most transactions. It is submitted to an environmental search provider together with a plan of the property and the associated fee.

Key term: environmental search

An environmental search is usually a desk-top report that compiles data and outlines whether the property is likely to be classed as 'contaminated land' under the Environmental Protection Act 1990. It may also give further information, eg in relation to ground stability and flooding.

Exam warning

For SQE1, you should be aware of the need to inform a buyer of the provisions of the Environmental Protection Act 1990 in relation to contaminated land. The Act gives the local authority power to carry out investigations and designate land as contaminated, requiring it to be remediated. The overriding principle under the Act is that the 'polluter pays' for remediation of contamination that it causes. The problem is that if the polluter cannot be found, is insolvent, or no longer exists, liability may fall on the owner or occupier.

Revision tip

Although the local search (CON29 and CON29O) will reveal whether the land has already been designated as contaminated and any associated notices served, the environmental search will reveal whether such designation is likely in the future.

Adverse results will require investigation and it may be necessary to commission a more detailed investigation/survey, involving a site visit and the taking and analysis of samples. An indemnity insurance policy, provided at the seller's expense, may also be a solution to cover the potential risks involved. In any event, the results should be reported to the buyer, their mortgagee, and potentially the surveyor, as the usual concerns will apply (see above).

Flood search

A **flood search** is made routinely in most transactions. It is submitted to a private search provider together with a plan of the property and the associated fee.

Key term: flood search

A flood search reveals whether the property is, or is likely to be, affected by river/coast/surface water or groundwater flooding. A basic flood search may be incorporated within an environmental search.

If a property is close to a river or the coast, then the need for a flood search will be self-evident. However, groundwater and surface water flooding (eg in the event of heavy rainfall) can happen in any location. Therefore, a flood search is always advisable, in conjunction with enquiries of the seller.

Aside from the potential for inconvenience and disruption, a key concern will be whether buildings insurance covering flooding as an insured risk will be available at reasonable rates. A government scheme, known as Flood Re provides some assurance that insurance will be available for owner-occupiers of residential properties. However, it does have some limitations (eg it does not cover properties built after 1 January 2009, buy-to-let and commercial properties, and most leasehold blocks).

A further and more detailed report may need to be commissioned if a risk is identified and a basic environmental report may contain such recommendations. In all cases, adverse results will need to be reported to the client, the client's mortgagee, and their surveyor.

Chancel repair liability search

A **chancel repair liability search** is made routinely in most transactions (even where it may not strictly be necessary – see below). It is submitted to a private search provider together with a plan of the property and the associated fee.

Key term: chancel repair liability search

This search reveals whether the property is, or is likely to be, affected by liability to contribute towards the costs of repairing and maintaining the chancel (a specific part) of a medieval parish church that may happen to be in the vicinity.

Whether a chancel repair liability search is strictly necessary will depend on the date of the last disposition (eg transfer) for value. Prior to 13 October 2013, chancel repair liability was an overriding interest on both first registration and for registered dispositions (see **Chapter 2**), so it was automatically binding on a buyer for valuable consideration. The position changed on and after this date:

- In *registered land*, chancel repair liability is no longer an overriding interest and requires protection by a *notice in the charges register* (see **Chapter 2**). Notices can now only validly protect chancel repair liability if there has been no transfer for value on or after 13 October 2013.
- In *unregistered land*, chancel repair liability is no longer an overriding interest and requires protection by reference in the title documents (see **Chapter 2**) or a *caution against first registration*. Cautions can now only validly protect chancel repair liability if there has been no transfer for value on or after 13 October 2013. An index map search (see **Index map search (SIM)**) will reveal any cautions against first registration.

If there is *no notice or caution* against first registration, upon the next transfer for value on or after 13 October 2013, liability will no longer be protected.

Therefore, if there is *no notice or caution* against first registration/reference in the deeds *and there has been a prior transfer for value* on or after 13 October 2013, there will be no liability.

If there is *no notice or caution* against first registration *and no previous transfer for value* on or after 13 October 2013, there is the remote possibility of a notice or caution being entered before completion and registration of title.

In any event, there is also the possibility of a protective unilateral notice being entered in due course, which a buyer would need to contest. This is because HM Land Registry does not guarantee the validity of any right to register a notice and may therefore enter one even if the applicant is not entitled to it (eg because of a prior disposition for value).

Despite the relatively low risks involved, some firms routinely carry out chancel repair liability searches, with an indemnity insurance policy being recommended if potential liability is uncovered. Insurance is usually available at a relatively small cost, so sometimes it is more cost effective simply to put this in place and not even undertake a search.

A suggested approach to questions on chancel repair liability is set out in **Figure 3.1**, and **Practice example 3.1** brings some of these points together.

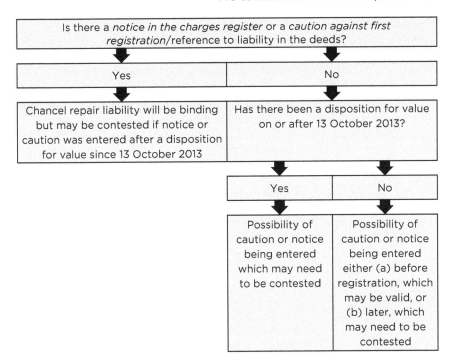

Figure 3.1: Chancel repair liability on a purchase for valuable consideration

Practice example 3.1

You act on the purchase of a freehold property with registered title, and the chancel repair liability search has revealed potential liability. There is no reference to such liability in the title.

How will you deal with this?

If there has been a prior transfer for value on or after 13 October 2013, the potential liability should not be binding on the buyer. If there has been no prior transfer for value on or after 13 October 2013, the potential liability could be binding on the buyer if a notice is registered before completion and registration of title. In any event, there is the possibility that a notice may still be entered, as HM Land Registry will not take steps to assess the validity of such an application. It may be more cost effective to insure against the potential risk.

Mining searches

A **mining search** should be made for transactions involving properties in mining areas. It is submitted to the Coal Authority or via a private search provider, together with a plan of the property and the associated fee.

Key term: mining search (form CON29M)

A mining search reveals details of past and proposed mining activity within the proximity of the property, including underground workings and any mine shafts (treated or untreated – eg 'capped' to allow safe build-over) as well as any subsidence claims.

The first step will be to ascertain whether the property is in a former mining area, by consulting the Law Society's Coal Mining Directory or checking the postcode on the Coal Authority's website. The reservation of mines and minerals within the title (see **Chapter 2**) should also be a good indication of this.

Other mining searches may also be required in some areas (see **Table 3.4**).

Table 3.4: Other mining searches

Substance	Area(s)	Search provider
Tin	Cornwall, Devon, and Somerset	Cornwall Mining Consultants
Clay	Cornwall, Devon, and Dorset	Kaolin and Ball Clay Association
Limestone	Dudley, Sandwell, Walsall, Wolverhampton, and Telford and Wrekin	Relevant local authority
Brine/salt	Cheshire and Greater Manchester	Cheshire Salt Search

The usual concerns relate to mining activity, and the impact on structural stability is a key concern for a buyer and their mortgagee.

Canal and River Trust/Environment Agency/Natural Resources Wales search

If the property is situated next to a canal or a river, a **Canal and River Trust/ Environment Agency/Natural Resources Wales search** may be made, accompanied by a plan and the necessary fee.

Key term: Canal and River Trust/Environment Agency/ Natural Resources Wales search

This is a search of the Canal and River Trust (for canals), the Environment Agency (for rivers in England) or Natural Resources Wales (for rivers in Wales) to ascertain liability for the repair, rebuilding, or maintenance of the waterways, banks, and towpaths, any adverse rights over the property, and the ownership of boundaries. The search may also reveal details of past flooding.

Commons registration search

If the property has been constructed recently on a greenfield site, is on the edge of an urban area, or has open space adjacent to or within the vicinity of it, a **commons registration search** will be essential (as an optional enquiry as part of the local search – CON29O, question 22).

> **Key term: commons registration search**
>
> This search reveals whether the property is designated as common land or a town or village green, to which the general public have access and possibly rights of use. If so, development or enclosure of the land will not be permitted, and its use and value etc will inevitably be affected.

Highways search

If there are any concerns that the property does not immediately abut a highway maintainable at public expense, a **highways search** can be commissioned of the local highways authority, accompanied by a plan and the required fee.

> **Key term: highways search**
>
> A search of the local highways authority which confirms the precise extent of the publicly maintainable highway, so far as it relates to the property.

Although the CON29 part of the local search reveals whether the roads abutting the property are maintainable at public expense, it does not necessarily cover verges and pavements. Therefore, if there is a significant gap between the property and the road (eg a grass verge), a highways search should be undertaken. These gaps are commonly known as 'ransom strips' as the owner of the land may be able to prevent access being made and could potentially demand a fee to sell the land or grant access. This is particularly important when acquiring land for development.

Railways

If a property is located close to a railway line, Network Rail will need to be consulted about any proposed development work close to the boundary. Specific enquiries should also be made of the seller as to whether any notices have been served by Network Rail and whether any payments have been paid, made, demanded, or are anticipated in respect of the maintenance of boundary features.

If the results of the local search reveal a proposed rail scheme (eg HS2 – www .hs2.org.uk), they will usually state where further information may be obtained.

Index map search (SIM)

If the title to the property or part of it is or appears to be *unregistered*, an **index map search** should be submitted to HM Land Registry, together with a plan and the fee, to verify this.

Key term: index map search

A search of the index map (SIM) to ascertain details of any registered title(s) affecting the property, any pending applications for registration, and cautions against registration.

A SIM should also be undertaken if mines/minerals are reserved from the title (see above and **Chapter 2**) and can be useful for complex sites (eg where there are a number of registered titles, to make sure that all land is within the relevant titles).

Land charges searches

If the title to the property is unregistered, **Land charges searches** should be made against all relevant estate owners (see **Chapter 2**).

Key term: land charges searches

A search of the land charges register held by the Land Charges Department in Plymouth, using form K15 to identify land charges that could be binding on a buyer.

Company search

In *both* registered and unregistered land, if the seller is a company, a **company search** must be made at Companies House.

In *unregistered land*, company searches should also be made against all corporate owners referred to in the epitome of title (see **Chapter 2**).

If *acting for a lender*, a company search should be made against the *buyer*.

Key term: company search

A company search checks whether the company is in existence, subject to any insolvency proceedings or procedures, and whether it has granted any fixed or floating charges over its assets (see *Revise SQE: Business Law and*

Practice and **Chapter 5**). At this stage, it should also be checked whether the company is able to enter into the transaction under its constitutional documents and who the officers/directors are.

Bankruptcy/insolvency search

Although usually pre-completion searches (see **Chapter 5, Insolvency searches – registered and unregistered land**), bankruptcy/insolvency searches may also be undertaken at the pre-exchange stage and repeated pre-completion. They are necessary where the buyer is borrowing to fund the acquisition.

Summary

Table 3.1 provides a summary of pre-contract searches and enquiries, and **Practice example 3.2** brings some of these points together.

Practice example 3.2

You act on the purchase of a freehold property with registered title in the Metropolitan Borough of Sandwell, near to Dudley. The property is in an established industrial and former coal mining area and in the centre of town, adjacent to the highway. There is a railway line and a canal nearby and both the seller and the buyer are individuals. The buyer is borrowing from a commercial lender to fund the acquisition.

Which searches and enquiries should you undertake?

You should undertake enquiries of the seller/enquiries before contract and recommend a personal inspection/survey. You should also carry out a local search (in two parts, considering any appropriate optional enquiries), water/drainage search, environmental search (particularly as this is an industrial area), and flood search. You should undertake a chancel repair liability search (as there is no information on the last disposition for valuable consideration), a coal mining search (the property is in a former mining area), a limestone search (the property is in Sandwell), a Canal and River Trust search (due to the canal), a railways search if development works are proposed (due to the railway), and a bankruptcy-only search (as the buyer is borrowing to fund the acquisition). A highways search should not be necessary as the property abuts the highway, and an index map search and Land charges searches should not be relevant as the title is registered. A company search should not be required as the property is registered, and both the buyer and seller are individuals. A commons registration search should not be a concern based on the description of the location.

RESULTS OF SEARCHES AND ENQUIRIES

For SQE1, you should be aware of some of the key problems commonly revealed from search and enquiry results/replies and the potential solutions. All problems should be investigated and reported to the client, their mortgagee and, if relevant, the surveyor.

Planning permissions and building regulations approvals

The buyer's solicitor should seek, from the seller's solicitor, copies of all planning permissions, building regulations approvals, and the associated certificates of compliance/completion certificates (see **Core principles of planning law**), in respect of works carried out on the property (as referred to in the local search and replies to pre-contract enquiries). Additional enquiries should be made as to whether permissions have been implemented/works completed and planning conditions complied with. It should also be asked whether any notices have been served or whether any action is anticipated.

The buyer's solicitor should also consider the need for planning permission in respect of proposed works or a change of use.

Adoption of roads

If the property does not abut a highway maintainable at public expense, then it should first be ascertained whether the property enjoys suitable ancillary rights in the title documents (see **Chapter 2**).

The risk to a buyer is that the local authority may seek to adopt the roadway in the future and the frontagers (the owners of properties served by the roadway) may be liable for the costs of bringing it into an adoptable condition.

Exam warning

Adoption of roads is a common issue for newbuild properties. The developer should agree in the contract to make them up to an adoptable standard without cost to the buyer. If the roads are not to remain private (see **Revision tip** below), there should also be an agreement in place under s 38 Highways Act 1980 between the developer and the local highways authority, supported by a financial bond to cover the developer's obligations should they become insolvent before bringing the highway up to an adoptable standard. In the absence of an agreement and bond, a mortgage lender may seek to make a retention from the mortgage advance to cover the potential cost.

Adoption of sewers

If foul and surface water from the property do not drain to public sewers, enquiries should be made about the alternative arrangements (eg there may be a private septic tank).

Tree preservation orders

If trees on the property are subject to a tree preservation order, details of the order and the protected trees should be ascertained. The buyer should also be made aware that it will usually be a criminal offence to lop or fell protected trees.

Smoke control order

A smoke control order is a very common and relatively uncontroversial type of local land charge, which is not normally a concern to a buyer. The practical implications are that only smokeless or other authorised fuels may be combusted on the property.

Listed buildings and conservation areas

If the property is a listed building or is in a conservation area (see **Listed buildings** and **Conservation areas**), this will mean that the use and development of the property may be limited, and it will be more difficult to make changes that would otherwise be relatively straightforward to make.

Occupiers

Any non-owning adult occupiers may have a beneficial interest in the property or other statutory rights (see **Chapter 2**). They should therefore be required to sign a waiver/release of their rights and an agreement to vacate on completion. This is usually dealt with as a special condition within the contract (see **Chapter 4**).

NATIONAL LAND INFORMATION SERVICE

The National Land Information Service (NLIS) is a collaboration between local authorities in England and Wales, HM Land Registry, water companies, and other organisations such as Companies House, the Environment Agency, and the Coal Authority. It brings information held by them together to make the search process easier and more cost effective. The information can be accessed through service providers known as 'licensed channels'.

CORE PRINCIPLES OF PLANNING LAW

For SQE1, you need to understand the definition of 'development' under planning legislation, as well as when planning permission and/or building regulations approval are required. You also need to appreciate the enforcement powers and time limits under planning and building control legislation, as well as be able to provide solutions to planning problems uncovered as part of the conveyancing process.

Planning permission is generally required for development (which includes construction and building works, as well as some changes of use), and building regulations approval is also required for most building works. Investigation of the planning and building regulations position is important, as obligations (including conditions attached to planning permissions) run with the land, so will bind a buyer. It follows that the benefit of them will also usually pass to a buyer.

A buyer's solicitor must therefore check whether all permissions and approvals are in place, whether there are any conditions attached to planning permissions, and whether they have been complied with. They must also check whether the property is listed or is within a conservation area and that all necessary permissions and approvals are in place. In addition, a solicitor must also be able to advise on the need for permissions and approvals for future works or changes of use.

Definition of development – when planning permission is required

Planning permission is required for **development** (s 57(1) Town and Country Planning Act 1990 (TCPA 1990)), so it is important to understand its statutory definition.

Key term: development

Development 'means the carrying out of building, engineering, mining or other operations in, on, over or under land, or the making of any material change in the use of any buildings or other land' (s 55 TCPA 1990).

Therefore, development covers two key areas: the carrying on of building works etc. (*operational development*), including demolition, rebuilding, structural alterations or additions (eg extensions), and other operations normally undertaken by a person carrying on business as a builder (s 55 (1A) TCPA 1990); and a material change of use (*change of use*).

Revision tip

It is a requirement of SQE1 that you are aware of the definition of development as it is referred to in the Assessment Specification.

Matters that do not constitute development

There are excluded from the definition, **matters that do not constitute development**.

Key term: matters that do not constitute development

These do not usually require planning permission and include (amongst others) the following:

- The carrying out for the maintenance, improvement, or other alteration of any building, of works which (a) affect only the interior of the building; or (b) do not materially affect the external appearance of the building (s 55 (2)(a) TCPA 1990) (*internal works*). (Note there is an exception for the development of larger mezzanine floors).
- The use of any buildings or other land within the curtilage of (ie immediately surrounding) a dwellinghouse for any purpose incidental to the enjoyment of the dwellinghouse as such (*incidental use*) (s 55(2)(d) TCPA 1990).
- Change of the primary use within the same use class (see below) (a *non-material change of use*) (s 55(2)(f) TCPA 1990).

Practice example 3.3 brings some of these points together.

Practice example 3.3

You act for a client who proposes to convert their spare bedroom by installing fitted office furniture for home working.

What is the planning position?

The work should not constitute development as it is interior-only and will not materially affect the external appearance of the building. The use as a home office will only involve business use which will be incidental/ancillary to the main residential use, so it should not constitute a material change of use.

Use classes

For SQE1, you should be aware of the main **use classes**.

Key term: use classes

The Town and Country Planning (Use Classes) Order 1987 (TCP(UC)O) (as amended) divides uses into the following broad categories:

* B – *General industrial* (B2) and *storage or distribution* (B8).
* C – *Residential uses* (including hotels, houses, residential institutions, and houses in multiple occupation).
* E – *Commercial, business and service* (including shops (other than shops for the sale of hot food but including the sale of food and drink for consumption on the premises), financial, professional, health and medical services, offices, light industrial and research/development).
* F – *Schools, places of learning and/or worship and non-residential institutions and community facilities* (including small essential shops in remote areas with no other similar facility within 1km).

A change of use *within* the same use class does not require planning permission.

If a use does not fall within one of the use classes, then express planning permission will always be required. This includes pubs, bars, night clubs, hot food takeaways, bingo halls, cinemas, concert halls, dance halls, and live music venues. These are often referred to as *sui generis* uses from the Latin meaning 'unique' or 'of its own kind'.

A change of use *between* classes usually requires express planning permission, although this may come under permitted development in some circumstances (see **Matters that do not require express planning permission**).

Revision tip

It is important to be aware that the use classes under the TCP(UC)O can change from time to time under statutory instrument. The most recent significant changes in England were made in 2020, and so it is important to check for updates prior to sitting the SQE1 assessments. The classes do vary in Wales (see www.gov.wales), but the detail is outside the scope of this book. It is also important to distinguish between *matters that do not constitute development* and *matters that do not require express planning permission*. Express planning permission is not required for both, but the latter still constitute development.

Matters that do not require express planning permission

Matters that do not require express planning permission are generally permitted under the Town and Country Planning (General Permitted Development) Order 2015 (the GPDO).

Key term: matters that do not require express planning permission (permitted development)

These are matters that do not require express planning permission, but still constitute development. They include (*inter alia*), the following:

- Small extensions, improvements or other alterations *within the curtilage of a dwelling house* (eg erection of a porch, an extension or conservatory). *It is important to note that these are subject to limitations and conditions, the detail of which is outside the scope of this book.*
- *Minor operations* (eg painting the exterior of a building and the erection of fences (subject to height limitations)).
- Certain *changes between use classes*. The detail of these is beyond the scope of this book and they are subject to change. In practice, the most up to date version of the GPDO should be checked on each occasion.

Although the GPDO automatically gives permission for certain permitted development, this is subject to there being an **Article 4 direction** in place.

Key term: Article 4 direction

An Article 4 direction revokes the GPDO in certain areas (in whole or in part) and will be revealed in the local search results. In such areas, express planning permission will always be required for development (including development which would otherwise normally be permitted under the GPDO), and more minor works.

Revision tip

Permitted development under the GPDO and Article 4 directions are key concepts that you should be aware of for the purposes of SQE1. It is not necessary to know the detail behind the GPDO, as, in practice, it would be normal to consult the GPDO where required. The detail is beyond the scope of this book and is also different in Wales (see www.gov.wales). However, you should be aware of the key principles.

Figure 3.2 provides a summary of the need for planning permission and **Practice example 3.4** brings some of these points together.

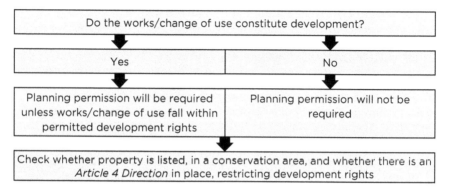

Figure 3.2: The need for planning permission

Practice example 3.4

You act for a client who proposes to erect a conservatory in their rear garden.

Will planning permission or any other relevant permission(s) or approvals be required?

The works will constitute development, although the erection of the conservatory *may* come under permitted development rights, for which express planning permission will not be required. The GPDO should be checked to see if the proposed development will fall within the relevant conditions and limitations. It should also be checked whether the property is listed, in a conservation area, or whether an Article 4 direction is in place. If listed, additional restrictions will apply, and if an Article 4 direction is in place or the property is in a conservation area, permitted development rights will likely not apply and express planning permission may be required. Although express planning permission will most likely otherwise not be required, the development may still require building regulations approval, which is a separate and distinct requirement.

Enforcement of planning law

For the purposes of SQE1, it is important to know the key enforcement powers available to the local authority and the time limits for the exercise of them.

As a precursor to taking action, the authority may enter the property and/or issue a **planning contravention notice**.

Key term: planning contravention notice

This is a request for information about any operations or activities on the property and potential breaches of planning control. It is an offence to fail to respond within 21 days of the notice or to provide false or misleading information in response to it.

If the local authority is satisfied that there has been a breach of planning control, it may issue a **completion notice, enforcement notice, stop notice, breach of condition notice**, or request an **injunction**.

Key term: completion notice

A planning permission for operational development will usually have a date by which it should be implemented (ie works commenced). If the local authority is concerned that development has stalled and that it will not be completed within a reasonable time, it may serve a completion notice. The notice requires the development to be completed within a specified reasonable time, failing which the planning permission will lapse.

Key term: enforcement notice

An enforcement notice may be issued where the local authority is satisfied that there has been a breach of planning control and that it is expedient for it to be issued. The notice should specify the breach and what steps are required to remedy it/which activities are to cease, and it must be served on the owner, occupier, and anyone with an interest in the property. It takes effect not less than 28 days after issue. It is a criminal offence to fail to comply with an enforcement notice, for which a fine will be payable, although a right of appeal may be available.

Key term: stop notice

A stop notice may only be issued following service of an enforcement notice. It requires the activities alleged to be in breach of planning control to cease, pending the enforcement notice taking effect or being appealed. A temporary stop notice (valid/effective immediately for 28 days) may also be issued if the local authority is satisfied that it is expedient for the activities to cease immediately. Contravention of a stop notice or temporary stop notice is a criminal offence, for which a fine may be payable. There is no right of appeal, although the validity and propriety of the decision to issue the notice may be challenged by way of judicial review.

Key term: breach of condition notice

A breach of condition notice may be issued by the local authority in the event of a breach of the conditions attached to a planning permission. It requires compliance with the conditions within a specified period. It is a criminal offence to fail to comply with a breach of condition notice and a fine may be payable. There is no right to appeal a breach of condition notice although the validity and propriety of the decision to issue the notice may be challenged by way of judicial review.

Key term: injunction

The local authority may apply to the court for an injunction when it considers it expedient to do so for an actual or apprehended breach of planning control. This is a discretionary, equitable remedy so may not always be granted if it is not necessary, proportionate or appropriate (eg if suitable alternative remedies would be available).

Time limits

For SQE1 it is important to understand the general time limits for the taking of enforcement action in the event of breach of planning control, which are as follows:

- *Operational development* – 4 years from substantial completion.
- *Unauthorised change of use to a single dwelling house* – 4 years from breach.
- *Any other breach* – (ie any other change of use or breaches of conditions) 10 years of the breach.

After these dates have passed, enforcement action may not normally be taken.

Practice example 3.5 brings together some of the points on enforcement.

Practice example 3.5

You act for a client who is purchasing a freehold house. Six years ago, a significant extension was built, for which conditional planning permission was obtained and implemented.

What is the position concerning enforcement of planning law?

The works constituted development and clearly did not fall within permitted development rights. The buyer will become liable for any breaches of planning law, following purchase. Although this is operational development, action may still be taken for breach of planning conditions within ten years of the breach. The building regulations position should also be ascertained.

Building control

Building regulations approval is a separate and distinct requirement to planning permission. Although most forms of operational development may also require building regulations approval, it may also be required for works that do not constitute development (eg interior works), or for which planning permission may not be required (eg small extensions).

Key term: building regulations approval

Building regulations approval is required for works of construction or significant alterations or extensions to buildings in order to ensure that they meet standards as to health and safety, design, permitted materials, and methods and standards of workmanship and construction.

Revision tip

Building regulations approval will usually be required for garage conversions, even though planning permission may not be necessary.

Works where building regulations approval is required include electrical installations, plumbing installations (not like-for-like replacements of bathroom fixtures), replacement windows and doors, heating systems, and replacement roofs.

Revision tip

Building regulations approval will not generally be required for conservatories if they are small (less than 30 square metres), are separated from the property with external quality walls, doors, and windows, and have an independent heating system. However, the electrical installations and any replacement glazing would be a separate matter.

Compliance with building regulations control involves an initial approval being granted to the proposed plans, with a building control officer inspecting the works and issuing a *certificate of compliance* (formerly known as a *completion certificate*) when the works are completed.

Revision tip

A system of self-certification of building regulations (competent person schemes) is applicable to certain trades and professions regulated by trade bodies. Most notably these include window installation (for replacement windows from 1 April 2002) provided through the Glass and Glazing Federation Self-Assessment scheme (FENSA), as well as other schemes for plumbing, heating, and electrical installations. Newbuild properties may also be subject to independent (e.g. NHBC) building control (in addition to defects insurance) rather than local authority building control.

Enforcement time limits

The time limit for the taking of enforcement action in the event of breach of building regulations control is two years from the completion of the work. An enforcement notice may also be issued within one year of completion of the work, requiring the works to be altered or removed. The local authority may also request an injunction *at any time* if the works are unsafe (s 36(6) Building Act 1984).

As a matter of course, copy building regulations approvals and certificates of compliance should be obtained in respect of all relevant works (as identified in the results of the local search and by enquiries before contract).

If all documentation is not in place, a suitable indemnity insurance policy may be an option to cover potential enforcement action being taken. However, it will not usually cover personal injury or business interruption.

Alternatively, a regularisation certificate (retrospective approval) may be requested from the local authority, indicating the work required to bring the property up to standard. This is an alternative course of action as it will usually be a condition of any indemnity insurance policy that approaches have not been made of the local authority.

However, as the power to request an injunction is not time limited, the buyer's surveyor should be asked to inspect the works and the buyer's mortgagee must be informed. The issue of structural soundness/safety could have an impact on use, enjoyment, value, marketability, and value as security for lending purposes.

Practice example 3.6 brings together some of these points.

Practice example 3.6

You act for a client who is purchasing a freehold detached house. The single integral garage was converted to a family room three years ago and the double glazing was changed throughout at the same time. The property is not listed or in a conservation area.

What is the position concerning planning permission and building regulations approval?

The garage conversion is not likely to constitute development provided that the conversion work was internal. It should be checked whether an Article 4 direction is in place. However, building regulations approval would be required as a separate and distinct requirement. Building regulations approval would also have been required for the replacement windows and a copy of the FENSA compliance certificate should be obtained. If either compliance certificate is not in place, indemnity insurance may be considered, although the works will be

immune from enforcement action. However, if any of the works are
unsafe, the local building control authority's power to take out an
injunction will be unlimited in time. The issues should be reported to
the buyer, the mortgagee, and their surveyor (if applicable).

Listed buildings

It is important for a buyer to ascertain whether the building and its curtilage is
listed as having special architectural and historic interest. This will be revealed
by the results of the local search.

The listing of the property will mean that listed building consent will be
required in addition to planning permission and may also be required for
internal works. The GPDO may also not apply to the property, so matters for
which express planning permission may not usually be required will require
express planning permission.

A copy of the listing should be obtained to uncover its extent and the nature
of the restrictions. The higher the listing, the more restrictions there will be.
Grade I is the highest listing followed by grade II* and grade II.

Conservation areas

It is important for a buyer to ascertain whether the property is situated in a
conservation area. This will be revealed by the results of the local search. The
designation of conservation areas serves to protect the special architectural
and historic interest of an area.

If a property is in a conservation area, additional planning restrictions will
usually be in place to curtail rights under the GPDO (eg restrictions on external
appearance). Consent will also be required to cut down, top or lop trees on
the property and for demolition of the property in any circumstances.

Further information regarding the precise restrictions should be obtained
from the local planning authority.

■ KEY POINT CHECKLIST

This chapter has covered the following key knowledge points. You can use these
to structure your revision, ensuring you recall the key details from each point:
* The buyer's solicitor usually carries out pre-contract searches and
  enquiries and some are generally required/recommended for all
  conveyancing transactions.
* Additional/optional pre-contract searches and enquiries may be applicable,
  relevant, or advisable for different types of conveyancing transactions.

- It is important to interpret and report to the buyer, lender and sometimes the surveyor, on the results of searches and enquiries, finding solutions for problems.
- Adverse search results may have ongoing financial and practical implications, including an impact on the value of the property, its use, enjoyment, and marketability as well as its value as security for lending purposes.
- Planning permission is generally required for 'development', which includes operational development and a material change of use.
- Some development may automatically be allowed without planning permission, under permitted development rights. However, sometimes such rights may be withdrawn on a local basis under an Article 4 direction.
- Additional restrictions may apply with listed buildings and within conservation areas.
- Building regulations approval is a separate and distinct requirement from planning permission for building works to ensure that such works meet standards of construction and safety.
- The local planning authority and building control departments have a range of enforcement powers with different time limits.
- If there have been breaches, solutions must be found (eg retrospective consent/approval or indemnity insurance).

■ KEY TERMS AND CONCEPTS

- enquiries before contract (**page 52**)
- personal inspection (**page 53**)
- local land charges search (**page 54**)
- enquiries of the local authority (**page 54**)
- water/drainage search (**page 55**)
- environmental search (**page 56**)
- flood search (**page 57**)
- chancel repair liability search (**page 57**)
- mining search (**page 60**)
- Canal and River Trust/Environment Agency/Natural Resources Wales search (**page 60**)
- commons registration search (**page 61**)
- highways search (**page 61**)
- index map search (**page 62**)
- Land charges searches (**page 62**)
- company search (**page 62**)
- development (**page 67**)
- matters that do not constitute development (**page 67**)
- use classes (**page 68**)
- matters that do not require express planning permission (permitted development) (**page 69**)

- Article 4 direction (**page 69**)
- planning contravention notice (**page 71**)
- completion notice (**page 71**)
- enforcement notice (**page 71**)
- stop notice (**page 71**)
- breach of condition notice (**page 72**)
- injunction (**page 72**)
- building regulations approval (**page 73**)

■ SQE1-STYLE QUESTIONS

QUESTION 1

A solicitor acts on the purchase of a freehold property used for residential purposes. The property is not a listed building or in a conservation area and there is no Article 4 direction in place. The client plans to carry out internal works to the property so that it can be used for commercial purposes and has asked whether planning permission will be required.

Which of the following best describes the position?

A   The client will not require express planning permission for the internal works as they do not constitute 'development'. However, the change of use does constitute 'development' and express planning permission will be required.

B   The client will not require planning permission for the internal works or the change of use as they do not constitute 'development' for planning purposes.

C   The client will require express planning permission for the internal works and the change of use as they both constitute 'development' for planning purposes.

D   The client will not require planning permission for the internal works as they fall within the definition of 'permitted development'. However, the change of use does constitute a material change of use and express planning permission will be required.

E   The client will not require planning permission for the internal works or the change of use as they both constitute 'permitted development' for planning purposes.

QUESTION 2

A solicitor acts on the purchase of a modern freehold residential property. The seller built a conservatory and installed replacement windows approximately one year ago and the buyer has plans to carry out some internal structural alterations. The property is not listed, is not in a conservation area, and there is no Article 4 direction in place.

Which of the following best describes the position?

A   Planning permission would not have been required for the erection of the conservatory, as it does not constitute development. However, building regulations approval would have been required for both the conservatory and the replacement windows. The internal structural alterations will not require planning permission as they do not constitute development, but they will require building regulations approval.

B   Planning permission would not have been required for the erection of the conservatory if it fell within the limits of permitted development. However, building regulations approval would have been required for both the conservatory and the replacement windows. The internal structural alterations will not require planning permission as they fall within permitted development, but they will require building regulations approval.

C   Planning permission would not have been required for the erection of the conservatory if it fell within the limits of permitted development. However, building regulations approval may have been required for the conservatory and will have been required for the replacement windows. The internal structural alterations will not require planning permission as they do not constitute development, but they will require building regulations approval.

D   Planning permission would not have been required for the erection of the conservatory if it fell within the limits of permitted development. However, building regulations approval would have been required for the conservatory. The internal structural alterations will not require planning permission as they do not constitute development, but they will require building regulations approval.

E   Planning permission would not have been required for the erection of the conservatory if it fell within the limits of permitted development. However, building regulations approval would have been required for the replacement windows. The internal structural alterations will not require either planning permission (as they do not constitute development) or building regulations approval.

QUESTION 3

A solicitor acts on the purchase of a vacant freehold commercial property and it transpires that there are some planning issues. The seller constructed a large extension three years ago without planning permission or building regulations approval. The client's surveyor has also discovered that although planning permission was obtained for another extension on the property six years ago, some of the conditions attached to it have either been breached or have not been complied with. The buyer has plans to change the use from general industrial to a nightclub.

Which of the following best describes the position?

A The buyer cannot be pursued for any breaches of planning or building control as the burden will not pass to them. However, they will require planning permission for the proposed material change of use.

B The buyer may be pursued for the operational development carried out without planning permission, but not for the associated breach of building control as the relevant time limit has now passed. However, an injunction may still be sought by the local authority if the building is unsafe. The buyer can also be pursued for the breaches of planning conditions as the relevant time limit has not passed. They will require planning permission for the proposed material change of use.

C The buyer may be pursued for the operational development carried out without planning permission and the associated breach of building control. The buyer can also be pursued for the breaches of planning conditions as the relevant time limit has not passed. They will require planning permission for the proposed material change of use.

D The buyer may be pursued for the operational development carried out without planning permission but not for the associated breach of building control as the relevant time limit has now passed. However, an injunction may still be sought by the local authority if the building is unsafe. The buyer can no longer be pursued for the breaches of planning conditions as the relevant time limit has now passed. They will require planning permission for the proposed material change of use.

E The buyer may be pursued for the operational development carried out without planning permission but not for the associated breach of building control as the relevant time limit has now passed. However, an injunction may still be sought by the local authority if the building is unsafe. The buyer can no longer be pursued for the breaches of planning conditions as the relevant time limit has now passed. They will not require planning permission for the proposed material change of use.

QUESTION 4

A solicitor acts on the purchase of a very old freehold property in England, 'Church View', title to which is unregistered. The property is in an extremely poor state of repair and condition, and it will require complete renovation. Although the property is in a rural area and abuts open fields, there is a petrol station and there are commercial properties nearby. There is also a river running directly behind the rear garden. Access is gained from a private road and there is a large grass verge between the property and the highway.

Mines and minerals are excluded from the title under an earlier conveyance. The buyer, seller, and all estate owners referred to in the epitome of title are individuals and the buyer is borrowing to fund the acquisition.

Which of the following best describes the appropriate searches of third parties and survey in these circumstances?

A   Enquiries of the seller, personal inspection, local search (with commons registration search), water and drainage search, mining search, environmental and flood search, chancel repair liability search, Environment Agency search, a highways search, and a basic valuation survey.

B   Enquiries of the seller, personal inspection, index map search, Land charges searches, local search (with commons registration search), water and drainage search, mining search, environmental and flood search, chancel repair liability search, Environment Agency search, a highways search, and a full structural survey.

C   Enquiries of the seller, personal inspection, index map search, Land charges searches, local search (with commons registration search), water and drainage search, mining search, environmental and flood search, chancel repair liability search, Environment Agency search, a highways search, and a home buyer's valuation and report.

D   Enquiries of the seller, personal inspection, local search, water and drainage search, mining search, environmental and flood search, chancel repair liability search, Environment Agency search, a highways search, and a full structural survey.

E   Index map search, Land charges searches, local search (with commons registration search), water and drainage search, mining search, environmental and flood search, chancel repair liability search, Environment Agency search, a highways search, and a home buyer's valuation and report.

QUESTION 5

A solicitor has been instructed on the purchase of a newbuild residential property from a national developer. As the property is not yet constructed, the local search has revealed that the road abutting the proposed property and foul and surface drainage services have yet to be adopted. The buyer is concerned about build quality and structural defects as the developer has a poor reputation.

Which of the following best describes the position?

A   The solicitor must ensure that the developer is under an obligation to make up the roads and mains water/drainage facilities to an adoptable standard and that appropriate agreements and supporting bonds are in place for the water/drainage facilities and also the roads, unless suitable private arrangements are in place. They must also ensure that an offer of appropriate structural defects insurance is available on exchange.

B   The solicitor need not be concerned about the roads provided that appropriate easements are to be contained in the transfer to the buyer. However, they must ensure that the developer is under an obligation to make up the mains water/drainage facilities to an adoptable standard and that appropriate agreements and supporting bonds are in place. They must also ensure that an offer of appropriate structural defects insurance is available on exchange.

C   The solicitor must ensure that the developer is under an obligation to make up the roads and mains water/drainage facilities to an adoptable standard and that appropriate agreements and supporting bonds are in place. The buyer should be advised to undertake a full structural survey of the property, once constructed.

D   The solicitor should advise the client's surveyor to assess the state and condition of the road as the buyer may be liable for the cost of making up the same to an adoptable condition. The buyer must ensure that an appropriate agreement and supporting bond is in place for the mains water/drainage facilities to be made up to an adoptable standard.

E   The buyer may proceed as the local authority and local water authority will be obliged to adopt the roads and mains water/drainage facilities following completion without cost to the buyer. The buyer should be able to rely on the usual easements in the transfer in any event. The solicitor should ensure that an appropriate offer for structural defects insurance is available on exchange of contracts.

■ ANSWERS TO QUESTIONS

Answers to 'What do you know already?' questions at the start of the chapter

1) The pre-contract searches and enquiries that are relevant to all conveyancing transactions are enquiries of the seller/enquiries before contract, personal inspection/survey, local search (in two parts), water/drainage search, environmental search, and flood search.

2) These matters will be revealed by the local search and the water/drainage search respectively.

3) False. Only work classed as development will require express planning permission, and in some cases, development will fall within permitted development rights. Building regulations approval is a separate and distinct requirement from planning permission and may be required even where planning permission is not.

4) True. A small rear extension or conservatory will usually come within permitted development rights unless they have been revoked by an Article 4 direction (eg in a conservation area) or the property is listed. However, building regulations approval is a separate and distinct requirement and may be required.

Answers to end-of-chapter SQE1-style questions

Question 1

The correct answer was A. The client should not require express planning permission for the internal works as they do not constitute 'development'. Option B is partially correct in this respect, but option C is incorrect. Options D and E are incorrect in that the client will not require planning permission for the internal works as they do not constitute 'development', not because they fall within the definition of 'permitted development'. However, the change of use does constitute 'development' (being a material change of use) and express planning permission will be required. Option B is incorrect on this point and options C and D are correct. A material change of use (not otherwise permitted) is not permitted development; therefore, option E is incorrect in this respect.

Question 2

The correct answer was C. Planning permission would not have been required for the erection of the conservatory if it fell within the limits of permitted development. From the facts, it cannot be ascertained with certainty whether it would fall within permitted development rights. Options B, D, and E are correct in this respect. However, option A is incorrect as such works would still have constituted development. Building regulations approval *may* have been required for the conservatory. However, from the facts it cannot be ascertained with certainty whether building regulations approval would have been required. In the circumstances, further enquiries should be raised. Therefore, options A, B, and D are incorrect on this point and option E does not mention the conservatory. Building regulations approval would have been required for the replacement windows (usually in the form of a FENSA certificate). Options A, B, and E are correct on this point, but option D does not mention the replacement windows. The internal structural alterations will not require planning permission as they do not constitute development, but they will require building regulations approval. Options A and D are correct and options B and E are only partially correct on this point. Option B is incorrect as such works do not require planning permission because they do not constitute development, rather than because they constitute permitted development. Option E is also incorrect as it fails to acknowledge that building regulations approval will be required for these works.

Question 3

The correct answer was B. The buyer may be pursued for the operational development carried out without planning permission as action can be taken within four years of completion. Options C, D, and E are also correct on this point, but option A is incorrect as the burden for breaches of planning control will pass to the buyer. The buyer may not be pursued for the associated breach of building control as the relevant time limit has now passed. However, an injunction may still be sought by the local authority if the building is unsafe. Options D and E are correct in this respect. Option A is incorrect as the burden will pass and option C is insufficiently detailed/precise on the position. The buyer can also be pursued for the breaches of planning *conditions* as the relevant time limit has not passed. Option C is correct on this point, although options D and E are incorrect. The client will require planning permission for the proposed material change of use as it is a change to a sui generis use, which always requires express planning permission. Options A, C, and D are also correct on this point, although option E is incorrect. A material change of use will always require express planning permission unless it falls within permitted development rights.

Question 4

The correct answer was B. Enquiries of the seller, personal inspection, local search, water and drainage search, environmental and flood search are advisable for all transactions. A chancel repair liability search should also be undertaken as there is no information on the last disposition for value and, as the property is unregistered, it is highly unlikely there will have been one since 13 October 2013 (it would have triggered first registration). The name of the property also suggests there may be a nearby church! An Environment Agency search is recommended due to the nearby river and a highways search would be recommended due to the potential 'ransom strip'. A full structural survey would be recommended due to the state and condition of the property, rather than a basic valuation or a home buyer's valuation and report. An index map search will be required as the property is unregistered and there is also a mines/minerals reservation in the title (meaning that a mining search is also recommended). Land charges searches will be required as the title is unregistered. A commons registration search would also be recommended based on the location of the property. All other options omit one or more of these searches or suggest the incorrect type of survey. A bankruptcy-only search will be undertaken pre-completion, but it may also be undertaken now and repeated later, if necessary.

Question 5

The correct answer was A. The solicitor must ensure that the developer is under an obligation to make up the roads and mains water/drainage facilities to an adoptable standard. Options B and C are therefore partially correct (option B as regards the water/drainage facilities).

Appropriate agreements and supporting bonds must be in place for the water/drainage facilities and the roads, unless suitable private arrangements are in place (it is common for roads to remain private on new developments). Options B and D are correct as regards the mains water/drainage facilities, although option C is incorrect as it does not acknowledge the possibility of the roads remaining private. The buyer will be able to rely on the easements within the transfer, but the solicitor should still ensure that the developer is under an obligation to construct the roads and water/drainage facilities to an adoptable standard. Therefore, options B and E are incorrect in this respect. Option E is also incorrect as the local authority and local water authority will not be obliged to adopt the road and mains water/drainage facilities following completion without cost to the buyer unless appropriate agreements are in place. Option D is incorrect as the solicitor should not need to advise the client's surveyor to assess the state and condition of the road provided that suitable arrangements are in place so that the buyer will not be responsible for the cost of making up the same to an adoptable condition. The solicitor must also ensure that an offer of appropriate structural defects insurance is available on exchange, and options B and E are also correct in this respect. Option C is incorrect as the buyer would not normally be advised to undertake a full structural survey of a newbuild property, once constructed.

■ KEY CASES, RULES, STATUTES, AND INSTRUMENTS

The SQE1 Assessment Specification does not require you to know any statutory authorities or specific case names for this topic. Specific sections of statutes are set out for ease of reference.

4

The draft contract and exchange of contracts

■ MAKE SURE YOU KNOW

This chapter provides an overview of the preparation for, and exchange of contracts. It deals with the key conditions contained in the Standard Conditions of Sale and the Standard Commercial Property Conditions, as well as the purpose of, and matters covered by, special conditions. It considers key points relating to the deposit and how it is held (as stakeholder or agent), insurance and the passing of risk, as well as the basics of VAT in a contract (dealt with in more detail in **Chapter 10**). The chapter will also consider the purpose and process of reporting to the client, and acting for a lender (including lender requirements and the purpose of a certificate of title). It then goes on to deal with the timing for issuing the certificate of title to a lender and then the practice, method, and authority to exchange and the consequences of exchange. For the SQE1 assessments, you will need to understand the detail of each of these elements as well as how they fit into the bigger process (see **Chapter 1**).

■ SQE ASSESSMENT ADVICE

For SQE1, you are required to understand what a typical contract for the sale and purchase of a property contains, who prepares the contract, and why and how it may be varied in particular circumstances. You also need to understand the importance of reporting to the client, the lender's certificate of title, and the process of exchange and its consequences.

As you work through this chapter, remember to pay particular attention in your revision to:
• The importance and key provisions of the Standard Conditions of Sale and the Standard Commercial Property Conditions.
• The need for special conditions and what they usually deal with.
• The important matters of the deposit, the obligation to insure and the passing of risk, and the basics of VAT in a contract.
• The purpose and process of reporting to the client.
• Acting for a lender and adhering to their requirements.
• When to prepare the certificate of title for a lender, its importance and purpose, and what it usually contains.
• Pre-exchange steps and the practice, method, and authority to exchange.
• The consequences of exchange.

■ WHAT DO YOU KNOW ALREADY?

Attempt these questions before reading this chapter. If you find some difficult or cannot remember the answers, remember to look more closely at that topic during your revision.

1) True or false? The safest option for a buyer is always for the deposit to be held as stakeholder.
   [Form of contract and the standard conditions, page 87]

2) Who usually bears the risk of damage and destruction of the property following exchange of contracts?
   [Form of contract and the standard conditions, page 87]

3) What are the VAT implications on the sale of a residential property?
   [Form of contract and the standard conditions, page 87]

4) Which Law Society formula should be used for exchange of contracts by telephone, where each solicitor holds the part contract signed by their own client and there is no chain of transactions?
   [Practice, method, and authority to exchange, page 106]

THE PURPOSE OF AND NEED FOR A CONTRACT

As we saw in **Chapter 1**, the first key milestone in a property transaction is exchange of contracts. At this stage, both parties become bound to complete on the agreed completion date and the buyer gains an equitable interest in the property. Before then, a great deal of work will have been undertaken, including deduction and investigation of title (see **Chapter 2**) and pre-contract searches and enquiries (see **Chapter 3**). However, until exchange of contracts, the parties are usually free and able to withdraw, without penalty.

The contract therefore serves the important purpose of *locking the parties into the deal* by making it *legally binding*. It gives them some certainty that title will pass and completion will take place, sets out the obligations of the parties and provides for remedies in the event of a delay or failure to complete. It follows from this that the solicitors acting for both parties must take care in agreeing the form of contract and only exchange when all pre-contract matters have been resolved to their satisfaction.

Although it is always necessary to have a transfer by deed of the legal interest in the property on completion, it is not strictly always necessary to have a contract in a conveyancing transaction. It is common in commercial transactions for parties to proceed straight to completion (eg on the grant of a commercial lease (see **Chapter 7**)) or to exchange contracts and complete on the same day (known as a simultaneous exchange and completion). However, in residential transactions, where the parties will often be moving from one property to the next on the same day, a gap between exchange and completion serves the useful purpose of giving the parties time to prepare to move and arrange for removals, and giving their solicitors time to deal with pre-completion matters (see **Chapter 5**). A contract is also useful where a condition needs to be fulfilled, or work needs to be carried out, before completion can take place. For example, if the property is a newbuild and needs to be constructed by the seller, or fitting out works need to be carried out by the buyer or a tenant.

DRAFTING AND AGREEING THE CONTRACT

In most conveyancing transactions, the contract is prepared by the seller's solicitor (following their deduction and investigation of title) (see **Chapters 1 and 2**) and sent to the buyer's solicitor for approval. The buyer's solicitor then approves and, if necessary, amends the contract. If amendments are required, they must be communicated to the seller's solicitor, who will need to decide whether they are acceptable, and produce two clean copies in readiness for exchange.

Form of contract and the standard conditions

The form of contract used will depend on the nature of the property and the transaction, as well as the firm's standard practice. In straightforward residential transactions, it is common practice to use a standard form of contract that is largely pre-printed. However, in more complex transactions, particularly those involving commercial properties, it is common to use a more bespoke word-processed form of contract, usually based on a standard precedent, or in the firm's style.

Whichever type of contract is used, it will normally be comprised of, and include the following:
- The particular details of the transaction (also known as the particulars of sale, see **Table 4.1**).
- The incorporation of **standard conditions**.
- The addition of **special conditions**.

Key term: standard conditions

Property transactions are so commonplace that it is not necessary, appropriate, or a good use of conveyancers' time to draft and negotiate fully bespoke terms and conditions on each transaction. It is therefore usual to incorporate either the **Standard Conditions of Sale** or the **Standard Commercial Property Conditions** into the contract, by reference.

Key term: Standard Conditions of Sale (SCs)

The SCs are usually used for straightforward residential transactions and, sometimes, straightforward commercial transactions (eg the sale of a small property with vacant possession). The current edition is the fifth edition, which was produced in 2018.

Key term: Standard Commercial Property Conditions (SCPCs)

The SCPCs are usually used in most transactions involving commercial properties. Part 1 provides the usual standard conditions that apply in all cases and Part 2 provides additional conditions that may be incorporated, where appropriate. The current edition is the third edition, which was produced in 2018.

Key term: special conditions

These are additional conditions that are relevant to the particular transaction and are agreed between the parties (see **Special conditions**, below).

Revision tip

The SCs and the SCPCs are updated from time to time. Although for the purpose of SQE1 you do not need to know them all in detail, you should check whether there is a new version of either or both at the time you sit the SQE1 assessments to see whether the key conditions referred to in this volume have changed. Copies of the SCs and SCPCs are available to view at www.lawsociety.org.uk.

For the purposes of SQE1, you should be familiar with the standard pre-printed form of contract that incorporates the SCs. A similar version is available incorporating the SCPCs, and you can view specimens of both at www.lawsociety.org.uk. The contract contains three parts: particulars of sale (on the front page); the relevant standard conditions; and special conditions (with some pre-printed options and room for additional special conditions).

Table 4.1 sets out the particulars of sale for a contract incorporating the SCs, with the key points on what to include. It would be helpful to have a specimen of the contract in front of you when considering this.

Table 4.1: Particulars of sale

Date	The date should be left blank and inserted on exchange.
Seller	The information in the proprietorship register (for registered land – see **Chapter 2**), or the conveyance to the seller (for unregistered land – see **Chapter 2**) should usually be used here.
Buyer	The buyer or buyers' name(s) and current address(es) should be inserted here.

Table 4.1: (Continued)

Property (freehold/ leasehold)	Delete/strike through either *freehold* or *leasehold* (see **Chapter 1**), as appropriate.
	For the sale of the *whole* of *registered land* comprised within a title, use the details from the property register (see **Chapter 2**). This is usually the full postal address.
	For the sale of the *whole* of the land comprised within the root of title (see below) in *unregistered land*, describe the property with reference to it (eg [address] more particularly delineated and edged red on a plan annexed to a conveyance dated [] and made between (1) [seller in the document] and (2) [buyer in the document] (the 'Conveyance')).
	For a sale of *part* of land comprised within a *registered or unregistered title,* the description will require adjustment to make it clear it is a sale of part only, and a HM Land Registry compliant plan will be required (see **Revision tip**, below).
Title number/ root of title	Delete/strike through either *title number* (if title is unregistered) or *root of title* (if title is registered), as appropriate (see **Chapter 2**).
	Insert the relevant title number for *registered land* or 'The Conveyance' (or other root document) for *unregistered land.*
Specified incumbrances (See **Key term**, below)	For *unregistered land*, insert 'The covenant(s) [etc] contained, mentioned or referred to in the Conveyance [or specify other root document]'.
	For *registered land*, adverse incumbrances should be referred to, but existing mortgages should *not* be included, as they should be discharged on completion. (eg If there were four entries in the charges register, the first two containing restrictive covenants, and the second two containing details of an existing mortgage (see **Chapter 2**) insert 'The covenants contained in entry numbers 1 and 2 of the charges register of the title').
Title guarantee (full/limited) (See **Key term**, below)	Delete/strike through either *full* or *limited*, as appropriate.
Completion date (see **Revision tip**, below)	The date should be left blank and inserted on exchange. It is important to consider the issue of synchronisation here (see **Chapter 1**).
Contract rate (See **Key term**, below)	Typically, insert 'The Law Society's interest rate from time to time in force'.

Table 4.1: (Continued)

Purchase Price	Insert the agreed purchase price here.
Deposit (See **Key term**, below)	Insert the agreed deposit here.
Contents price (if separate)	If a separate price has been agreed for chattels/fittings at the property (see **Chapter 1**), insert the agreed price here.
Balance	This should be the balance payable on completion.

Revision tip

The sale of a newbuild property will usually be a sale of part of the land comprised within a registered title. On any sale of part (or transfer of unregistered land that is to be registered for the first time), it is important to ensure that any plan of the property is HM Land Registry compliant. For the purposes of SQE1, you need to be aware of this requirement, although you do not need to know the detail behind it. See *HM Land Registry Practice Guide 40*, for further information.

Key term: specified incumbrances

Specified incumbrances are *adverse* title matters that the property is sold subject to (as opposed to rights and covenants that the property has the *benefit* of). They include covenants (both positive and restrictive – see **Chapter 2** and **Special conditions**, below) and adverse easements (ie easements that benefit other land, but burden the property – see **Chapter 2**).

It is important to specify the relevant incumbrances for a number of reasons:
- With the exception of positive covenants (see **Special conditions**), they will usually run with the land, and therefore burden a buyer.
- It makes it expressly clear that the buyer is taking subject to them.
- Under both sets of standard conditions (SC 3.1.1 and SCPC 4.1.1), the seller agrees to sell free from incumbrances, other than those specified in SC 3.1.2 and SCPC 4.1.2 respectively (which include incumbrances specified in the contract).
- The buyer will not usually be able to raise requisitions about the specified incumbrances after exchange of contracts (SC 4.2.1 and SCPC 7.2.1 – see **Chapter 2**).

Revision tip

Although in registered land the relevant specified incumbrances are usually set out in the charges register (see **Chapter 2**), it is important to check the property register (see **Chapter 2**), as adverse matters may be included within positive rights, which benefit the property (see **Practice example 4.1**). In any event, it is important to ensure that charges of a financial nature (usually mortgages) are specifically excluded from the definition of specified incumbrances.

Practice example 4.1

You act on the purchase of a freehold property with registered title:

- The charges register contains four entries. The first two refer to adverse matters affecting the property, including a wayleave agreement (a type of easement granted to a service provider) and restrictive covenants. The final two refer to an existing mortgage.
- The proprietorship register (see **Chapter 2**) contains a restriction protecting the mortgagee's rights (providing that no disposition may be made without the mortgagee's consent – see **Chapter 2**).
- Entry number two of the property register states that the property has the benefit of the rights granted by, but is subject to the rights reserved in, a conveyance (copy filed).

What should be the definition of specified incumbrances in these circumstances?

It should be 'the matters referred to in entry numbers 1 and 2 of the charges register and entry number 2 of the property register'. Entry 2 of the property register needs to be mentioned as adverse matters are mixed in with ancillary rights, which benefit the property. Entry numbers 3 and 4 of the charges register should not be referred to as the buyer will not be buying the property subject to the mortgage, and an undertaking should be given to discharge it on completion (see Chapters 2 and 5). HM Land Registry will automatically remove the restriction when the mortgage is discharged to enable the buyer to be registered as proprietor.

Key term: title guarantee

Title guarantee refers to implied covenants for title that are inserted into the transfer under the Law of Property (Miscellaneous Provisions) Act 1994 (the LP(MP)A 1994). They relate to the guarantee that the seller can give about the title and incumbrances and assistance they will give to transfer it. Ultimately, title guarantee depends on the *status of the seller* and the three main options are **full title guarantee**, **limited title guarantee**, and **no title guarantee**.

In the case of *both* full and limited title guarantee, the seller covenants that:

- They have the right to dispose of the property.
- They will, at their own cost, do all they reasonably can to give the title *they purport to give* (sometimes referred to as 'further assurance').

The *title they purport to give* is, in registered land (see **Chapter 2**), the same class of title the seller has, or in the case of unregistered land being registered for the first time (see **Chapters 2 and 5**), all reasonable assistance to enable the buyer to be registered as proprietor.

For the purposes of SQE1, it is important to know the different types of title guarantee and the circumstances in which each one would be applicable or appropriate.

Key term: full title guarantee

- Full title guarantee is usually given when the seller owns the whole legal and equitable interest in the property (eg they are an owner-occupier).
- In addition to the matters stated above, the seller covenants that the property is free from all charges, incumbrances, and third party rights other than those they do not and could not reasonably be expected to know about.

Key term: limited title guarantee

- Limited title guarantee is usually given when the seller does not own the whole legal and equitable interest in the property and has limited knowledge about it. This would include a sale by a trustee or personal representative (see **Chapter 2** and *Revise SQE: Wills and the Administration of Estates*).
- In addition to the matters stated above, the seller covenants that they have not, since the last disposition (eg transfer) for value, charged or incumbered the property or granted any third party rights. They also covenant that they have not allowed any such charges, incumbrances, or third party rights to be created and that they are not aware of anyone else having done so since the last disposition for value.

Key term: no title guarantee

No title guarantee is usually given when the seller has no knowledge at all about the property and is simply disposing of it in a professional capacity. This could include a sale by a trustee in bankruptcy or a mortgagee in possession.

Exam warning

Candidates often confuse or conflate the concepts of title guarantee and class of title (see **Chapter 2**). The former relates to the *status of the seller* and hence what they may warrant about their right to dispose of the property and further assurance they can give to help to transfer the title. However, the latter relates to the quality of the *title itself* and the level of state guarantee as to its validity against third party rights.

Excluded from the covenants for title are matters to which the disposition is expressly made subject (ie referred to in the contract), matters known to the buyer at the time of the disposition, and, in the case of registered land, matters on the registers of title (s 6 LP(MP)A 1994 – see **Chapter 2**).

Key term: contract rate

The contract rate is the rate of interest that will be paid by the defaulting party on the purchase price (less the deposit paid (see **Key term**) if the buyer is in default) in the event of late completion (see SC 7.2.2, SCPC 10.3.2 and **Chapter 5**).

The contract rate is intended to be a penalty and is typically set at 2–5% above the base lending rate of a high street bank. The most straightforward way to deal with this is to insert *'The Law Society's interest rate from time to time in force'* (currently 4% above Barclays Bank base rate), and this is provided for as the default provision in any event under both sets of standard conditions (SC and SCPC 1.1.1(e)).

Alternatively, the seller's solicitors will use another bank (typically their own bank) to set the rate (eg '4% above the base lending rate of Lloyds Bank plc'). Although the rate is a matter of negotiation, typically 4% above base rate is usually settled on in most cases. If a specific bank is referred to, it may be advisable to add the words *'or should the bank cease to publish such a rate, such other comparable rate as the Seller shall reasonably require'*.

Key term: deposit

The deposit is a sum representing part of the purchase price that is paid by the buyer on exchange of contracts as a demonstration of commitment to the purchase. It is typically 10% of the purchase price, and this is what is provided for in the standard conditions (SC 2.2.1 and SCPC 3.2.1).

The seller may forfeit and keep the deposit and any accrued interest in the event of failure to complete, following service of a notice to complete (see SC 7.4 and SCPC 10.5 and **Chapter 5**). Likewise, if the seller is in default, the buyer may demand repayment of the deposit with accrued interest (see SC 7.5 and SCPC 10.6).

Although a deposit of 10% is provided for in the standard conditions, the parties may agree to a lower deposit (often 5%). In this case, this should be added as a special condition (see **Special conditions,** below) to vary the relevant standard conditions. If using the SCs, it would also be advisable to include a provision that if the deposit is less than 10%, the balance up to the 10% will become payable immediately upon default (this is provided for in SCPC 9.8.3). However, if a buyer fails to complete, they may not necessarily have the funds available.

A key question with regard to the deposit is whether it should be held as **stakeholder** or **agent**. For the purposes of SQE1, you should understand the appropriate standard conditions and be able to determine which would be most appropriate in particular circumstances.

Key term: stakeholder

- Under the standard conditions, the deposit is held by the seller's solicitor as stakeholder until completion and it cannot be handed over until completion. On completion, it may be released to the seller with accrued interest (SC 2.2.6 and SCPC 3.2.2).
- *This is the safest option for a buyer, as it avoids the possibility of the deposit being dissipated by the seller.*
- However, under the SCs (not the SCPCs) there is an exception. If, before completion, the seller agrees to buy another property in England and Wales for their residence, they may use all or any part of the deposit as a deposit in that transaction. Therefore, it can be used on a related purchase in some circumstances (SC 2.2.5).

Key term: agent

- Alternatively, the deposit may be held by the seller's solicitor as agent and a special condition will need to be inserted into the contract (unless SC 2.2.5 applies).
- *This is much more risky for the buyer as the deposit can be released immediately to the seller and used for any purpose whatsoever.* The risk of this is that the seller may dissipate the funds, disappear or become bankrupt, making the return of the deposit practically impossible.

Under the SCs, the deposit is usually paid by electronic transfer or client account cheque (SC 2.2.4). However, under the SCPCs, it must be paid by electronic transfer (SCPC 3.2.2). If the parties agree to payment by client account cheque and there will be insufficient time for the cheque to clear between exchange and completion, the seller's solicitor may agree for the buyer's solicitor to hold the deposit to the order of the seller's solicitor (making it payable on demand).

Revision tip

On the purchase of a newbuild property, it may not be possible to agree a fixed completion date, particularly where the property is still in the course of construction. This can cause issues with synchronisation (see **Chapter 1**). Therefore, it is usual to provide that completion will take place on notice (ie a number of working days following notice of completion of construction). The buyer's solicitor should include a longstop date in the contract to allow the buyer to withdraw in the event of a significant delay.

Special conditions

The parties are free to agree appropriate special conditions, which depend on the nature of the transaction and what has been agreed between them.

For the purposes of SQE1, you should be familiar with the usual special conditions on the standard pre-printed form of contract that incorporates the SCs. These can be deleted or amended, if required, and they are summarised in **Table 4.2**.

Table 4.2: Special conditions

Special condition	Content	Action required
1	This incorporates the SCs and the terms within them into the contract.	None.
2	This combines the terms of the contract, the SCs and the agreement to transfer with the appropriate title guarantee.	None.
3	This provides for: (a) the sale including the chattels/fittings set out on the list attached, for the contents price, and (b) the exclusion of fixtures set out on the list attached.	Remember that chattels/fittings do not usually run with the land, but fixtures do (see **Chapter 1** and **Practice example 4.2**). It is therefore necessary to contract out of the normal rules, if required.
		If no chattels/fittings are *included*, option (a) may be deleted. If no fixtures are to be *excluded*, option (b) may be deleted.
		An appropriate list or list(s) must be added and it is common to use the Fittings and Contents Form (see **Chapter 3**) for this purpose.
		If fixtures are to be removed, an appropriate special condition should be added that the item(s) will be removed on or before completion and that any damage will be made good to the reasonable satisfaction of the buyer.
4	This provides two alternatives as regards vacant possession. Either: (a) the property is sold with vacant possession, or (b) the property is sold subject to the following leases or tenancies.	One alternative must be deleted and if option (b) is retained, details of the tenancy/tenancies or lease(s) should be set out.

Table 4.2: (Continued)

5	This optional provision amends the standard time for completion (2 PM) under SC 6.1.2 and 6.1.3, usually to an earlier time (eg 12 PM).	If there is not a chain of transactions (see **Chapter 1**), this provision should be deleted. If there is a chain of transactions, it should be adjusted to allow sufficient time to complete all transactions on time on the same day (eg completion of a sale by 12 PM and the associated purchase by 1 or 2 PM).
6	This is a standard provision stating that the parties can generally only rely on *written representations* passing between the parties or their solicitors.	None. However, the parties (particularly the buyer) should be asked whether any oral representations have been made pre-contract, and consideration should be given as to whether they should be formalised in writing.
7	Occupier's consent – this provides from any adult occupiers: (a) an agreement to the sale of the property, (b) a release/waiver of any rights in the property (including any included fixtures and contents), and (c) an agreement to vacate the property on the completion date.	This clause should be retained if there are any adult occupiers at the property apart from the seller(s), so that they may also sign the contract. Otherwise, it may be deleted (see **Practice example 4.2**).

Practice example 4.2 brings these points together.

Practice example 4.2

You act on the purchase of a residential property, with vacant possession, adopting the SCs. There is no chain of transactions as the seller will be moving into rented accommodation and the buyer has no property to sell. It has been agreed that the seller will remove a garden statue that is cemented to the terrace in the garden and that a freestanding fridge-freezer will be included in the sale. The seller lives at the property with her 25-year-old son.

How will you provide for the above in the special conditions (SPCs) within the contract?

The two alternatives for SPC 3 should be retained as a fitting/chattel (the fridge-freezer) is being included and a fixture (the statue) is being

removed. **An additional special condition will need to be added to deal with the statue's removal by the seller on or before completion with any damage being made good. SPC alternative 4(b) will need to be removed and SPC 4(a) retained as the sale is being made with vacant possession. SPC5 should be deleted as there is no chain of transactions and SPC7 should be retained, with the son's details inserted so that he may also sign the contract.**

Bespoke additional special conditions may also need to be added to deal with the following:

- An **indemnity covenant** to be given by the buyer in the transfer.
- The appointment of an additional trustee to receive the proceeds of sale, to effect overreaching (see **Chapter 2**).
- The provision of an indemnity insurance policy in respect of any defect in title, which it has not been possible to remedy (see **Chapter 2**).
- Payment of a reduced deposit, or for the deposit to be held as agent.
- Removal of fixtures (including timing and making good any damage caused).
- VAT, insurance, and the passing of risk (see **Insurance and the passing of risk**, and **VAT**, below).
- Additional provisions relating to sales of part (eg grant of easements, reservation of easements, imposition of covenants, declarations, and necessary definitions). In such circumstances, it is best practice to simply add a special condition that the transfer (usually a TP1 – see **Chapter 5**) will be in the form of the draft annexed (with it being agreed before exchange). It is also good practice to provide that any mortgagee's consent to the terms of the proposed transfer and the release/discharge of the part sold (see **Chapter 5**) will be provided if either or both cannot be obtained before exchange.

Revision tip

A sale of a newbuild property by a developer will usually be a sale of part of the land within a registered title. The draft contract will be different, as it will usually provide for the construction of the property to the agreed specification. Care should be taken by the buyer's solicitor to ensure all agreed extras are included, the developer is obliged to construct the property in a good and skilful manner, using good quality materials and any rights to vary them are not unreasonable. The contract should also provide that an NHBC (see **Chapter 1, Structural defects insurance policy**) or equivalent offer of cover will be provided on exchange and that the cover note/policy documentation will be provided on completion. The standard form draft transfer will also usually be provided at the pre-contract stage.

Key term: indemnity covenant

An indemnity covenant is a covenant to be inserted into the transfer (see **Chapter 5**) that the buyer will observe and perform covenants affecting the title and will indemnify the seller in respect of any future breach. An agreement to enter into the covenant within the transfer is usually agreed at this stage.

For SQE1, you need to be aware of the need for an indemnity covenant in given circumstances as summarised below:

- Restrictive covenants usually run with the land and bind a buyer, but positive covenants usually do not (see **Chapter 2**).
- If the seller is the original covenantor, or they gave an indemnity covenant to the then seller on their purchase of the property (see **Chapter 2**), the seller should insist that the buyer provide an indemnity covenant. This is because the seller may continue to be liable under positive covenants following sale (either due to privity of contract (see **Revise SQE: Contract Law**) as the original covenantor, or as a result of the previous indemnity).
- An indemnity covenant is automatically provided for (under SC 4.6.4 and SCPC 7.6.5) where these circumstances apply. However, it is standard practice to include a specific obligation to enter into an indemnity covenant in the transfer at this stage and to include restrictive as well as positive covenants.

Revision tip

It can easily be ascertained whether the seller gave an indemnity to the seller from whom they originally purchased the property by looking at the proprietorship register (in the case of registered land) or the conveyance to the seller (in the case of unregistered land) (see **Chapter 2**).

Exam warning

It is important to be able to distinguish between *indemnity covenants* and *indemnity insurance* (see **Chapter 2**). Candidates often conflate the two concepts.

Practice example 4.3 brings these points together.

Practice example 4.3

You act on the purchase of a registered freehold property, which is subject to both positive and restrictive covenants. The SCs have been adopted.

Will an indemnity covenant be required?

The restrictive covenants will usually bind the buyer. However, the seller may continue to be bound by the positive covenants if they were the original covenantor or they entered into an indemnity on their purchase (this would be shown in the proprietorship register). If either of these situations applies, SC 4.6.4 will provide for an indemnity to be incorporated into the transfer. It would make sense to agree an express indemnity at this stage (using a standard precedent indemnity clause) for eventual incorporation into the transfer. The indemnity would usually include all of the specified incumbrances (including positive and restrictive covenants).

Insurance and the passing of risk

Under the standard conditions, the risk of damage to and/or destruction of the property passes to the buyer on exchange of contracts (SC 5.1.1 and SCPC 8.1). Therefore, in such an event, the buyer would still be bound to complete, notwithstanding the damage or destruction.

A *buyer* of a freehold property must therefore be advised to put buildings insurance 'on risk' immediately from exchange. It will also usually be a requirement of their lender that suitable insurance is in place and the buyer should be made aware of any specific requirements of the lender as to the nature of the policy (see **Lender requirements**). For example, it will usually need to be for the full reinstatement value and cover a comprehensive list of insured risks.

A *seller* should be advised to maintain their buildings insurance until completion, notwithstanding that risk passes. Although the seller will usually be under no contractual obligation to the buyer to insure (under SC 5 or SCPC 8), the seller will usually be under an obligation to keep the property insured under the terms of any existing mortgage. There is also the risk that the sale may not proceed to completion.

A solicitor who gives incorrect advice as to the passing of risk and the responsibility for insurance is likely to be liable in negligence should their client suffer loss as a result.

SC 5.1 and SCPC 8.2 also outline the rights and obligations of the parties if the seller accepts responsibility to insure the property under the terms of the contract, or if the property is *leasehold* and the seller is obliged to insure under the lease. These include an obligation on the seller to maintain the insurance policy (which the buyer can inspect). They must also do what they can to maintain the policy including if, for example, the landlord is responsible (see **Chapter 6**). In both circumstances, they must also pay over any insurance proceeds received that have not yet been applied in repair/reinstatement and assign any rights to the buyer on completion, holding anything actually received on trust.

Revision tip

On the sale of a newbuild property in the course of construction, the seller will usually retain the risk and responsibility for insurance, varying the standard conditions accordingly.

In advising both parties to maintain insurance, there is the likelihood of the same property being insured twice. In such circumstances, if the buyer cannot recover the full amount because of the seller's insurance (where they were under no contractual obligation to insure) the purchase price will be reduced accordingly (SC 5.1.5 and SCPC 8.2.4).

VAT

It is important to ascertain and appreciate the VAT position when acting for both sellers and buyers in a property transaction. This is dealt with in more detail in **Chapter 10**; however, the key provisions from a contractual perspective are summarised in **Table 4.3**.

Table 4.3: VAT in the contract

Type of transaction	VAT position	Contractual provision
Residential property	VAT is not normally payable (*VAT exempt*).	SC 1.4 reflects this and provides that the purchase price and contents price are inclusive of VAT (in other words no VAT will be paid on top).
The position as regards *commercial property* transactions firstly depends on whether the property is classed as an *old* or a *new* property: • New properties are those which were completed up to 3 years ago. • Old properties are those which were completed more than 3 years ago.		
New commercial property	Automatically *standard rated* (meaning that VAT should be paid on the purchase price).	It should be made clear that the purchase price is exclusive of VAT, which may be charged in addition thereto. Appropriate to adopt SCPC 2 (see below).
Old commercial property	*Exempt* from VAT (meaning no VAT is payable) *unless* an *option to tax* has been exercised by the seller (see **Chapter 10**).	

Table 4.3: (Continued)

	If option to tax is exercised: The *exempt supply* turns into a *standard rated supply* and VAT should be paid on the purchase price.	As for a new commercial property (see above).
	If option to tax is not exercised: VAT should not be payable (it remains an *exempt supply*).	Appropriate to use SC 1.4 or add a similar special condition to a contract incorporating the SCPCs. A safer option for the seller would be to incorporate SCPC Part 2, Condition A1 (see below).

SCPC 2 warrants that VAT is payable at the standard rate on top of the purchase price and a VAT invoice will be provided on completion. Using the un-amended SCs for a standard rated transaction would be inappropriate as the seller would still have to account to His Majesty's Revenue and Customs (HMRC) for the VAT, meaning they would in effect receive 20% less for the property.

SCPC Part 2, Condition A1 provides a warranty that VAT is not payable and that the seller will not exercise the option to tax the property. However, if the law changes between exchange and completion, making it a taxable supply, VAT will be payable on completion and a VAT invoice will be provided by the seller. Although this is a safer option for the seller, as the buyer bears the risk of a change in the law, the buyer may resist this, particularly if they will not be able to recover the VAT or would rather not have the delay in recovery from HMRC. Remember, that the part 2 conditions in the SCPCs only apply if they are expressly incorporated.

Practice example 4.4 brings some of these points together.

Practice example 4.4

You act on the sale of a commercial property that was built over twenty years ago. An option to tax has been made by the seller.

How should VAT be dealt with in the contract?

It would be appropriate to use SCPC 2 here. The same would be appropriate had the property been completed less than three years ago. If an option to Tax had not been made, the seller could use SC 1.4 or a similar special condition. Although in such circumstances it would be safer to use SCPC Part 2, Condition A1, this may be resisted by the buyer.

PURPOSE AND PROCESS OF REPORTING TO THE CLIENT

It is always necessary to report to the client in a conveyancing transaction before exchange of contracts and it is best practice to do this in person (supported with an attendance note), as well as in writing.

The report should cover the areas referred to in **Table 4.4**.

Table 4.4: Reporting to the client

The results of investigation of title	Most importantly, ancillary rights, as well as any adverse rights and covenants should be related to the buyer (see **Chapter 2**).
The results of searches and enquiries	All relevant issues should be related to the buyer (see **Chapter 3**).
The contract	The key terms and its effect and implications should be outlined for the seller and the buyer (see above).
The mortgage	The key terms should be outlined to the buyer, including the interest rate and any conditions attached to the mortgage (eg early repayment charges). More generally, the client should understand the consequences of default, including the mortgagee's rights and remedies of possession and sale, the client's obligations to keep the property insured and in good condition and to comply with planning law and other statutory provisions. They must also understand that mortgagee's consent will usually be required to carry out structural alterations and additions or to let out the property or share occupation.
The need for the buyer to inspect the property and to be satisfied as to its state and condition	See **Chapters 1 and 3**.

Revision tip

The report must clearly relate relevant points to the practical implications. Simply stating the position without comment would be negligent (eg stating that there are mine entries within the boundaries). Therefore, for example, any impact of matters on the value of the property, its use, enjoyment, marketability, and its value as security for lending purposes should be clearly reported upon.

ACTING FOR A LENDER AND LENDER REQUIREMENTS

When acting for a lender as well as the buyer, it is important to appreciate that you have two clients, and lenders will have specific, as well as more general requirements. This can give rise to conduct issues (see *Revise SQE: Ethics and Professional Conduct*).

Lender requirements

Your first step should be to consider the instructions and documentation received from the lender and make a careful note of any specific requirements or conditions attached to the borrowing or the release of funds (eg expiry of the offer). These can vary from lender to lender, but they will usually be set out in the instruction letter and mortgage offer (or facility letter for commercial lending). You should not exchange contracts unless all conditions have been fulfilled or you are satisfied that you will be able to fulfil the conditions before completion.

Most lenders will require a first legal mortgage to be registered against the property as security for the advance (see *Revise SQE: Land Law*). They will also need to be sure that title to the property is good and marketable, with all necessary ancillary rights, and free from any materially adverse rights, covenants, restrictions, or liabilities that could have an impact on the value of the property, its use, enjoyment, and its value as security for lending purposes.

The UK Finance Mortgage Lenders' Handbook

It is important to be aware of the **UK Finance Mortgage Lenders' Handbook**, which applies to most main high street lenders in residential, and sometimes commercial, lending.

Key term: UK Finance Mortgage Lenders' Handbook

The UK Finance Mortgage Lenders' Handbook (the 'Handbook') was previously known as the Council of Mortgage Lenders, Lenders' Handbook and provides key information relating to the requirements of conveyancers in secured lending for most high street lenders. Part 1 outlines general requirements, which apply to all lenders that are members of UK Finance. Part 2 deals with the specific requirements of particular lenders, and part 3 outlines requirements when acting for a lender only.

Revision tip

For SQE1 it is necessary to know the importance of the Handbook, but it is not necessary to know its provisions in detail. A copy can be found at www.ukfinance.org.uk.

Any mortgage must be made by deed (s 52 LPA) and the lender will usually provide a partially pre-printed deed for completion and execution by the buyer/borrower. The document will be dated on completion (see **Chapter 5**).

A standard requirement of most lenders is that any adult occupier of the property (other than the borrower(s)) must sign a waiver of their rights in the property. This is to facilitate a smooth exercise of the power of sale (see *Revise SQE: Land Law*) in the event of default. Any occupier must be separately advised in order to avoid any suggestion of duress or undue influence (see *Revise SQE: Ethics and Professional Conduct*).

PURPOSE AND IMPORTANCE OF A CERTIFICATE OF TITLE AND TIMING OF ITS ISSUE

The **certificate of title** is an essential part of fulfilling a lender's requirements.

> **Key term: certificate of title (COT)**
>
> The certificate of title (sometimes referred to as a report on title) is a formal document addressed to the lender from the lender's/buyer's solicitor confirming it is safe to lend. It also confirms that:
> * The charge will be registered (usually as a first legal charge).
> * The buyer's title to the property will be good and marketable, with all necessary ancillary rights, and free from any materially adverse rights, covenants, restrictions, or liabilities that could have an impact on the value of the property, its use, enjoyment, and its value as security for lending purposes.

The purpose of a COT *for the lender* is clear. Ultimately, a mortgagee will want to be sure that their charge will be duly registered and that, should it exercise its power of sale, it will be able to sell the property and recover what is owed. If title to the property is defective in some way, they may not be able to sell the property and a potential buyer may not be able to secure borrowing.

The purpose of a COT *for the buyer* is also clear in that it includes a request for the mortgage advance to enable completion to take place.

As for *timing* of the COT, if there are no disclosures to be made (ie the COT will be clean and unqualified) the report may be made at the pre-completion stage (see **Chapter 5**). However, if there are any issues that need to be reported to the lender and which may influence the decision to provide the advance, these should be reported before exchange of contracts.

> **Revision tip**
>
> It is important to qualify any COT given if disclosures are made. Qualifications can be made in a separate document, but it is important to cross refer to it in the main document, to avoid any doubt that the disclosures were made. Any lender will be looking to make a claim against their instructed solicitors if relevant disclosures were not made and their security has been affected.

In residential transactions involving high street lenders, a standard form COT approved by UK Finance is usually used. In some commercial transactions, a more detailed COT known as the City of London Law Society COT may be used.

Revision tip

On the purchase of a newbuild property, it is a standard requirement of the Handbook that the COT should not be submitted until the completed UK Finance Disclosure of Incentives Form has been received from the developer and an NHBC or equivalent cover note is available (see www.ukfinance.org.uk).

PRE-EXCHANGE STEPS

At this stage, the *seller's solicitor* should take the following steps leading up to exchange:
* Prepare two identical clean copies of the contract and send one to the buyer's solicitor.
* Arrange for the contract to be signed by or on behalf of the seller and by any non-owning adult occupier.
* Agree a completion date in principle with the client and other solicitor.
* Request a **redemption statement** from the mortgagee made up to the proposed completion date, with a daily rate of interest thereafter.

The *buyer's solicitor* should undertake the following steps:
* Check there are no outstanding points regarding investigation of title, survey, and searches and enquiries.
* Check there are no outstanding points/conditions regarding the mortgage.
* Arrange for the contract to be signed by or on behalf of the buyer.
* Report to the client.
* Report to the lender.
* Obtain cleared funds for the agreed deposit and confirmation regarding the balance due.
* Advise client regarding insurance (see above).
* Agree a completion date in principle with the client and other solicitor.

Key term: redemption statement

This is a statement from a mortgagee setting out the amount required to redeem the mortgage(s). When requesting it, it is important to ensure that it relates to all accounts secured by the relevant charge(s). The statement should be sought *before exchange of contracts* to ensure there will be sufficient funds available on completion to fulfil the undertaking to discharge the charge(s) (see **Chapter 5**).

PRACTICE, METHOD, AND AUTHORITY TO EXCHANGE

Due to the importance and significant consequences of exchange of contracts, it is important to seek the client's written authority to do so. Most importantly, the client must be aware that they will be locked into the agreed terms and the completion date.

The contract must incorporate all agreed terms and be signed by or on behalf of the parties. This means that a solicitor may sign a contract on behalf of a client, but clear written authority to sign the specific contract should be obtained. It is possible to exchange two separate copies of the contract (usually one part signed by each party) provided that they are identical (Law of Property (Miscellaneous Provisions) Act 1989, s 2).

Although exchange of contracts may take place in person or by post/ document exchange (when the last part is posted) it is common to adopt **Law Society Formula A, B,** or **C** for exchange of contracts by telephone. As each formula contains undertakings, they may only be used by qualified practitioners. For SQE1, you should know which formula would be most appropriate in given circumstances.

Key term: Formula A

Formula A is used when *one solicitor holds both parts of the signed contract* (usually the seller's solicitor). In this case the buyer's solicitor will usually have sent over their part signed contract and a client account cheque in respect of the deposit to be held to their order. The deposit is released on condition the seller's solicitor undertakes that:

- They hold both parts of the signed contract (and the client account cheque in respect of the deposit).
- They will insert the completion date.
- They will hold their client's part contract to the order of the buyer's solicitor.
- They will send their client's part contract out to the buyer's solicitor that day by first class post, document exchange or personal delivery.

Key term: Formula B

Formula B is the most popular of the formulae and is used when *each solicitor holds their client's own signed part of the contract*. Each solicitor undertakes:

- They hold their client's signed contract (and for the buyer's solicitor, the client account cheque in respect of the deposit).
- They will insert the completion date.
- They will hold their client's signed part to the other's order and will send it out to them that day by first class post, document exchange or personal delivery (together with the deposit cheque held by the buyer's solicitor).

Key term: Formula C

Formula C is used in *chain transactions* where the deposit is sent further up the chain and all transactions need to be synchronised.

- *Part one*: The solicitor at one end of the chain telephones the next one in line and each confirms that they hold part contract signed by their client. The solicitor at the end of the chain undertakes to exchange if they are called back by the other within a specified time *on that same day* (they are said to unconditionally and irrevocably 'release' their part contract for the specified time). This is repeated along the chain until a Formula B exchange takes place at the other end.
- *Part two*: There are then exchanges back along the chain.

Revision tip

When using any of these formulae it is necessary to record any agreed variations to them. For example, there is an undertaking to send the deposit by client account cheque, so if the funds are sent electronically (an option under the SCs, but compulsory under the SCPCs) this should be recorded. Likewise, if exchange takes place late in the working day, it may need to be agreed that the part contract and any deposit will be sent out on the following day.

Following exchange of contracts, a file note should be made recording the following:
- Names of the solicitors effecting the exchange.
- Date and time of exchange.
- Formula used and any agreed variations to it.
- Deposit.
- Completion date.

If Formula C is adopted, a note must be made of each conversation (the agreement to release) and the actual exchange.

Part one: Agreement to release
- The date and time of the conversation.
- The individuals involved and details of two others who may exchange in their absence.
- Formula to be used and any agreed variations.
- The proposed completion date.
- The end of the release period.
- Who to pay the deposit to.

Part two: Exchange
- The time.
- Identities of the parties.

Following exchange by any of the methods outlined above, the following actions should be taken:
- Prepare file notes/correspondence.
- Diarise the completion date.
- Inform clients and the estate agents.

CONSEQUENCES OF EXCHANGE

The consequences of exchange are as follows:
- The parties become committed under a binding contract to complete on the agreed completion date.
- The seller retains legal ownership, although the buyer gains an equitable interest under an estate contract (see *Revise SQE: Land Law*). Effectively, the seller holds the property on constructive trust for the buyer. They must take reasonable care of the property so that it can be transferred in the same condition, but they remain responsible for any outgoings and may keep any rent or profits until completion.
- Risk and the responsibility to insure the property both usually pass to the buyer under the SCs (see above).
- If the buyer occupies the property before completion, they do so as licensee (SC 5.2.2) although mortgagee's consent would be required and this is not recommended.

Strictly speaking, the buyer's interest under the contract should be protected through the registration of a Class C (iv) Land Charge (in unregistered land) or a Notice (in registered land) (see **Chapter 2**). However, this is only really done in practice where there are more than 6 weeks between exchange and completion.

■ KEY POINT CHECKLIST

This chapter has covered the following key knowledge points. You can use these to structure your revision, ensuring you recall the key details from each point:
- The contract is drafted by the seller's solicitor and usually incorporates the particulars of sale, standard conditions (either the SCs or the SCPCs) and special conditions.
- The deposit may be held as stakeholder or agent, and stakeholder is the safest option for a buyer. Under the SCs, the deposit is usually held as stakeholder unless the seller has a related purchase.
- The risk of damage or destruction of the property usually passes to the buyer on exchange of contracts, as does the responsibility for insurance. The seller should also be advised to maintain their policy until completion.

- The sale of a residential property is usually exempt from VAT, so the contract should provide that the purchase price is inclusive of VAT. The sale of an old commercial property is exempt from VAT, with the option to tax. If the option has not been exercised, the contract should provide that the purchase price is inclusive of VAT. If the option has been exercised, or on the sale of a new commercial property, the contract should provide that the purchase price is exclusive of VAT, which will be charged in addition thereto.
- It is very important to report to the client before exchange on all aspects of the transaction and acquire their authority to exchange.
- When acting for a lender, all of their requirements must be adhered to, both specifically and generally.
- The certificate of title should be prepared and issued before completion to confirm to the lender that it is safe to lend, confirm the title is good and marketable and request funds. If a qualified report is to be given, the issues should be disclosed before exchange of contracts.
- Following completion of pre-exchange steps, exchange of contracts should take place; if by telephone, using the appropriate Law Society formula A, B, or C.
- Following exchange of contracts, the beneficial interest in the property passes to the buyer and the transaction becomes legally binding.

■ KEY TERMS AND CONCEPTS

- standard conditions (**page 87**)
- Standard Conditions of Sale (**page 87**)
- Standard Commercial Property Conditions (**page 88**)
- special conditions (**page 88**)
- specified incumbrances (**page 90**)
- title guarantee (**page 91**)
- full title guarantee (**page 92**)
- limited title guarantee (**page 92**)
- no title guarantee (**page 92**)
- contract rate (**page 93**)
- deposit (**page 93**)
- stakeholder (**page 94**)
- agent (**page 94**)
- indemnity covenant (**page 98**)
- UK Finance Mortgage Lenders' Handbook (**page 103**)
- certificate of title (**page 104**)
- redemption statement (**page 105**)
- Formula A (**page 106**)
- Formula B (**page 106**)
- Formula C (**page 107**)

■ SQE1-STYLE QUESTIONS

QUESTION 1

A solicitor acts on the sale of a freehold residential property, where contracts have been exchanged. The property is subject to an existing mortgage in favour of a high street lender and the buyer will grant a new mortgage to a high street lender on completion. The contract incorporates the Standard Conditions of Sale (Fifth edition) and there are no relevant special conditions.

Which of the following best describes the position regarding the passing of risk and the responsibility for insurance?

A   The seller retains the risk of damage or destruction and must insure the property under the standard conditions.

B   The risk of damage or destruction passes to the buyer and they must insure the property under the standard conditions.

C   The risk of damage or destruction passes to the buyer and they must usually insure the property to fulfil their lender's requirements.

D   The risk of damage or destruction passes to the buyer but both parties should usually insure the property in order to fulfil the requirements of their respective lenders.

E   The risk of damage or destruction remains with the seller but both parties should usually insure the property in order to fulfil the requirements of their respective lenders.

QUESTION 2

A solicitor acts on the purchase of a freehold residential property, where the buyer would like to pay a reduced deposit of 5%. The draft contract incorporates the Standard Conditions of Sale (Fifth edition).

Which of the following best describes the position as regards the deposit?

A   The standard conditions provide that a deposit of 10% of the purchase price must be paid and that the deposit will be held by the seller's solicitor as agent.

B   The standard conditions provide that a deposit of 10% of the purchase price must be paid and that the deposit will be held by the seller's solicitor as stakeholder.

C   A special condition will need to be added to deal with the payment of the reduced deposit and also provide that the deposit will be held by the seller's solicitor as agent.

D   A special condition will need to be added to deal with the payment of the reduced deposit and also provide that the deposit will be held by the seller's solicitor as stakeholder.

E   A special condition will be required to deal with the payment of the reduced deposit and the deposit will be held by the seller's solicitor as stakeholder unless the seller has a related purchase of a property in the UK.

QUESTION 3

A solicitor acts on the purchase of a freehold residential property, which is registered at HM Land Registry with absolute title. The seller is acting as personal representative of the deceased sole proprietor.

Which of the following best describes the position regarding title guarantee?

A   The seller should give full title guarantee, otherwise the buyer will not be able to be registered with absolute title.

B   The seller would be expected to give limited title guarantee in these circumstances and it should not affect the class of title.

C   Limited title guarantee would be appropriate here. The seller will covenant that the property is free from all charges, incumbrances and third party rights other than those they do not and could not reasonably be expected to know about. The class of title should not be affected.

D   Limited title guarantee would be appropriate here as the seller covenants that they have the right to dispose of the property with the 'further assurance' that they will, at their own cost, do all they reasonably can to give the title they purport to give. The class of title should not be affected.

E   Full title guarantee would be appropriate here as the seller covenants that they have the right to dispose of the property with the 'further assurance' that they will, at their own cost, do all they reasonably can to give the title they purport to give. The class of title should not be affected.

QUESTION 4

A solicitor acts on the sale of a freehold commercial property, which was constructed approximately 18 months ago.

Which of the following best describes the VAT position and how best to deal with it in the contract?

A   The transaction will automatically be standard rated. The contract will need to include an obligation on the buyer to pay VAT on top of the purchase price and it would be appropriate to use the Part 1 Standard Commercial Property Conditions of Sale.

B   The transaction will be VAT exempt, meaning no VAT will be payable on the purchase price. It would be appropriate to use the un-amended Standard Conditions of Sale.

C   The transaction will be VAT exempt, meaning no VAT will be payable on the purchase price, unless the seller has exercised the option to tax. If the seller has done so, it would be appropriate to use the Part 1 Standard Commercial Property Conditions of Sale.

D   The transaction will be VAT exempt, meaning no VAT will be payable on the purchase price, unless the seller has exercised the option to tax. If the seller has not done so, it would be appropriate to use the Part 2 Standard Commercial Property Conditions of Sale.

E   The transaction will automatically be standard rated. The contract will need to include an obligation on the buyer to pay VAT on top of the purchase price and it would be appropriate to use the Part 2 Standard Commercial Property Conditions of Sale.

QUESTION 5

A solicitor has been instructed on the purchase of a freehold property, the title to which contains both restrictive and positive covenants, as well as a registered mortgage in the charges register. It is proposed that the contract will adopt the Standard Conditions of Sale (Fifth edition).

Which of the following best describes the position as regards the specified incumbrances?

A   The specified incumbrances should include the covenants as well as the mortgage, and the seller will be entitled to an indemnity covenant in respect of them.

B   The specified incumbrances should include only the covenants and the seller will be entitled to an indemnity in respect of them.

C   The specified incumbrances should include only the covenants and the seller will be entitled to an indemnity in respect of them if they were the original covenantor or they gave an indemnity on their purchase.

D   The specified incumbrances should include the covenants as well as the mortgage, but the seller will only be entitled to an indemnity covenant in respect of the covenants if they were the original covenantor.

E   The specified incumbrances should include only the covenants and the seller will be entitled to an indemnity in respect of them if they gave an indemnity on their purchase.

■ ANSWERS TO QUESTIONS

Answers to 'What do you know already?' questions at the start of the chapter

1) True. This means that the deposit may not be released to the seller until completion. Under the standard conditions of sale, the deposit is usually held as stakeholder, unless the seller has a related purchase in the UK.

2) Under the standard conditions, on the sale of a freehold property the risk of damage and destruction of the property following exchange of contracts usually passes to the buyer. The buyer should therefore be advised to insure the property. It will also usually be a requirement of any lender that insurance is in place and the seller should be advised to maintain their policy of insurance until completion.

3) The sale of a residential property is usually exempt from VAT.

4) Law Society Formula B should be used in these circumstances.

Answers to end-of-chapter SQE1-style questions

Question 1

The correct answer was D. The risk of damage or destruction of the property in these circumstances passes to the buyer (SC 5.1.1) and the seller is under no contractual obligation to insure the property (SC 5.1.2). Therefore, options A and E are incorrect in these respects. Although the buyer should be *advised* to insure the property to protect their own interests and fulfil the usual lender requirements, it is not a contractual obligation for them to do so. Therefore, option B is incorrect on this point. Option C is therefore partially correct, but option D is most correct since both parties will be under an obligation to insure to protect their respective lenders.

Question 2

The correct answer was E. Although the standard conditions do provide that a deposit of 10% of the purchase price is payable on exchange of contracts (making options A and B partially correct), a special condition may be added varying this to deal with the payment of a reduced deposit (making options C and D partially correct). The general position is that the deposit will be held as stakeholder (not agent), unless the seller has a related purchase of a property in the UK. Therefore, option A is incorrect and option B is only partially correct on this point. The special condition will not have to deal with the deposit being held as stakeholder or agent as the default position should apply and stakeholder is safer for the buyer. Therefore, options C and D are also incorrect here.

Question 3

The correct answer was B. The seller would not be expected to give full title guarantee in these circumstances as they do not own the whole legal and equitable interest in the property, and they will usually have limited knowledge about it. Therefore, options A and E are incorrect in this respect. Title guarantee concerns the status of the seller, rather than the quality of the title itself, therefore the class of title should not be affected (making option A incorrect on this point and options C, D, and E partially correct). Option C is also incorrect as the covenants referred to relate to full title guarantee. Options D and E are incorrect as the covenants referred to do not relate exclusively to full or limited title guarantee – they apply in both cases.

Question 4

The correct answer was A. This is the sale of a 'new' commercial property and it will automatically be standard rated. Therefore, options B, C, and D are incorrect in this respect, although option F is partially correct. It would be most appropriate to use the Part 1 SCPCs as they oblige the buyer to pay VAT on top of the purchase price. It would be inappropriate to use the Part 2 SCPCs as the same contain a warranty that VAT is not payable by the buyer, which would leave the seller out of pocket. Therefore, option E is incorrect on this point. If the property were an old commercial property, the sale would be exempt, but with the option to tax by the seller. If the option to tax had been exercised, it would be advisable to use the Part 1 SCPCs (see option C). If not, it would be advisable to use the Part 2 SCPCs (see option D). The sale of a residential property is usually exempt and it would be most appropriate to use the SCs (see option B).

Question 5

The correct answer was C. The specified incumbrances should include the covenants, but exclude the mortgage as it will usually be discharged on completion and hence the buyer will not take subject to it. Therefore, options A and D are incorrect in this respect and options B and E are partially correct. The seller will only be entitled to an indemnity in respect of covenants for which they may remain liable after completion (SC 4.6.4). Therefore, this would exclude the mortgage, but would include covenants for which the seller was either an original party or for which an indemnity was given on purchase. Therefore, options A and B are incorrect on this point and options D and E are only partially correct.

■ KEY CASES, RULES, STATUTES, AND INSTRUMENTS

The SQE1 Assessment Specification does not require you to know any statutory authorities or specific case names for this topic. Specific sections of statutes and standard conditions are set out for ease of reference.

5

Pre-completion, completion, and post-completion matters

■ MAKE SURE YOU KNOW

This chapter provides an overview of pre-completion, completion, and post-completion matters. It deals with the key pre-completion requirements, searches, and steps, including drafting and agreeing the form of transfer deed and the formalities for its execution. It then deals with completion itself (methods and effect) and post-completion steps (including the discharge of mortgages, Stamp Duty Land Tax (SDLT)/Land Transaction Tax (LTT) (see also **Chapter 10**) and HM Land Registry formalities). Finally, the chapter considers remedies for delayed completion, including contractual compensation, common law damages, notice to complete, and rescission. For the SQE1 assessments, you will need to understand the detail of each of these elements as well as how they fit into the bigger process (see **Chapter 1**).

■ SQE ASSESSMENT ADVICE

For SQE1, you are required to understand the stages of pre-completion, completion, and post-completion. You need to appreciate what each aspect entails for both the solicitor acting for the seller and the solicitor acting for the buyer/lender. You also need to be aware of the key remedies for a delay or failure to complete.

As you work through this chapter, remember to pay particular attention in your revision to:

- The key pre-completion steps and searches, including drafting and agreeing the form of transfer deed and the formalities for its execution.
- How completion is effected.
- Post-completion steps, including the discharge of any mortgage(s), SDLT/ LTT and HM Land Registry formalities.
- What remedies may be available for failure to complete.

■ WHAT DO YOU KNOW ALREADY?

Attempt these questions before reading this chapter. If you find some difficult or cannot remember the answers, remember to look more closely at that topic during your revision.

1) Which form of transfer deed would be appropriate for the sale of the whole of the land comprised within a registered title?

   [Form of transfer deed, page 117]

2) True or false? When acting on the purchase of a property with registered title by a company from another company, an OS1 search must always be made in the name of the buyer. Bankruptcy-only searches must also be made against the companies.

   [Pre-completion searches and enquiries, page 121]

3) What are the time limits for submission of an SDLT/LTT return and for submission of an FR1 and AP1?

   [Post-completion, page 130]

4) True or false? There is no immediate right under the standard conditions to rescind the contract in the event of a delay in completion, although contractual compensation may be payable.

   [Remedies for late completion, page 134]

INTRODUCTION TO COMPLETION

The second key milestone in a property transaction is completion (see **Chapter 1**). The *equitable interest* in the property passes at exchange of contracts (see **Chapter 4**), when the parties become bound to complete on the agreed completion date. At completion, the *legal interest* is transferred, through completion of the transfer deed (subject to registration at HM Land Registry), the balance purchase price is paid, and the keys are handed over. There will be pre-completion matters that need to be attended to following exchange of contracts, and post-completion matters required to conclude the matter.

THE TRANSFER DEED

The first major step following exchange of contracts is for the buyer's solicitor to produce the draft **transfer deed** and to send it to the seller's solicitor for approval and execution.

Key term: transfer deed

The transfer deed is needed to transfer the legal estate to the buyer. Although a contract is not always required in a conveyancing transaction (see **Chapter 4**), a transfer deed will *always* be required to transfer legal ownership. This is because a conveyance of land, or of an interest in it, will usually be void for the purposes of creating a legal estate unless it is made by deed (s 52 Law of Property Act 1925 (LPA)).

Drafting the transfer deed: responsibilities and timing

The usual convention is that the buyer's solicitor produces the draft transfer deed, using the information from the contract and title/deeds and, if not sending it electronically, provides two hard copies to the seller's solicitor. The seller's solicitor then approves and/or amends the draft transfer. If it is approved as drawn, the seller's solicitor will use one copy (usually referred to as the top copy or engrossment) as the final copy/version and arrange for it to be executed (see **Execution**, below).

Strictly speaking, Standard Condition of Sale (SC) 4.3.2 and Standard Commercial Property Condition (SCPC) 7.3.2 provide a timetable for drafting, approving, and providing a clean copy of the transfer deed (see **Chapter 4** for more on SCs and SCPCs). However, these provisions are rarely referred to in practice as the parties invariably act expeditiously following exchange of contracts.

Form of transfer deed

In *registered land* (see **Chapter 2** for more on registered/unregistered land), the HM Land Registry standard forms of transfer deed *must* be used. These are usually **form TR1** or, in some circumstances, **form TP1**.

Key term: form TR1

Form TR1 is used for the transfer of the *whole* of the land comprised within a registered title or titles. It is also often used for the transfer of the whole of the land comprised within an unregistered title or titles (see **Revision tip**, below).

Key term: form TP1

Form TP1 is used for the transfer of *part* of the land comprised within a registered title or titles. It is also often used for the transfer of part of the land comprised within an unregistered title or titles (see below).

Revision tip

In the case of registered land, the HM Land Registry standard forms of transfer *must* be used (see Rule 58 of The Land Registration Rules 2003). The relevant standard form of transfer *may* also be used for the transfer of unregistered land. Although it is possible to use an old-fashioned conveyance instead (ie a bespoke document, rather than a standard form – see **Chapter 2**), it is standard practice not to. For the purposes of SQE1, you should be familiar with forms TR1 and TP1 and you can view specimens of both at www.gov.uk. Most importantly, you should know which form would be appropriate in given circumstances and how they differ.

Revision tip

Although it is the usual convention that the buyer's solicitor drafts the transfer deed, this may vary in some circumstances:

- In a *straightforward sale of whole*, the seller's solicitor may produce the draft transfer as part of the pre-contract documents (see **Chapters 2–4**), so that it can be agreed before exchange.
- On a *sale of part*, it can be more straightforward for the seller's solicitor to draft the transfer and provide in the contract that the transfer will be in the form of the annexed draft (see **Chapter 4**). This avoids having to duplicate new easements, covenants (see **Chapters 2 and 4**), and declarations in the contract and makes the process more efficient.
- A *sale of newbuild property* by a developer will typically be a sale of part of the land comprised within a registered title. Therefore, for the reasons stated above, the usual convention of the buyer's solicitor drafting the transfer will be dispensed with.

Drafting forms TR1 and TP1

As stated above, the transfer deed is drafted using the information from the contract and registered title or title deeds. **Table 5.1** sets out the sections of form TR1 with the key points on what to include.

Table 5.1: Completing form TR1

TR1 panel number	Description	Comments
1	Title number(s)	Insert from contract/official copies. Leave blank if title unregistered.
2	Property	Insert from contract/official copies/title documents.
3	Date	This should be left blank and only inserted on the completion date. It is standard practice to write '*Do not date*' in pencil in this panel, with additional instructions, if sending it to the client for execution.
4	Transferor	Insert from contract/official copies/title documents.
5	Transferee for entry in the register	Insert from contract.
6	Transferee's intended address(es) for service	This will usually be the property address, but may be the buyer's home or business address (eg if they are buying an investment property), or a company's registered office. Up to three addresses may be given, one of which must be a postal (rather than electronic) address.

Table 5.1: (Continued)

7	Transfer	This is the main operational part of the transfer – it simply declares that the transferor transfers the property to the transferee.
8	Consideration	The consideration (purchase price, not including any separate price for chattels) must be stated here in both words and figures (including any VAT (see **Chapters 4 and 10**)).
9	Title guarantee	This should reflect what was agreed in the contract – full, limited, or no title guarantee (see **Chapter 4**).
10	Declaration of trust	In the case of co-ownership, this should be completed based on the clients' instructions on how the beneficial interest should be held (see **Chapters 1 and 2**). There are three options: joint tenants, tenants in common in equal shares, or another way (eg tenants in common in unequal shares – in which case the percentage shares should be specified). It is also possible to use HM Land Registry form JO to declare the beneficial interest, but it is standard practice to use this panel instead.
11	Additional provisions	These should be inserted as provided for in the contract. On a sale where the seller remains liable for covenants (see **Chapters 2 and 4**), an indemnity covenant will usually be added here. The seller will be entitled to this in any event under SC 4.6.4 and SCPC 7.6.5.
12	Execution	See **Execution**, below.

Revision tip

Form TP1 looks very similar, but contains additional panels for the following:

- The title number(s) of other titles affected by the transfer.
- Additional provisions: Definitions (eg of the retained land), rights granted for the benefit of the property, rights reserved for the benefit of other land, restrictive covenants by the transferee, restrictive covenants by the transferor, and agreed declarations. Declarations can include declarations as to light and air (see **Chapter 2**) and that the rule in *Wheeldon v Burrows* and s 62 LPA 1925 are excluded from the transfer – see *Revise SQE: Land Law*.

Drafting a full TP1 is outside of the scope of this book, but for the purposes of SQE1, you should be aware of what they usually contain. In practice, great care needs to be taken in the drafting and negotiation of the additional provisions, although precedents are widely available.

It is imperative to include a HM Land Registry compliant plan on a sale of part (see *HM Land Registry Practice Guide 40* and **Chapter 4**).

Execution

It is important that the transfer is correctly executed as a deed so that it validly conveys the legal estate (see above).

For newly granted deeds, the requirements are as follows:
• It must be *clear on the face of it that it is a deed*.
• It must be *signed* by the parties and *delivered* (ie intended to take effect – although the word delivered does not need to be used if it is clear on the face of it that it is a deed: it is presumed delivered on execution).
• The signature also needs to be *attested*, ie witnessed by an independent adult witness (ie not a family member or a party to the transaction) who should also sign, printing their name, address, and occupation below.

It is no longer a requirement for deeds executed by individuals to be sealed (see **Chapter 2**).

A company may execute by affixing the company seal if this is provided for in its articles of association (see **Revise SQE: Business Law and Practice**). Otherwise, the company acting by two directors, or by two directors and another person who is the company secretary, may execute it. In other words, if someone is both a director and the company secretary, they cannot sign twice. Alternatively, a single director may execute it on behalf of the company by signing in the presence of an independent witness (see Companies Act 2006, s 44).

It is also best practice for any plan(s) annexed to the transfer deed to be signed by the signatories, although these signatures do not need to be attested.

Revision tip

HM Land Registry Practice Guide 8 on execution of deeds contains useful guidance and some examples of execution clauses.

The seller/transferor must *always* execute the transfer. However, the buyer/transferee only needs to execute it if they are entering into new covenants (eg an indemnity covenant – see **Chapter 4**) or agreeing to any new declarations within the deed (eg a declaration of trust in the case of co-ownership – see **Chapter 2**). If the buyer needs to execute the transfer, it is best practice for it to be executed by them first (sometimes called executed in escrow) and then sent to the seller's solicitor for execution by the seller, or for the transfer to be executed in two parts. A seller's solicitor will usually be *very* reluctant to hand over such an important executed document before completion and may be negligent if they did.

PRE-COMPLETION SEARCHES AND ENQUIRIES

The buyer's solicitor will also undertake **pre-completion searches and enquiries** and, for SQE1, it is important to understand why they are carried out and what the results may reveal.

Key term: pre-completion searches and enquiries

These are undertaken by the buyer or the buyer's solicitor. Some are undertaken in all circumstances and the others will depend on the status of the seller and/or buyer and whether title to the land is registered or unregistered. They serve to update information provided before exchange and to confirm the solvency of the seller and the buyer, as well as arrangements for completion.

Figure 5.1 provides a useful overview of which searches and enquiries are required in which circumstances.

Pre-completion HM Land Registry search: registered land

In the case of *registered land*, a **pre-completion HM Land Registry search** must be undertaken.

Key term: pre-completion HM Land Registry search

This search serves two very important purposes:
- It 'updates' the official copies provided and investigated pre-exchange, to confirm whether any adverse entries (eg incumbrances; see **Chapters 2 and 4**) have been made to the title since the issue date.
- It provides the buyer's solicitor with a thirty working-day priority period to submit the HM Land Registry application to register the transfer (and any mortgage). Provided that the application is submitted in time, it will take priority over any other submitted applications.

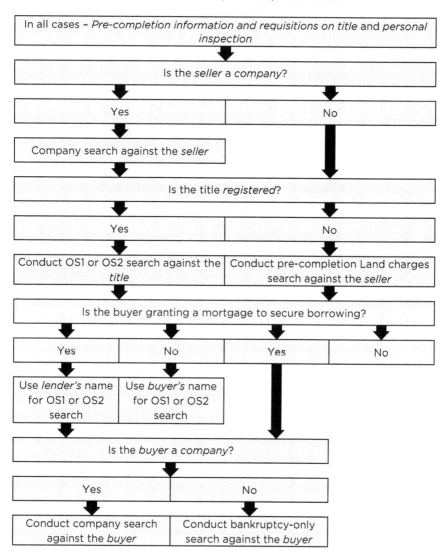

Figure 5.1: Pre-completion searches and enquiries – an overview

For SQE1, the most common types of pre-completion HM Land Registry searches that you need to be aware of are an **OS1 search** and an **OS2 search**.

Key term: OS1 search

An OS1 is an official search with priority of the *whole* of the land in a registered title. This is the most common search and is used when all of the land in the title is being transferred.

Key term: OS2 search

An OS2 is an official search with priority of *part* of the land in a registered title. This is used when part of the land in the title is being transferred (eg a sale of part, which would typically include the sale of a property on a new development). A plan must usually be submitted with an OS2 application as the whole of the title will not be affected. On the purchase of a newbuild property, there may also be an estate plan that has been pre-approved by HM Land Registry, in which case the plot number may be entered instead.

Exam warning

Both types of search should be made against the title number from the *search from date* on the official copies (not the *edition date* – see **Chapter 2**) and *should be made in the name of the lender if there is a mortgage involved on the purchase*. Searching in the name of the lender/mortgagee gives *both* the buyer's and the lender's applications (for the transfer and mortgage respectively) priority, whereas a search in the name of the buyer (normal where there is no mortgage on the purchase) would protect them only. This is a crucially important point that is not always appreciated by candidates.

The results will be provided on form OS1R or OS2R, as appropriate, and will clearly set out whether there have been any adverse entries since the search from date (providing a new edition of the register, if so). If any adverse entries are revealed, requisitions (see **Chapter 1**) should be made of the seller. The priority period will also be clearly set out. It is crucially important to diarise this date and the run up to it so that the HM Land Registry application is lodged in good time. Failure to do so could result in a professional negligence claim against the solicitor/firm, if loss is suffered (see **Practice example 5.1**).

Practice example 5.1

A solicitor acts for a lender (the first lender) on its taking of a first legal mortgage over a property with registered title. They undertook the correct OS1 search with a priority period that expired at 12 P.M. yesterday, but they failed to submit the HM Land Registry application in time. They are also aware of a second charge in favour of another lender (the second lender), to which the first lender provided consent. The second lender had the benefit of an OS1 priority search for the 30 working-day period following the expiry of the first lender's priority period.

What are the implications for the first lender's charge?

Had the first lender's HM Land Registry application been submitted on time, any application from the second lender would have been held over until expiry of the first priority period. The second lender's

application will now take priority (meaning the second charge will be registered as a first charge) and the solicitor will have been negligent in not submitting the application in time to protect the first lender's priority.

Pre-completion Land charges search: unregistered land

In the case of *unregistered land*, a full **pre-completion Land charges search** must usually be undertaken against the *seller(s)*.

Land charges searches (using form K15) will already have been undertaken at the pre-contract stage (see **Chapters 2 and 3**) against all known estate owners referred to in the epitome of title documents (see **Chapter 2**) since 1926.

Key term: pre-completion Land charges search

This search is made against the *seller(s) only* in unregistered land on form K15. The results (on form K18) give the buyer a 15 working-day priority period to complete the transaction (see **Revision tip**, below). This means that they will not take subject to any land charges registered against the name of the seller(s) after the date of the search, provided that *completion* takes place within the priority period.

If the matter can be *completed* within 15 working days of the pre-contract Land charges search (see **Chapters 2 and 3**), then it will not need to be repeated. It is not necessary to search against the names of former estate owners again at this stage.

Any adverse entries must be dealt with accordingly (see **Chapters 2 and 3**).

Revision tip

It is important to appreciate the difference in the nature of the priority periods afforded by an OS1/OS2 search and a pre-completion Land charges search. The former gives priority to the *HM Land Registry application*, whereas the latter gives priority to the *completion date*, as opposed to the date by which the application for first registration should be submitted (see **Registration at HM Land Registry**, below).

Insolvency searches: registered and unregistered land

In the case of *registered and unregistered land*, where a *buyer who is an individual* (as opposed to a company) is borrowing to fund the purchase, a bankruptcy search must be made against them, for the benefit of the lender (who will be keen to ensure that they are not subject to bankruptcy proceedings):

• In *registered land*, a **bankruptcy-only search** will be undertaken.

- In *unregistered land*, a bankruptcy-only search may be undertaken or, for convenience, the buyer may be added to the pre-completion Land charges (K15) search when searching against the seller.

Key term: bankruptcy-only search

A bankruptcy-only search is a more limited form of Land charges search, which searches for bankruptcy entries only. It is made on form K16.

If any adverse entries are revealed against the relevant name(s), the buyer should be asked to confirm that the entries do not relate to them. The buyer signing a simple certification by way of an endorsement on the form usually achieves this.

In the case of *registered and unregistered land*, where a *buyer who is a company* (as opposed to an individual) is borrowing to fund the purchase, a company search must be made against them, for the benefit of the lender (who will be keen to ensure that they are not subject to insolvency proceedings). In addition to the matters referred to below, the articles of association must be checked to ensure that the company has power to borrow money (see *Revise SQE: Business Law and Practice*).

Company search: registered and unregistered land

In the case of *registered and unregistered land*, where the seller is a company, a **company search** must be made against them.

Key term: company search

A company search checks whether the company is in existence, subject to any insolvency proceedings or procedures, and whether it has granted any fixed or floating charges over its assets (see *Revise SQE: Business Law and Practice*).

The seller's solicitor must be asked to provide an undertaking to discharge any fixed charges on or before completion and to provide written confirmation that any floating charges have not become fixed through crystallisation (see below and *Revise SQE: Business Law and Practice*).

Procedural link

For SQE1, you should appreciate the differences between individual and corporate insolvency and the different types of charges that may be granted by companies (see *Revise SQE: Business Law and Practice*).

Company searches have no priority period, so it is wise to undertake them as close as possible to completion. In cases of real concern as to the insolvency status of a company, or where a transaction is of particularly high value, a telephone search may be made of the Registry of Winding-up petitions at the Companies Court.

Personal inspection: registered and unregistered land

It is wise to remind the client of the need to carry out a personal inspection of the property prior to completion to check the following:

- The general state and condition.
- For occupiers who may have overriding interests (see **Chapter 2**).
- That all relevant fittings to be transferred are present.
- That no fixtures have been removed (other than those agreed upon under the contract).
- Whether there are any issues or problems that remain to be resolved under the terms of the contract.

A personal inspection is particularly relevant with newbuild properties where it is important to ensure that the property has actually been built and whether there are any issues with small defects (snagging) that will require resolution.

Completion information and undertakings

It is at this stage that the buyer's solicitor must also raise pre-completion requisitions on title of the seller's solicitor. They usually deal with key practical issues surrounding completion and it is common practice to use the standard Law Society Conveyancing Protocol form, **Completion information and undertakings**. A sample can be viewed at www.lawsociety.org.uk. Please note that a new edition of the form (4th edition) was issued on 9 January 2023.

Key term: Completion information and undertakings form

This form is raised by the buyer's solicitor, for completion by the seller's solicitor. It deals with the following practical matters concerning completion:

Q1 – Vacant possession and key arrangements.

Q2 – What deeds and documents will be handed over on completion.

Q3 – Place and method of completion, with an *undertaking* (see **Procedural link**, below) to adopt the Law Society's Code for Completion by Post 2019 (the 'Code') (see **Completion**, below).

Q4 – Amount payable on completion and the seller's solicitor's bank details.

Q5 – *Undertaking* (see below) to redeem or discharge specified/listed mortgage(s) on or before completion and to send form **DS1**, **DS3**, the **receipted charge**(s), or confirmation that the notice of release or discharge in electronic form has been given to HM Land Registry, as and when it is received. If the Code is not adopted, the seller's solicitor must confirm they are the duly authorised agent of the proprietor of every mortgage or charge for which an undertaking has been given to redeem or discharge (this is a standard requirement of the Code).

Key term: DS1

Form DS1 is a form executed by the lender confirming that a charge over the whole of a registered title has been discharged. Alternatively, confirmation that an electronic DS1 (e-DS1) has been sent or confirmation of direct electronic discharge (ED) may be provided by some large lenders.

Key term: DS3

Form DS3 is a form executed by the lender confirming that a charge has been discharged over part of a registered title. It should always have a plan annexed to identify the part of the title that has been released.

Key term: receipted charge

A receipted charge (or original mortgage with a vacating receipt endorsed on it) is provided in the case of a charge over unregistered land (see **Chapter 2**).

Procedural link

The Completion information and undertakings form contains undertakings at questions 3 and 5. For SQE1 you should familiarise yourself on undertakings within the context of Property Practice (see *Revise SQE: Ethics and Professional Conduct*). Most importantly, the seller's solicitor should seek a redemption statement (see **Chapter 4**) from the lender(s) before giving the relevant undertakings, in order to ensure there will be sufficient funds from the proceeds of sale. Depending on the terms of the redemption statement obtained prior to exchange of contracts, it may be necessary to update it, again requesting a daily rate of interest to deal with any delay.

Revision tip

Although charges over the whole of a title(s) in registered land may be discharged electronically (using an e-DS1 or ED), there are no equivalent processes for discharges of part.

Summary of pre-completion searches and enquiries

For SQE1, you need to know, with precision, which pre-completion searches and enquiries are applicable in different circumstances. **Table 5.2** provides a useful summary.

Table 5.2: Summary of pre-completion searches and enquiries

Search	When relevant	Who/what to search against	Purpose	Priority period
Land Registry pre-completion search (OS1 – whole or OS2 – part)	Registered title	Title number In favour of *buyer* if no mortgage In favour of *lender* if transfer and/or mortgage	Update official entries and provide priority	30 working days to submit HM Land Registry application
Pre-Completion Land charges search (K15)	Unregistered title	Seller(s)	To take free of entries arising until completion	15 working days to complete
Bankruptcy-only search (K16)	Registered and unregistered title *and* buyer is an *individual* granting a mortgage	Buyer(s)/Borrower(s)	Verify solvency for lender	As K15 search
Company search	Registered and unregistered title *and* buyer is a *company* granting a mortgage or charge	Buyer(s)/Borrower(s)	Verify solvency for lender and power to borrow	N/A
Company search	Registered and unregistered title and *seller* is a *company*	Seller(s)	Verify existence and solvency of seller(s) and existing charges	N/A
Personal inspection	Registered and unregistered title	Buyer(s) to inspect the property	Check for changes since exchange of contracts	N/A
Pre-completion information and undertakings	Registered and unregistered title	Raised of the seller's solicitor	Confirm completion arrangements (including discharge of charge(s))	N/A

Financial matters

Once the buyer's solicitor has confirmation of the balance due, they should:

- (If not already submitted) issue the certificate of title to the lender (or its solicitor) with any additional information required (eg a copy of the executed mortgage, pre-completion search results).
- Request the balance due from the client, in the form of a financial statement (including the balance due to the seller's solicitor on completion, professional charges, disbursements to date, and anticipated disbursements (eg SDLT/LTT, HM Land Registry fees, and telegraphic transfer fees), less any funds paid on account).

Both of the above should be undertaken in good time to enable funds to be transferred, and it is particularly important to be aware of how much notice the lender will require.

COMPLETION

At completion:

- The balance purchase price is transferred to the seller's solicitor.
- The deposit is released (if held as stakeholder – see **Chapter 4**).
- The transfer deed and buyer's mortgage deed are dated.
- The seller's solicitor then immediately sends the amount required to redeem any existing mortgage(s) to the mortgagee(s) by way of telegraphic transfer, in fulfilment of their undertaking to do so (see **Post-completion**, below).

Practice and procedure

On the day of completion, it is good practice for the buyer's solicitor to telephone the seller's solicitor to confirm that the balance purchase monies have been sent over. Under both sets of standard conditions, the funds should be sent by bank transfer (SC 6.7 and SCPC 9.7). The seller's solicitor should telephone the buyer's solicitors to acknowledge the funds, when received, and agree the release of the deposit and completion by dating the transfer deed. The buyer's solicitor will date the mortgage and it is usually the seller's solicitor who holds and dates the transfer deed (unless it has been executed in two parts).

In the event of a synchronised sale and purchase (see **Chapter 1**) the purchase follows the sale along the chain.

Date, time, and place of completion and the Law Society's Code for Completion by Post

In the rare event that no completion date is set on exchange of contracts, the date will be twenty working days after the date of the contract (SC 6.1.1 and SCPC 9.1.1).

Unless the time for completion is amended by way of special condition (see **Chapter 4**), the time for completion will be 2 P.M. If the funds have not been received by then, completion is treated as having taken place on the next working day (see SC 6.1.2 and 9.1.2 and **Remedies for late completion**, below).

Completion usually takes place at the office of the seller's solicitor (SC 6.2.2 and SCPC 9.2.2). It is rare for completion to take place through attendance in person and it is usual to adopt the **Law Society's Code for Completion by Post** (it is compulsory if the Protocol (see **Chapter 1**) is adopted).

> **Key term: Law Society's Code for Completion by Post ('the Code')**
>
> The Code provides that the seller's solicitor acts as unpaid agent for the buyer's solicitor in completing the transaction and undertakes to send the completion documents out by first class post or through the document exchange (DX) system on the day of completion, at the buyer's risk. The most recent version of the Code is 2019, and it can be viewed at www.lawsociety.org.uk. It is important to check the latest version of the Code at the time you sit the SQE1 assessments. Any variation to the undertaking to send the documents out on the same day must be agreed.

The purchase monies will be held to the order of the buyer's solicitor (meaning they are not yet released to the seller's solicitor) until completion is agreed, following which any title deeds and documents will be held to the order of the buyer.

There is an implied undertaking that the seller's solicitor will carry out the instructions of the buyer's solicitor on completion, so it is important to specify what is expected and what documents must be handed over (eg examined deeds from the epitome of title on a sale of part of unregistered land).

Effect of completion

The effect of completion in *unregistered land* is that legal title passes to the buyer. However, in *registered land*, legal title does not technically pass until the disposition (ie the dealing with/the transfer of the title) is completed by registration (see **Chapter 1**).

POST-COMPLETION

Following completion, the main tasks of the *seller's solicitor* after sending the redemption monies to any mortgagee(s) will be to:
- Send the dated transfer deed and other title deeds and documents (if any) to the buyer's solicitor.

- In *registered land* subject to an existing mortgage: complete form DS1 or DS3 (as appropriate – see above) and send it to the relevant mortgagee(s), unless they have confirmed that they will be discharging the charge electronically.
- In *unregistered land* subject to an existing mortgage: Send the original legal mortgage back to the mortgagee with a request for the vacating receipt to be endorsed on it.
- Send appropriate evidence of discharge (executed DS1, DS3, receipted charge/mortgage, or confirmation of electronic discharge) to the buyer's solicitor as soon as it is received, to fulfil the undertaking given.
- Account to the client for the balance due (following deduction of estate agent's fees where authority has been given to pay them, costs, and disbursements (including official copy fees and bank transfer charges)), seek formal release of the undertaking(s) given, make any necessary accounts transfers, and close the file.

Revision tip

In the case of particularly high value transactions, where the lender is not a member of UK Finance (see **Chapter 1**), a buyer's solicitor should obtain confirmation that the value of the mortgage does not exceed the level of professional indemnity insurance of the seller's solicitor. If it does, the buyer's solicitor should either insist on increased cover or that evidence of discharge be provided on completion.

Following completion, the main tasks of the *buyer's solicitor* will be to:
- Check the documents received from the seller's solicitor.
- Deal with the SDLT/LLT formalities (see below and **Chapter 10**).
- If the buyer is a company and there is mortgage or other charge(s) in favour of a lender, register the charge(s) at Companies House within 21 days.
- Register the disposition at HM Land Registry or apply for first registration, as appropriate (see **Registration at HM Land Registry**, below).
- Check the title information document (newly issued official copies) received from HM Land Registry to make sure the transfer and any charge have been registered correctly, and if a first registration, that there are no errors or omissions in the registration.
- Send a copy of the title information document to the lender together with any other documents required in accordance with its instructions.
- Send a copy of the title information document to the client together with any other title deeds and documents not required by the lender.
- Make any necessary accounts transfers and close the file.

Submission of SDLT/LTT return and payment of tax due

For properties in *England*, the SDLT return (form SDLT 1) must be completed and sent to His Majesty's Revenue and Customs (HMRC) within 14 days of completion.

For properties in *Wales*, the LTT return (form LTR) must be completed and sent to the Welsh Revenue Authority (WRA) within 30 days of completion.

Both forms may be submitted in paper form or online.

It is important to diarise the relevant dates as there are penalties (including fines and interest) for non-submission and late payments.

A form SDLT5 (in England) or a WRA certificate will be received when the relevant return has been made and duty paid. It is required to go with the application to register the disposition or property at HM Land Registry (see below).

Registration of charge at Companies House

Although it is not a strict requirement under the law to register a charge granted by a company borrower at Companies House, it is considered *vitally important* due to the potential consequences of failure to register. It is therefore an extremely important requirement of lenders in practice.

Any such charge should be registered at Companies House within 21 days of its creation by sending form MR01, a certified copy of the charge and the relevant fee.

Failure to register has very serious consequences – the charge will be void against a creditor, liquidator, or administrator of the borrower. As such, there is the potential for a negligence claim in the event of failure to register, and a court order would be required to file it late (see **Revise SQE: Business Law and Practice**, where this is dealt with in more detail).

Registration at HM Land Registry

In the case of *registered land*, the disposition should be registered at HM Land Registry using form AP1 (an application to change the register) within the priority period of the OS1/OS2 search.

The following documents should be sent with the application (set out in chronological order) to register the discharge (if applicable), transfer, and charge (if applicable):
• Evidence of discharge.
• Transfer.
• SDLT/LTT certificate.
• Mortgage.
• Certificate of registration at Companies House (if applicable) together with confirmation that it is the same charge to which the Companies House registration relates.

- **Form DI** to disclose any overriding interests.
- Relevant fee.

> ### Key term: form DI
> The disclosable overriding interests form, used to disclose any overriding interests known to the buyer (eg short leases – see **Chapter 7**).

Solicitors and other professional conveyancers may send certified copies of the documents, rather than the originals, with an AP1 application (see above) or FR1 application (see below).

In the case of *unregistered land*, an application should be made to HM Land Registry using form FR1 (an application for first registration) within two months of completion. Failure to register means that the transfer becomes void as regards the transfer of the legal estate (s 7 Land Registration Act 2002).

The following documents should be sent with the application (set out in chronological order and listed on form DL (documents list), in duplicate) to register the title, transfer, and charge (if applicable):

- Documents from the epitome of title (including Land charges searches).
- Pre-contract searches, enquiries, and replies.
- Contract.
- Requisitions on title and replies.
- Pre-completion search certificates.
- Transfer.
- Receipted mortgage.
- SDLT/LTT certificate.
- Mortgage.
- Certificate of registration at Companies House (if applicable) together with confirmation that it is the same charge to which the Companies House registration relates.
- Form DI (as above).
- Relevant fee.

> ### Revision tip
> For most AP1 and FR1 applications it is also necessary to provide details of conveyancers acting for all parties or verification of the identity of unrepresented parties (see *HM Land Registry Practice Guide 67*).

Summary of post-completion applications and time limits
For SQE1, you need to know, with precision, which post-completion applications are relevant and applicable in different circumstances. **Table 5.3** provides a useful summary.

Table 5.3: Summary of post-completion applications and time limits

Application	When relevant	Time limit
SDLT return	Land transaction in England	14 days of completion
LTT return	Land transaction in Wales	30 days of completion
AP1	Application to register a disposition of a registered title	Within priority period of OS1 or OS2 search
FR1	Application for first registration of property with unregistered title	Within 2 months of completion

REMEDIES FOR LATE COMPLETION

For SQE1, it is important to know the implications and remedies available in the event of late completion and to be able to apply them to factual scenarios.

If completion does not take place by the agreed time (typically 2 P.M. – See **Chapter 4**) on the agreed date, then there is no immediate right to rescind the contract (see *Revise SQE: Contract Law*). This is because time is not of the essence of the contract until a **notice to complete** is served (SC 6.1 and SCPC 9.1). However, completion is treated as having taken place on the next working day and **contractual compensation** *may* be payable (SC 7.2 and SCPC 10.3).

Exam warning

Under the SCs, either the seller or buyer may be required to pay contractual compensation for late completion. However, *only the buyer* may be required to pay it under the SCPCs. This is an important distinction and could therefore form part of an assessment question.

Key term: contractual compensation

Contractual compensation is payable on actual completion at the contract rate (see **Chapter 4**) on the balance purchase price (less the deposit if the buyer is in default) for the period during which the party was in default (see **Practice example 5.2**).

Common law damages, based on normal contractual principles for breach of contract (see *Revise SQE: Contract Law*) may also be claimed for consequential losses such as additional legal, removal, and storage costs.

Revision tip

The rules on calculation of contractual damages are outside the scope of this book. However, the important thing to be aware of is that there can be *no double recovery*. Therefore, any *contractual compensation* would need to be deducted from the total amount of common law contractual damages.

Key term: notice to complete

A notice to complete can be served by either the seller or the buyer, provided that they are ready and able to complete and the time for contractual completion has passed (SC 6.8.1 and SCPC 9.8.1). The effect is to make time of the essence of the contract, and it gives the party in default ten working days to complete following service (SC 6.8.2 and SCPC 9.8.2).

If the notice is not complied with, the party serving the notice has the *option* (not an obligation) to rescind the contract. The deposit may be forfeited with accrued interest (if the buyer is in default) or repaid with accrued interest (if the seller is in default) (SC 7.4 and 7.5 and SCPC 10.5 and 10.6). Under SCPC 9.8.3, if the deposit was less than 10% of the purchase price, the buyer must pay the balance immediately on service of the notice to complete.

In the event of rescission, the non-defaulting party retains their rights to other rights and remedies, including damages (SC 7.4.3 and 7.5.3 and SCPCs 10.5.3 and 10.6.3).

Summary of remedies for late completion

For SQE1, you need to know, with precision, which remedies for late completion are relevant and applicable in different circumstances. **Table 5.4** provides a useful summary and **Practice example 5.2** brings some of these points together.

Table 5.4: Summary of remedies for delayed completion

Remedy	Entitlement	Limitations
Rescission	No immediate entitlement although notice to complete may be served	Notice to complete must be served first
Notice to complete	May be served by a party who is ready and able to complete – gives 10 working days to complete	May be served by either party On expiry the deposit may be forfeited/must be repaid, with interest
Contractual compensation	May be claimed after the date for contractual completion has passed	Either party may claim under the SCs Under the SCPCs, *only the seller* may claim Can be no double recovery
Common law damages	May be claimed by either party	Can be no double recovery

Practice example 5.2

In a contract for the sale of a property incorporating the SCs, the buyer is unable to complete for six days. The contract rate is 4.5% and the purchase price is £600,000. A 10% deposit was paid on exchange of contracts.

What rights does the seller have?

There will be no immediate right to rescind the contract, although a notice to complete may be served. The following contractual compensation will be payable, and the seller may also claim common law damages (although double recovery will not be possible):

Purchase price	£600,000
Less	
Deposit	£60,000
=	£540,000 x 4.5%
=	£24,300
Divide by 365	(daily rate)
=	£66.58
x 6 days =	£399.48

■ KEY POINT CHECKLIST

This chapter has covered the following key knowledge points. You can use these to structure your revision, ensuring you recall the key details from each point:

• Generally, the transfer is drafted by the seller's solicitor and submitted to the buyer's solicitor for approval. It incorporates information from the contract and the title. It must always be executed by the seller (and sometimes the buyer).

• The buyer's solicitor will raise pre-completion searches and enquiries to update information from the pre-exchange stage, check the solvency of the buyer (and sometimes the seller), and finalise completion arrangements.

• Completion usually takes place using the Law Society's Code for Completion by Post.

• The main post-completion step for the seller is the discharge of any mortgage(s) to fulfil any undertaking given prior to completion.

• The main post-completion steps for the buyer include registration of the charge at Companies House (if applicable), the submission of the SDLT/LTT return, and HM Land Registry formalities.

• In the event of a delay in completion there is no immediate right to rescind. However, notice to complete may be served, giving the party in default ten working days to complete. Compensation *may* be payable at the contract rate, although the SCPCs do differ on this point. Common law damages may also be claimed although there can be no double recovery.

■ KEY TERMS AND CONCEPTS

- transfer deed (**page 116**)
- form TR1 (**page 117**)
- form TP1 (**page 117**)
- pre-completion searches and enquiries (**page 121**)
- pre-completion HM Land Registry search (**page 121**)
- OS1 search (**page 122**)
- OS2 search (**page 123**)
- pre-completion Land charges search (**page 124**)
- bankruptcy-only search (**page 125**)
- company search (**page 125**)
- Completion information and undertakings (**page 126**)
- DS1 (**page 127**)
- DS3 (**page 127**)
- receipted charge (**page 127**)
- Law Society's Code for Completion by Post (**page 130**)
- form DI (**page 133**)
- contractual compensation (**page 134**)
- notice to complete (**page 135**)

■ SQE1-STYLE QUESTIONS

QUESTION 1

A solicitor acts on the purchase of the whole of a freehold residential property that is registered at HM Land Registry and contracts have been exchanged. The buyer, who is an individual, will be borrowing to help finance the transaction and will grant a new mortgage to a high street lender on completion. The seller is a property development company.

Which of the following best describes the necessary pre-completion searches in these circumstances?

A   A Land charges search must be carried out against the seller and all previous estate owners referred to in the epitome of title, as well as a bankruptcy-only search against the buyer, and a company search against the seller.

B   A Land charges search must be carried out against the seller, as well as a bankruptcy-only search against the buyer, and a company search against the seller.

C   An OS1 search must be carried out in the name of the buyer, as well as a bankruptcy-only search against the buyer, and a company search against the seller.

D   An OS1 search must be carried out in the name of the lender, as well as a bankruptcy-only search against the buyer, and a company search against the seller.

E   An OS2 search must be carried out in the name of the lender, as well as a bankruptcy-only search against the buyer, and a company search against the seller.

QUESTION 2

A solicitor acts on the purchase by a company of a freehold commercial property in Wales, which forms the whole of the property comprised within a title registered at HM Land Registry. The company is borrowing to facilitate the acquisition, and the lender, for whom you also act, will require a first legal mortgage over the property.

Which of the following best describes the position as regards the post-completion steps and timescales?

A   The mortgage should be registered at Companies House within 21 days of completion, a Stamp Duty Land Tax (SDLT) return must be submitted to HMRC and duty paid within 14 days of completion, and form AP1 should be submitted to HM Land Registry within the priority period of the OS1 search.

B   The mortgage should be registered at Companies House within 21 days of completion, a Land Transaction Tax Return must be submitted to the Welsh Revenue Authority and duty paid within 30 days of completion, and form AP1 should be submitted to HM Land Registry within the priority period of the OS1 search.

C   The mortgage should be registered at Companies House within 21 days of completion, a Land Transaction Tax Return must be submitted to the Welsh Revenue Authority and duty paid within 14 days of completion, and form AP1 should be submitted to HM Land Registry within the priority period of the OS1 search.

D   The mortgage should be registered at Companies House within 21 days of completion, a Land Transaction Tax Return must be submitted to the Welsh Revenue Authority and duty paid within 30 days of completion, and form FR1 should be submitted to HM Land Registry within two months of completion.

E   The mortgage should be registered at Companies House within 21 days of completion, a Land Transaction Tax Return must be submitted to the Welsh Revenue Authority and duty paid within 30 days of completion, and form FR1 should be submitted to HM Land Registry within the priority period of the pre-completion Land charges search against the seller.

QUESTION 3

A solicitor acts on the sale of a residential property, title to which forms the whole of the property comprised within a title registered at HM Land Registry. The title is subject to a mortgage in favour of a high street lender, and an undertaking has been requested by the buyer's solicitor for them to discharge the charge and provide evidence of discharge.

Which of the following best describes the form(s) of discharge that may be appropriate?

A   Form DS1, e-DS1, or electronic discharge.

B   Form DS3.

C   Vacating receipt.

D   Form DS1.

E   Form DS3, an e-DS3, or an equivalent electronic discharge.

QUESTION 4

A solicitor acts on the purchase of a residential property, which forms the whole of the property comprised within a title registered at HM Land Registry.

Which of the following best describes the purpose of the OS1 HM Land Registry Search?

A   It is an important pre-contract search, which provides the buyer with a period within which their HM Land Registry application will be awarded priority over other applications affecting the title, and confirms whether any adverse entries have been made since the search from date on the official entries.

B   It is an important pre-completion search, which provides the buyer with a period within which their HM Land Registry application will be awarded priority over other applications affecting the title, and 'updates' the official copy entries received pre-exchange, confirming whether any adverse entries have been made since the search from date on the official entries.

C   It is an important pre-completion search, which provides the buyer with a period within which the transaction must be completed, and confirms that the seller is still the registered proprietor.

D   It is an important pre-completion search, which provides the buyer with a period within which the transaction must be completed, and 'updates' the official copy entries received pre-exchange, confirming whether any adverse entries have been made since the search from date on the official entries.

E   It is an important pre-completion search, which provides the buyer with a period within which their HM Land Registry application will be awarded priority over other applications affecting the title, and 'updates' the official copy entries received pre-exchange, confirming whether any adverse entries have been made since their edition date.

QUESTION 5

A solicitor has been instructed to act on the purchase of a freehold property. The contract incorporates the Standard Conditions of Sale (Fifth edition) and there are no relevant special conditions. Contracts have been exchanged and completion is due today. The buyer is ready and able to complete, although the seller has requested that completion be delayed.

Which of the following best describes the position if completion is delayed?

A   The buyer may immediately terminate or rescind the contract as time is of the essence in property transactions.

B   The seller cannot be required to pay contractual compensation.

C   Compensation will be payable by the seller at the contract rate.

D   Common law damages may be claimed on top of contractual compensation.

E   The deposit must be repaid immediately to the buyer.

◼ ANSWERS TO QUESTIONS

Answers to 'What do you know already?' questions at the start of the chapter

1) Form TR1.

2) False. Although an OS1 search (or OS2 search on a sale of part of a title or titles) may be made in the name of the buyer, if the buyer is borrowing to fund the purchase, the search must be made in the name of the lender. Bankruptcy-only searches only apply to individuals, so company searches would be appropriate here. A company search against the buyer will only be required if the buyer is borrowing to fund the purchase.

3) SDLT returns must be filed within 14 days of completion and LTT returns within 30 days of completion. An AP1 application must be filed within the 30 working-day priority period of the OS1/OS2 search, and an FR1 must be lodged within two months of completion.

4) True. There is no immediate right under the standard conditions to rescind the contract in the event of a delay in completion, although

contractual compensation may be payable. However, under the Standard Commercial Property Conditions only the *buyer* can be required to pay compensation.

Answers to end-of-chapter SQE1-style questions

Question 1

The correct answer was D. As title to the property is registered, an OS1 search must be undertaken to ensure no adverse entries have been made on the registers of title since the date of the official copies, and to give the HM Land Registry application priority. The OS1 search must be made in the name of the lender to protect both the buyer and the lender. Therefore, option C is incorrect in this respect. An OS2 search is not applicable as it is the whole, not part, of a registered title that is being sold. Therefore, option E is incorrect on this point. A bankruptcy-only search is always required for the lender's benefit when individual borrowing is involved, and a company search will be required against a company, whether it is buyer or seller in a transaction (in this case it is the seller). Options C and E are correct on these points. Option B correctly identifies the relevant searches in these circumstances had title been unregistered. In such circumstances, Land charges searches against the previous estate owners carried out at the pre-contract stage would not need to be repeated (see option A).

Question 2

The correct answer was B. Although it is not compulsory to register the charge at Companies House, the implications of failing to do so are so serious that it should be registered and such an obligation will inevitably form an important part of the lender's instructions. All the options are correct on this point. A Land Transaction Tax Return is the relevant tax return here (not an SDLT return as suggested in option A) as the property is in Wales. The filing period is within 30 days of completion (not 14 days as suggested in option C, although this is the relevant period for an SDLT return, as set out in option A). Options D and E are correct on this point. Form AP1 is the relevant HM Land Registry form here as title is registered, and it must be submitted within the priority period of the OS1 search (making options A and C partially correct). Form FR1 is the incorrect form (making options D and E incorrect) although the timescale for filing it is correct in option D. The priority period of a Land charges search (see option E) specifies the time by which the purchase must be completed (not the time by which the FR1 should be submitted to HM Land Registry).

Question 3

The correct answer was A. A form DS1, e-DS1, or electronic discharge would all be appropriate in these circumstances as they can be used to discharge a charge over the whole of a registered title. Option D is therefore partially correct. Option C is incorrect as a vacating receipt relates to a charge over unregistered land. Options B and E are incorrect as a DS3 relates to the release of part of the land from a registered charge, and there is no such thing as an e-DS3 or an equivalent electronic discharge in such circumstances.

Question 4

The correct answer was B. The OS1 is a pre-completion, rather than a pre-contract, search. Therefore, option A is the only option that is incorrect in this respect. The priority period relates to the time by which the HM Land Registry application should be submitted, not the period by which the transaction must have been completed (compare this with the pre-completion Land charges search in unregistered land). Therefore, options C and D are incorrect, but the others are correct on this point. The results confirm more than whether the seller is still registered as proprietor (as suggested in option C) and 'update' the official entries from the search from date (the specific date of the official entries), not the edition date (the date the register was last updated). Therefore, option E is incorrect, although options A and D are correct in this respect.

Question 5

The correct answer was C. This is because contractual compensation will be payable at the contract rate on the purchase price (less the deposit if the buyer had been in default). Option A is incorrect as there is no immediate right to terminate or rescind the contract in these circumstances and time is not usually of the essence until a notice to complete is served. Option B is incorrect as, under the SCs, either the seller or the buyer may be required to pay contractual compensation. However, under the SCPCs only the buyer can be required to pay contractual compensation. Option D is incorrect, as although common law damages may be payable in addition to contractual compensation, there can be no double recovery. Option E is incorrect, as the deposit must only be repaid after ten working days have passed following service of a notice to complete (which makes time of the essence of the contract).

■ KEY CASES, RULES, STATUTES, AND INSTRUMENTS

The SQE1 Assessment Specification does not require you to know any statutory authorities or specific case names for this topic. Specific sections of statutes and standard conditions are set out for ease of reference.

Structure and content of a lease

■ MAKE SURE YOU KNOW

This chapter provides an overview of the structure and content of a lease and the Code for Leasing Business Premises (the 'Code'). It deals with the key covenants relating to repair, insurance, alterations, user and planning, rent and rent review, and alienation. It also deals with the options for the term of the lease, as well as the importance and requirements of the Code.

For the SQE1 assessments, you will need to have an appreciation of each of these elements of a lease and the Code.

■ SQE ASSESSMENT ADVICE

For SQE1, you are required to understand the structure and key provisions of a commercial lease, as well as the requirements of the Code.

As you work through this chapter, remember to pay particular attention in your revision to:

- The structure of a lease.
- The options, key requirements, typical content, and detail of covenants relating to repair, insurance, alterations, user and planning, rent and rent review, and alienation, as well as the options for the term of a lease.
- The differences between absolute, qualified, and fully qualified covenants and the statutory modification of some covenants.
- The significance of the Code.

■ WHAT DO YOU KNOW ALREADY?

Attempt these questions before reading this chapter. If you find some difficult or cannot remember the answers, remember to look more closely at that topic during your revision.

1) True or false? It is usual in a commercial lease for the landlord to be responsible for the cost of repairing the premises.
   [Repair, page 147]

2) Why should a landlord be wary of unusually onerous tenant covenants within a lease?

[Structure and content of a lease: an overview, page 144; and Rent review, page 160]

3) True or false? It is possible in some circumstances for a tenant's covenant to be modified by statute.

[Alterations, page 154; and Alienation, page 163]

4) What is the status of the Code for Leasing Business Premises – is it voluntary or mandatory?

[Code for Leasing Business Premises, page 169]

STRUCTURE AND CONTENT OF A LEASE: AN OVERVIEW

For SQE1, it is important to be aware of the structure and content of a typical commercial **lease**, as dealing with commercial leases is often a large part of a typical commercial property solicitor's daily work.

Key term: lease
An estate in land granted by a landlord to a tenant whereby exclusive possession of a property is given to the tenant for a certain term (see *Revise SQE: Land Law*).

Table 6.1 indicates how a commercial lease will usually be structured.

Table 6.1: The usual structure of a commercial lease, and the key terms involved

Prescribed clauses	Key term: prescribed clauses Prescribed clauses appear at the beginning of the lease and are a compulsory requirement for leases granted on or after 19 June 2006, where the landlord's title is registered, and the lease is substantively registrable (see **Chapter 7**). They contain key information required by HM Land Registry for the purposes of registration (see *HM Land Registry Practice Guide 64*).
Commencement date and parties	The commencement date will be the date of grant of the lease. It does not have to be the same date that the term commences. The parties will be (1) the landlord, (2) the tenant, and (3) any guarantor(s).
Definitions and interpretation	The definitions help to save space within the lease by defining terms that appear repeatedly throughout it (eg Rent, Term, Premises, and Insured Risks). Defined terms usually have a capital letter at the beginning of each word. The interpretation provisions are standard and

Table 6.1: (Continued)

	provide, for example, that references to statutes and statutory instruments generally include them as amended from time to time. The effect of this is that a covenant by the tenant to comply with statutes relating to the use of the property would include future and amended statutes.
Grant of the lease	The grant is the main operative part of the lease. It provides that the landlord grants, and the tenant takes, the lease of the premises (as defined) for the term (see **Options for the term of a lease**, below), at the rent (see **Key term** and **Rent**, below). It also provides details of the rights granted to the tenant (ancillary rights) and rights reserved for the benefit of the landlord (excepted and reserved rights). These could include rights of access and parking and rights of entry for the purpose of carrying out repairs. The rights are typically more detailed in leases forming part of a multi-let property (eg a floor in an office block or shop within a shopping centre), where, for example, rights to use internal corridors and stairways etc will need to be included.
Rent and **rent review**	**Key term: rent** The rent usually includes the annual rent, which represents the amount paid for the tenant's occupation (ie the landlord's income). Other sums are sometimes reserved as rent (eg insurance rent, and in the case of multi-let buildings, service charge) as this makes forfeiture more straightforward (see **Chapter 8** and **Key term: provisos**, below). **Key term: rent review** Most leases will provide that the rent will be subject to a review or periodic reviews throughout the term.
Tenant's covenants	A significant part of the lease will be comprised of tenant's covenants for the benefit of the landlord, to protect their interests and sometimes their adjoining property.
Landlord's covenants	Landlord's covenants are usually limited to covenants for quiet enjoyment (whereby the landlord covenants to allow the tenant to have peaceful enjoyment and occupation of the property, without undue interference) and insurance (see **Insurance**, below). In multi-let properties these will usually extend to a covenant to provide additional services relating to the building and common parts (eg maintenance of the main structure) in exchange for the tenant paying a service charge.

Table 6.1: (Continued)

Provisos	Key term: provisos
	Provisos are conditions or qualifications attached to the grant of the lease. The main proviso is usually for re-entry/forfeiture, which allows the landlord to enter and repossess the property in the event of non-payment of rent, breach of covenant, or other specified circumstances (including the bankruptcy/insolvency of the tenant) (see **Chapter 8**).
Schedules	Schedules are used to improve the flow of a lease by separating key detail/information. Any schedule must be expressly referred to in the main body to be incorporated.
Execution clause	Leases must usually be executed as a deed, although leases not exceeding three years may be created informally (sections 52 and 54, Law of Property Act 1925 and see also **Chapters 2, 5, and 7**).

Landlord's concerns

On the grant of a lease, the landlord's main concern will be to ensure that their interests are protected. They will usually require a lease to be on **full repairing and insuring (FRI)** terms, so that the annual rent they receive is pure income (sometimes called a 'clear rent') and does not need to be used to pay for repairs etc. *Simply put, an FRI lease should 'pay for itself,' enabling the landlord to benefit from the full rental income and any capital gain that accumulates over time* (see **Chapter 10**). A lease which is on FRI and otherwise standard and acceptable terms is known as an **institutionally acceptable lease**.

Key term: full repairing and insuring (FRI) lease

An FRI lease is a lease that requires the tenant to be responsible for the costs of repairing and insuring the premises (see **Repair** and **Insurance**, below).

Key term: institutionally acceptable lease

An institutionally acceptable lease is one that is granted on acceptable FRI terms, such that it would be suitable as an investment for an institutional investor (eg a pension fund) who will be keen to get a steady stream of income (without deduction of other costs) and a capital gain over time.

For a lease to be on otherwise acceptable terms, it should be at a market rent (see **Rent review**) and on terms that sufficiently control the tenant, to protect the value of the landlord's investment and adjoining property. The marketability, value, and value for secured lending purposes of a property that is subject to a non-FRI, non-institutionally acceptable lease may also be adversely affected.

Revision tip

A landlord must take care not to include clauses that are unreasonably restrictive or onerous as they could have an adverse impact on rent review (see **Rent review**).

Tenant's concerns

The tenant's main concern on the grant of a lease will be to ensure that the lease is granted on reasonable and not unduly onerous terms, so that they may enjoy the premises without unnecessary restrictions. Undue restrictions and onerous liabilities may affect the tenant's day-to-day use and enjoyment of the property, their financial liability, and the marketability/transferability of the lease should they wish to deal with it in the future (see **Chapter 7**). A tenant's solicitor must therefore seek to amend the draft lease to protect the tenant's interests.

Revision tip

The process of commercial lease negotiation is complex and will usually involve the solicitor for the tenant making several amendments to the lease. For the purposes of SQE1, you should have a sound knowledge and understanding of the key provisions as a foundation for gaining hands-on experience of detailed negotiations in practice.

REPAIR

The tenant's repairing obligations will usually depend on the extent of the premises. Different concerns arise on negotiation, depending on the age of the premises, although responsibility for damage caused by an insured risk should *always* be excluded (see **Damage caused by insured risks**).

Extent of the premises: lease of whole or lease of part

Where a commercial tenant is taking a *lease of the whole of a building*, they will usually be responsible for the repair and maintenance of the whole of the premises (as defined, to include the landlord's fixtures (eg boilers and heating systems), structure, and exterior).

However, where the tenant is taking a *lease of part of a building*, they will typically be responsible for the repair and maintenance of the whole of the premises (as defined, to include the interior-only and exclude the structure, exterior, and common parts). However, the tenant will typically be required to contribute towards the costs of repairing and maintaining the structure, exterior, and common parts, often through the payment of a service charge. *Therefore, even a lease of part may effectively be on full repairing terms.*

Revision tip

The definition of the premises within the lease is key to ascertaining the extent of the tenant's repairing obligations, although their liability to meet the costs of other repairs may extend beyond this.

Negotiation of the clause

On the grant of a lease, the tenant should seek to qualify the wording of the repairing covenant, as follows:

- Avoid an obligation to 'put the property into repair,' as this is more onerous than 'keeping the property in repair.' The former phrase means that the tenant will be under a positive obligation to put the property into repair if it is not in repair at the date of the lease.
- Avoid an obligation to keep the property in 'good condition,' as this goes further than remedying disrepair.
- Exclude liability for fair wear and tear.
- Exclude liability for historic contamination (ie contamination not caused by the tenant), as this could technically be disrepair, as well as a breach of the tenant's obligation under the lease to comply with statute.

Revision tip

The results of any pre-contract environmental search should be consulted to see whether an exclusion for historic contamination would be reasonable (see **Chapters 3 and 7**).

Older properties

On the grant of a lease of an *older property*, the tenant will often seek to qualify the covenant by providing that the tenant will not be required to put or keep the premises in any better state of repair and condition than they are in at the date of the lease, as evidenced by a **schedule of condition** to be annexed to the lease.

Key term: schedule of condition

A report, usually prepared by a surveyor, detailing the state of repair and condition of the property prior to the grant of the lease. It is designed to evidence and set the minimum benchmark for the tenant's repairing obligations, above which the tenant is not required to improve the premises. Therefore, it is important for the schedule to be as detailed as possible and preferably for it to be prepared by a surveyor, who may be liable in negligence if it is not comprehensively prepared.

Newer properties

On the grant of a lease of a *newbuild or recently constructed property*, the tenant should also seek to exclude the tenant's liability to remedy inherent defects in the design and construction of the building, as these would technically be classed as disrepair. The landlord will often have recourse to warranties given by the professional team for several years after construction, so they may agree to limit the liability, at least whilst these are subsisting.

Damage caused by insured risks

In any event, the clause should exclude damage caused by a risk covered by the landlord's buildings insurance policy (see **Insurance**), unless and to the extent that the policy has been vitiated (invalidated) or insurance monies have not been paid due to the acts or default of the tenant or anyone at the premises with their authority. This is a key requirement of a repairing covenant that you should be aware of for the purposes of SQE1.

INSURANCE

Under a typical commercial lease, the landlord insures the property at the expense of the tenant.

Landlord's concerns

The landlord will wish to ensure that the property (or the whole building, in the case of a multi-let building), is fully insured against the usual **insured risks**, to protect the landlord's interest, capital investment, and obligations to any mortgagee. The landlord will also wish to be able to recover these costs from the tenant.

> **Key term: insured risks**
>
> The list of risks against which the landlord covenants to insure. They typically include (amongst others) fire, explosion, lightning, flood, storm, tempest, burst or overflowing pipes, and impact by vehicles or aircraft or articles dropped therefrom.

Tenant's concerns

The tenant's concerns will be to ensure that:

- The property (or the whole building, in the case of a multi-let building) is fully *insured* against damage or destruction caused by a comprehensive list of *insured risks*.
- The landlord is under an obligation to *repair or reinstate* in the event of such damage or destruction.

- They will not have to pay *rent* (and possibly other sums due to the landlord under the lease) when the premises are unsuitable for use or occupation after such damage or destruction.
- They have the *option to break* the lease if reinstatement is delayed.

A typical commercial lease will contain the following provisions:

Landlord's covenant to insure for the full reinstatement value against insured risks (as defined)

Insurance for the *full reinstatement value* is important, particularly for the tenant, so that there will not be a shortfall in the insurance proceeds in the event of a claim. Insurance should include the costs of demolition, site clearance, professional fees, and VAT. In the case of a multi-let building, insurance should extend beyond the premises, to the whole building.

It is in the interests of the tenant for the list of insured risks to be suitably *comprehensive*, as the tenant will be responsible for damage or destruction caused by **uninsured risks** (see **Practice example 6.1**). However, as the tenant will be paying towards the insurance policy, they must balance this risk against including risks that may be prohibitively expensive to insure against or unnecessary in some areas. For example, cover including damage caused by terrorist acts may be very expensive for a landmark building in a large city, or unnecessary for an industrial unit in a small town. It is therefore usual to add '*and such other risks as the Landlord shall reasonably require*' at the end of a reasonably comprehensive list and for the landlord to make such obligation subject to (a) exclusions, excesses, limitations, or other conditions imposed by insurers and (b) such insurance being available in the market on reasonable terms.

Key term: uninsured risks

Risks that the landlord does not covenant to insure against (either as a specified risk or a reasonable additional risk).

Practice example 6.1

Two separate commercial tenants in the same building occupy premises under FRI leases, where the landlord is obliged to insure against several risks, and *such other risks as it shall reasonably require*. Due to no fault of the tenants, or anyone at the building with their authority, the premises are destroyed by flood and subsidence respectively. The list of insured risks in both leases includes flood but does not specifically include subsidence.

Who is responsible for making good the damage caused?

As flood is an insured risk and nothing has been done to invalidate the policy of insurance, the landlord should be responsible for the damage. However, the obligation on the landlord to insure will usually be subject to exclusions, excesses, limitations, or other conditions and insurance against such risk being available in the market on reasonable terms. The tenant will need to check the terms of the policy and will be responsible if the risk is uninsured.

As subsidence is not a specified insured risk, the tenant will be responsible unless the landlord has in fact insured against this risk as a reasonable additional risk. If insured, the obligation to insure will be subject to the same matters referred to above (ie exclusions, excesses, etc).

Revision tip

If precontract searches and enquiries have revealed issues with mining, the list of insured risks should be checked to see if they include subsidence, landslip, and heave (where the ground pushes upwards). Likewise, if they have revealed a flood risk, the list should include flood. If these are not insured risks (either specifically or as a reasonable additional risk), the tenant will usually be responsible for remedying damage or disrepair in relation to them.

Tenant's covenant to pay the insurance rent

The tenant should covenant to pay the **insurance rent** (as defined).

Key term: insurance rent

The insurance rent is usually defined as including the policy premium and insurance premium tax for buildings insurance, in addition to insurance to cover for the landlord in the event of rent suspension (see below). The tenant will also often covenant to pay the cost of insurance valuations, and any excesses.

Landlord's covenant to apply the insurance proceeds/repair/reinstate

The landlord will normally covenant to apply the insurance proceeds (except sums received for loss of rent) in obtaining any necessary consents and repairing and reinstating the property (including the building, in the case of a multi-let property). A typical tenant's amendment is to provide that the landlord will make up any deficiency in the insurance proceeds out of their own funds, to protect them in the case of under-insurance. If reinstatement is impossible, it is typical in most commercial leases to provide that the insurance monies will belong to the landlord.

Rent suspension

A **rent suspension** provision is usually standard.

Key term: rent suspension

A provision in the lease that the tenant's obligation to pay annual rent or a fair proportion of it (eg if only part is damaged or destroyed) will be suspended when the premises (including the building, in the case of a multi-let property) are damaged or destroyed by an insured risk, to the extent that the premises are unsuitable or unfit for occupation or use.

The landlord should have no issues with a rent suspension for the duration of their loss of rent insurance policy, that the tenant will have funded as part of the insurance rent.

The tenant may also seek for other sums due under the lease and reserved as rent to be suspended (eg insurance rent and service charge).

Ideally, from the tenant's perspective, rent suspension should be unlimited, but it will often be limited to the period against which the landlord is obliged to insure for loss of rent. If the rent suspension is limited, then a tenant's right to termination at the end of the rent suspension period will be crucial (see below).

It is usual to provide that the rent suspension will not apply to the extent that the insurance policy has been vitiated by the tenant or anyone else at the property with their authority.

Termination

The lease should provide that the landlord will be able to terminate the lease should repair/reinstatement become impossible or impractical. The tenant should also insist that they have a right to terminate the lease following the end of the rent suspension period if the premises have not been repaired/reinstated, so that they do not have to start paying rent (and possibly other sums) again. The landlord will usually insist that such right is subject to them having complied with their obligations under the lease. As stated above, on termination, it is typical to provide that the insurance proceeds will belong to the landlord.

Exam warning

Due to its complexity, the interaction between the tenant's repairing obligations and the insurance provisions is likely to form part of an SQE1 question. You should therefore have a good working knowledge of how the provisions interrelate.

Figure 6.1 outlines the process for approaching questions on repair and insurance and **Practice example 6.2** brings these points together.

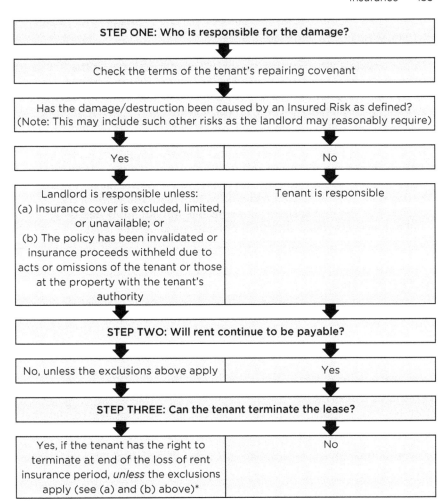

STEP ONE: Who is responsible for the damage?

Check the terms of the tenant's repairing covenant

Has the damage/destruction been caused by an Insured Risk as defined?
(Note: This may include such other risks as the landlord may reasonably require)

Yes | No

Landlord is responsible unless:
(a) Insurance cover is excluded, limited, or unavailable; or
(b) The policy has been invalidated or insurance proceeds withheld due to acts or omissions of the tenant or those at the property with the tenant's authority

Tenant is responsible

STEP TWO: Will rent continue to be payable?

No, unless the exclusions above apply | Yes

STEP THREE: Can the tenant terminate the lease?

Yes, if the tenant has the right to terminate at end of the loss of rent insurance period, *unless* the exclusions apply (see (a) and (b) above)*

No

*The landlord may also have the right to terminate if it becomes impossible or impractical to reinstate.

Figure 6.1: Insurance and repair

Practice example 6.2

A tenant of commercial premises under a typical FRI lease of the whole of a property carries out manufacturing processes that require the use of potentially explosive materials. The tenant fails to store the materials correctly, as required by the landlord's insurance policy, and the premises are destroyed by an explosion.

Who will be responsible for the damage, will rent continue to be payable, and may the tenant terminate the lease?

Under a typical FRI lease the tenant will covenant to repair the property, save for damage caused by an insured risk. It is highly likely that explosion will be an insured risk and that cover for such a risk will be available. However, it is also likely that by failing to store the materials correctly, the tenant will have vitiated the landlord's insurance policy and the insurance proceeds will be withheld. The tenant should have made itself familiar with the landlord's policy and adhered to its conditions. In such circumstances, the lease is likely to state that rent suspension will not apply, so the tenant must continue to pay rent. They will also be unable to terminate the lease in this situation as the rent suspension provisions will not apply and they will not have complied with their obligations under the lease.

ALTERATIONS

For SQE1, you should be aware of the need to deal with alterations, the different types of covenants, statutory modification of some covenants, the requirements of a licence to alter, and when a tenant may be entitled to compensation for improvements.

Tenant's concerns

Most tenants will wish to make alterations to the premises to suit their requirements, and they would usually like to have as few restrictions as possible. Unduly restrictive provisions on alterations could also have an impact on their ability to deal with the lease in the future (see **Alienation**, below).

Landlord's concerns

The main concern of the landlord will be that the tenant's alterations will not have an impact on the value of the property, its marketability, and its value as security for lending purposes. If, for example, alterations are very specific to the tenant's individual needs, they may make the property unattractive to future tenants. The landlord may also be concerned about the impact of significant alterations on other occupants/nearby property (eg noise or nuisance).

Except in the case of very short leases, a tenant will commonly have the right to make some alterations.

Types of covenant

In a typical commercial lease of the whole of a property, there will be an **absolute covenant** against structural and exterior alterations, and a **qualified** or **fully qualified covenant** against internal, non-structural alterations and changes to service media (eg electrical systems), with no consent being required to some very minor additions (eg installation of internal demountable partitioning).

Revision tip

For SQE1, you should be able to recognise each of the above types of covenant and be aware of their practical implications, and any statutory modification of them in the context of alterations, as well as user and alienation (see **User and planning**, and **Alienation**, below).

Key term: absolute covenant

An absolute covenant provides that such action is not permitted under any circumstances. In the absence of statutory modification (see below) the only way around this would be to approach the landlord for a one-off consent/the exercise of discretion, a deed of variation of the lease, or to proceed and risk forfeiture of the lease or other action by the landlord (see **Chapter 8**).

Key term: qualified covenant

A qualified covenant provides that such action is permitted, but with the landlord's prior consent.

Key term: fully qualified covenant

A fully qualified covenant provides that such action is permitted, but with the landlord's prior consent *and* that such consent is not to be unreasonably withheld.

Qualified covenants

A tenant's solicitor will usually seek to amend an absolute or qualified covenant, to a fully qualified covenant, also adding the words 'or delayed' after 'withheld'.

The tenant may also rely on section 19(2) of the Landlord and Tenant Act 1927 (LTA 1927), which provides that, where there is a *qualified covenant against alterations*, consent may not be unreasonably withheld for work classed as **improvements**. However, the landlord may require reasonable compensation for any reduction in value of its reversion (ie the landlord's interest in the property), payment of its legal and other costs, and (where reasonable) reinstatement at the end of the term.

Key term: improvements

Improvements in this context are those alterations that *increase the value or usefulness of the property from the tenant's point of view.* Therefore, the test is very subjective in favour of the tenant. It does not matter whether they reduce the value of the landlord's reversion.

Revision tip

Despite the statutory modification under s 19(2), it would be best practice for a tenant's solicitor to negotiate a fully qualified covenant in any event, to avoid any argument as to whether proposed works constitute improvements.

Absolute covenants

Even in the case of an *absolute covenant*, the tenant may still rely on the procedure under s 3 of the LTA 1927 to carry out works that would be *improvements* (see below). The procedure is as follows:

- The tenant serves a *notice* on the landlord with details of the proposals.
- The landlord has *three months* to object or to offer to carry out the works in return for a reasonable increase in rent.
- If the landlord *does not respond*, the tenant may proceed with the works.
- If the landlord *objects*, the tenant may apply to the court for an order authorising the improvements.
- If the tenant *rejects* the landlord's offer to carry out the works (*they are under no obligation to accept*), the tenant may not carry them out.

Exam warning

Improvements in this context are alterations that:
- Add to the letting value of the property.
- Are reasonable and suitable to the character of the property.
- Do not diminish the value of any other property of the landlord.

You should be aware of the different definitions for the different aspects of the LTA 1927.

Revision tip

If works are required to comply with the Equality Act 2010 (eg disabled access), an absolute covenant will also be statutorily modified to become fully qualified.

Licence to alter

Where consent is given, the landlord will mostly insist on a **licence to alter**.

Key term: licence to alter

A formal document providing consent to the proposed alterations, often with plans annexed. It usually deals with the carrying out of the works (including standards of workmanship and materials, and supervision by the landlord's surveyor), obtaining all other necessary consents, payment of costs, and reinstatement at the end of the term.

Compensation for improvements

Under s 1 LTA 1927, a tenant may be entitled to compensation for improvements made using the procedure under s 3 LTA 1927, which add to the letting value of the property. However, the procedure is rarely used, and in any event most leases will require removal of alterations at the end of the term, meaning that no compensation will be payable.

Figure 6.2 outlines the process for approaching questions on alterations and **Practice example 6.3** brings these points together.

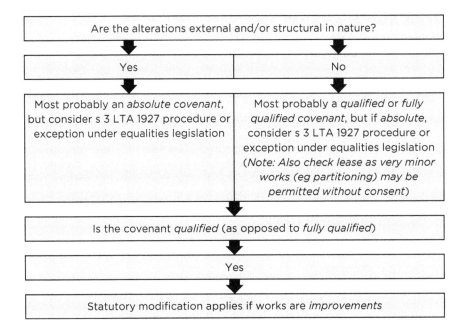

Are the alterations external and/or structural in nature?

Yes	No

| Most probably an *absolute covenant,* but consider s 3 LTA 1927 procedure or exception under equalities legislation | Most probably a *qualified* or *fully qualified covenant,* but if *absolute,* consider s 3 LTA 1927 procedure or exception under equalities legislation (*Note: Also check lease as very minor works (eg partitioning) may be permitted without consent*) |

Is the covenant *qualified* (as opposed to *fully qualified*)

Yes

Statutory modification applies if works are *improvements*

Figure 6.2: Alterations

Practice example 6.3

A tenant of a high street shop under a typical FRI lease wishes to carry out shop-fitting works and add an additional door to the rear loading bay. They also wish to install internal demountable partitioning to the first-floor offices.

What are the likely restrictions to the proposed works (assuming that no bespoke provisions have been negotiated)?

It is likely that there will be a qualified or fully qualified covenant against the shop-fitting works as these are internal non-structural alterations. In the case of a qualified covenant, the tenant may be able to rely on s 19(2) LTA 1927 to make the covenant fully qualified as the alterations are likely to be improvements. The internal demountable partitioning may be permitted without consent, but it will be necessary to check the terms of the lease. There is likely to be an absolute covenant against the installation of the additional door as this is a structural alteration. In such circumstances, the tenant could apply for a one-off consent or use the procedure under s 3 LTA 1927.

USER AND PLANNING

For SQE1, you should be aware of the need to deal with the clauses that concern the tenant's use (user) and the different types of covenants.

Landlord's concerns

A landlord will usually wish to limit the tenant's permitted use of the property, due to the potential impact on the use of adjoining property by the landlord or others. For example, in the retail context, a landlord may wish to prevent competition with its own business, or to provide a suitable mix of tenants in a parade of shops. In the industrial context, a landlord may not wish to mix light industrial and heavy industrial tenants, to avoid potential for nuisance. However, a very limited clause could have a negative impact on rent review for the landlord (see **Rent review**).

Tenant's concerns

The tenant would ideally like to have relatively few restrictions on user, as a very limited and precise user clause may have an impact on the future marketability of the lease or a change in business. It really is a question of balance, as an overly broad clause could inflate the rent payable on review (see **Rent review**).

Typical provisions

A typical clause will therefore specify a use and allow diversification within a specific use class or classes within the Schedule to the Town and Country Planning (Use Classes) Order 1987 (see **Chapter 3**). Alternatively, there may be a qualified or fully qualified covenant allowing variation of uses within the class(es), with the consent of the landlord.

Revision tip

It is important to be aware that, as use classes may change over time, the interpretation clause (see above) stating that references to statutes and statutory instruments include amended versions from time to time, should specifically exclude the use classes order.

Revision tip

If a qualified covenant is suggested by the landlord, conversion to a fully qualified covenant would be the best option for the tenant, as there is no statutory modification of user covenants.

However, there is some protection in section 19(3) of the LTA 1927 which provides that no fine or increased rent may be charged as a condition of giving consent, provided that no structural alteration is involved. The landlord may, however, charge its legal or other expenses in giving consent, together with a reasonable sum in respect of loss in value to the premises or neighbouring premises.

In some circumstances, the content of the user covenant may be dictated by covenants within the landlord's title or existing planning permissions. However, it is the tenant's responsibility to ensure that their proposed use complies with planning law, any covenants within the title, and other statutory provisions. This will usually be confirmed as a specific covenant or covenants within the lease.

Practice example 6.4 brings these points together.

Practice example 6.4

A tenant of a shoe shop has a lease that includes the following tenant's covenant:

> 'Not to use the Premises other than as a shop for the retail sale of goods other than hot food, or such other use within Class E of the Schedule to the Town and Country Planning (Use Classes) Order 1987 as the Landlord may previously approve'.

The tenant wishes to assign the lease to a tenant who proposes to use the shop to sell electrical goods.

What restrictions will apply to the proposed use?

No restrictions will apply as the new use will still be a shop for the retail sale of goods, other than hot food. If an alternative use within Class E were proposed (eg a restaurant), the landlord's consent would be required. The landlord would be under no obligation not to unreasonably withhold or delay consent as there is no statutory modification of qualified covenants in these circumstances. Section 19(3) of the LTA 1927 will also apply.

RENT

The lease will usually provide that:

- Rent is payable in advance, on a set day each month, or by four equal payments on the usual quarter days (25 March, 24 June, 29 September, and 25 December). However, at common law, rent will be payable in arrears unless the lease specifies otherwise.
- Rent is typically payable by standing order, or other electronic transfer, and the lease should include an obligation to pay any VAT properly payable (ie if the landlord has opted to tax – see **Chapter 10**).
- A proportionate sum of the rent is normally payable on completion, unless of course the grant of the lease falls on a rent payment date, then the full amount will be payable.

RENT REVIEW

Most leases will provide that the rent will be subject to review or periodic review throughout the term (eg every three to five years). The most common form of rent review is an **open market rent review** provision. However, it is also possible for the rent to increase to fixed amounts at set times, or for the rent review to be linked to either the tenant's turnover or to increases in a published index (eg the retail prices index – RPI). Index-linked rent reviews and fixed increases may be very simple to apply in practice, but they may not truly reflect the state of the property rental market at the time. A turnover rent review has the advantage that both parties have a vested interest in the success of the tenant's business. The detail of turnover rent reviews is beyond the scope of this book.

Key term: open market rent review

The rent is reviewed to the hypothetical open market rental value of the premises at the time of review, considering stated assumptions and disregards (see below). *The rental value must be hypothetical, as the tenant will not be vacating.* The review will usually be on an upwards-only basis, meaning that the reviewed rent will be the higher of the rent previously payable and the market rent at the time. Although upwards–downwards reviews may be better for the tenant, they are very unpopular with institutional landlords who look for a guaranteed income as part of their investment.

Assumptions and disregards

For SQE1, you should be aware of the typical **assumptions and disregards** and why they are commonly included. These are summarised in **Table 6.2**.

Key term: assumptions and disregards

The assumptions and disregards are designed to ensure that the reviewed rent under the terms of the hypothetical lease is fair to both parties.

Table 6.2: Open market rent review assumptions and disregards

Assumptions	
There is a willing landlord and a willing tenant	Without this, the rent review could not operate
The property is to be let with vacant possession	The hypothetical tenant would want vacant possession and would pay less for a property that was already occupied
The lease will be on the same terms, excluding the rent, but including the rent review provisions	The terms should reflect the reality
	A tenant would pay less for a lease with onerous tenant covenants, so the landlord should not be able to disregard their effect here
	It is fair for the existing rent to be disregarded, as it is the market rent at the time of review that is relevant
	A tenant would often pay more for a lease with a static rent throughout, so it is only fair there is the assumption that it will be subject to review if the lease provides for this
That the term will be equal to the unexpired residue of the term	This should really reflect the reality
	If the clause states that the term will be presumed to be a set number of years, this may or may not depress the rent, depending on the state of the market and the demand for shorter or longer leases

Table 6.2: (Continued)

That the tenant has complied with its covenants	The tenant should not benefit from its own breaches
	For example, if the tenant has let the property fall into disrepair it will have saved costs and would in turn benefit, as the hypothetical tenant would pay less for a property in a poor state of repair
That the property has been reinstated if it has been damaged or destroyed	A tenant would pay less for a property that has been destroyed, so it would be unfair to base the reviewed rent on the state of the premises at that specific time, when the landlord will be under an obligation to reinstate
Disregards	
The tenant's occupation	A tenant would pay more to avoid having to move
The goodwill of the tenant	The goodwill (eg customer base and reputation) will have been generated by the tenant so it should not be punished for having a successful business
The effect of voluntary improvements by the tenant	Voluntary improvements are those that the tenant was not obliged to carry out under the lease (eg to comply with legal requirements)
	This avoids the tenant paying for improvements twice (once through the actual costs and again through the rent)

The review process

The most popular method of determining the reviewed rent in modern leases is a provision that the parties will try to agree the reviewed rent between themselves first, with the rent being determined by an independent third party if they are unable to agree.

Older leases often contain more structured provisions, requiring the parties to serve formal notices and counter-notices as part of the negotiations. The reviewed rent is then deemed to be the rent in the last notice if the subsequent notice was not served. The modern system has much less inherent danger as it avoids these 'deeming provisions'.

It is usual to provide that the existing rent will continue to be payable until the reviewed rent is determined, and once agreed, the tenant will pay interest (at a non-penal rate) to compensate the landlord for the delay in receipt of funds. The lease will also provide for a memorandum of the review to be endorsed on both parts of the lease.

Practice example 6.5 brings some of these points together.

Practice example 6.5

The rent under a commercial FRI lease is subject to review, and the rent review provisions state that the hypothetical lease will be on the same terms, excluding the rent, but including the rent review provisions, and that the effect of tenant's voluntary improvements will be disregarded. The lease has ten years' unexpired term remaining and contains onerous alienation provisions and a very restrictive user clause. The tenant has made some voluntary improvements to the premises, with landlord's consent, but has not kept the premises in good repair under the terms of the lease.

How might you explain the possible impact of the onerous clauses, improvements, and disrepair on rent review?

The onerous/restrictive clauses should reduce the rent that a hypothetical tenant would pay for the premises, so the landlord will be prejudiced on review. The tenant will not be required to pay a greater rent due to the improvements that they have already paid for. There will most probably be an assumption that the tenant has complied with its covenants in the lease, so it should not be able to benefit from a reduced rent due to its own breach.

ALIENATION

The **alienation** provisions are particularly important to commercial leases and, for SQE1, it is essential to have a good working knowledge of the need for them, as well as their typical content, operation, and statutory modification.

Key term: alienation

Alienation concerns dealing with the tenant's interest under the lease.

The concerns of the parties

The landlord will usually wish to have control over who occupies, or has an interest in, the property other than the tenant, to protect its own interests. In all but the shortest of leases, the tenant will wish to be able to deal with its interest as freely as possible, so that the lease is marketable, and its interests are not unduly restricted.

Typical alienation clause

In the absence of express restriction, the tenant will be able to deal with their interest in any way they wish.

A typical alienation clause will therefore need to deal with *each of* the following:
- **Assignment.**
- **Underletting/subletting.**
- Charging/mortgaging (see also **Chapter 4**).
- **Sharing occupation.**
- **Parting with or sharing possession** or holding the lease on trust for another (see *Revise SQE: Trusts Law*).

Key term: assignment

The transfer of an existing lease (the unexpired residue) by the existing tenant (the assignor) to another tenant (the assignee) (see **Figure 6.3**, below, and **Chapter 7**).

Key term: underletting/subletting

The grant of a further lease carved out of an existing lease, which may comprise the whole or part of the premises contained within the existing lease, but for a shorter term than that of the existing lease. If granted for a longer term, it will take effect as an assignment (see **Chapter 7**). The existing lease becomes the headlease and the further lease is an underlease/sublease (see **Chapter 7** and **Figure 6.4**, below).

Key term: sharing occupation

Sharing occupation would include a licence, where exclusive possession is not given (so the occupant is sharing occupation, rather than legal possession) (see **Chapter 9**).

Key term: parting with or sharing possession

An important residuary category. This would include both formal as well as *informal* assignment and underletting, or other arrangements with the same effect.

Typically, there will be an absolute covenant against assignment, underletting, charging, sharing occupation, and parting with or sharing possession, with the usual exceptions, which are elaborated upon below.

Assignment of whole

Assignment of *whole only* (see **Figure 6.3**) is normally permitted, with landlord's consent. Assignment of part is usually prohibited as underleases are generally preferred for dealings with part.

Landlord grants lease of property to a tenant

Landlord

Tenant

During the term of the lease, the tenant transfers (usually the whole of) its interest to another tenant

Landlord

Tenant (Assignor)   Assignee

Figure 6.3: Assignment

In this context, there are three statutory modifications to be aware of and these are summarised in **Table 6.3**.

Table 6.3: Statutory modification of alienation covenants

s 19(1)(a) LTA 1927
This provides that a *qualified covenant* is automatically upgraded to a fully qualified covenant (consent is not to be unreasonably withheld).
This section applies to qualified covenants against assignment, underletting, charging, or parting with possession in all leases.
s 19(1A) LTA 1927
Allows the parties to specify *circumstances* and *conditions* to proposed assignments for insertion into the lease.
Conditions typically include the provision of an AGA (see **Chapters 7 and 8**) and guarantors. *Circumstances* typically include there being no outstanding sums under the lease and the landlord being satisfied with the assignee's covenant strength. The section provides that compliance with such circumstances and conditions would be reasonable, and the landlord would not be unreasonable in withholding consent if they were not complied with. If the landlord relies on other reasons, they must be reasonable.
This section only applies to qualified covenants against assignment in new leases (see **Chapter 8**).
s 1 Landlord and Tenant Act 1988 (LTA 1988)
For a *qualified covenant* the landlord must, within a reasonable time of a written application:
• give consent, unless it is reasonable not to do so.
• give written notice of the decision, specifying any conditions to the consent or reasons for withholding it.
Like s 19(1)(a), this section applies to qualified covenants against assignment, underletting, charging, or parting with possession in all leases.

Generally, whether or not refusal of consent is reasonable will be a question of fact. However, reasons must relate to the landlord and tenant relationship in the lease, and the landlord must act reasonably and not discriminatively. For example, the following could be good reasons: the tenant's proposed use and potential conflict with the landlord's business or tenant-mix policy; significant breaches of the lease; or concerns regarding the assignee's covenant strength.

Charging of whole

Charging/mortgaging will normally not be permitted for commercial leases, except a charge of the whole by way of floating charge (see **Revise SQE: Business Law and Practice**). In any event, the typical forfeiture clause in a commercial lease will be unsuitable for most lenders. This is because they typically provide for forfeiture on insolvency (which is when a lender would usually seek to repossess) and the lease is unlikely to have a capital value if it was not granted for a premium (meaning it would be unsuitable as security as it would not have a realisable sale value).

Sharing occupation

A corporate tenant will normally seek to permit sharing occupation with other companies within the same group. This is because if another company within the same group of companies as the tenant is in occupation, this could otherwise be a technical breach of the alienation provisions.

For similar reasons, a retail tenant may wish to have the opportunity to create concession arrangements with others.

Underletting of whole or part

Underletting/subletting (see **Figure 6.4**) of whole is often permitted with landlord's consent.

Landlord grants lease of property to a tenant

Landlord

Tenant

During the term of the lease, the tenant carves a further shorter lease of whole or part of the property out of the lease

Landlord (Now Head Landlord)

Tenant (Now Head Tenant and Landlord under the Underlease)

Tenant 2 (Undertenant)

Figure 6.4: Underletting

Where the premises lend themselves to underletting of part (eg two easily divisible, but semi-detached industrial units, or separate floors in an office block) this may be permitted with landlord's consent.

An underlease may be preferable to the parties for the following reasons:

Tenant:
- They may dispose of the whole or part of a property on a temporary basis.
- In a rising market, they may be able to make a profit from the underlease rent.
- They will not be liable under an Authorised Guarantee Agreement (AGA) (see **Chapters 7 and 8**) and will be able to take control in the event of default by the undertenant.
- In a falling market, they may be able to recover some of their costs by making some return on the property.

Landlord:
- The existing tenant will remain liable under the existing lease.

However, the risk to the landlord is that they will lose direct control over the occupation of the property, and they may become the landlord of an undesirable subtenant in the event of forfeiture, surrender, or disclaimer of the headlease (see **Chapters 8 and 9**) or the subtenant claiming security of tenure (see **Chapter 9**).

The following statutory qualifications apply to *qualified covenants against underletting* in all leases: s 19(1)(a) LTA 1927 (see above); s 1 LTA 1988 (see above).

The alienation clause will also typically provide conditions for any underletting. Some examples are set out below:
- The underlease is on the same terms as the headlease.
- The rent is not less than the rent payable under the headlease (or a proportionate part in respect of an underletting of part), payable at the same times and subject to review, at the same times and on the same basis. *The tenant will usually wish to provide that this will be the market rent (or proportionate market rent) so they can underlet in a falling market.*
- The underlease will be excluded from the provisions of Part II of the Landlord and Tenant Act 1954 (see **Chapter 9**).
- That there will be no further underleases.
- That the undertenant will enter into a direct covenant with the head landlord to observe and perform the tenant covenants in both leases so far as they relate to the premises, except the covenant to pay rent in the headlease (see **Chapter 7**).

Figure 6.5 provides a suggested approach to dealing with questions on assignment and underletting, and **Practice example 6.6** brings some of these points together.

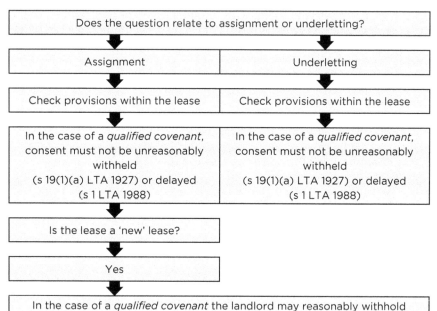

Figure 6.5: Alienation

Practice example 6.6

The tenant of business premises under a typical FRI lease wishes to assign the lease to a third party. The lease was granted in 1998 and part of the alienation clause reads as follows:

'The Tenant shall not assign the whole of this lease without the consent of the Landlord.'

What are the landlord's obligations following a request to assign the lease?

The qualified covenant will automatically be upgraded to a fully qualified covenant under s 19(1)(a) LTA 1927, so consent must not be unreasonably withheld. As this is a 'new lease', it is likely to contain circumstances and conditions to any proposed assignment and it will be reasonable for the landlord to rely on those under s 19(1A) LTA 1927. If the landlord refuses consent for another reason it must be reasonable to do so. The landlord must deal with any application expeditiously under s 1 LTA 1988.

OPTIONS FOR THE TERM OF A LEASE

The three main options for the term of a lease are a **fixed term**, **periodic tenancy**, or a **tenancy at will**.

Key term: fixed term

A fixed term tenancy is the most popular type of tenancy and can last for any fixed period of time (eg weeks, months, or years). Shorter leases are much more common in the current economic climate and tenants will often seek the right to break the lease (ie bring it to a premature end) at a specific time or times throughout the lease.

Key term: periodic tenancy

A periodic tenancy is a tenancy from one period to another (eg from week to week or month to month). Periodic tenancies may arise both expressly or impliedly and their term is determined by the frequency of payment of rent. They give a tenant greater flexibility, but they can usually be determined at common law by either party giving one full period's notice (eg one month for a monthly periodic tenancy). However, a yearly periodic tenancy requires six months' notice.

Key term: tenancy at will

A tenancy at will is a more precarious arrangement whereby the tenant occupies the premises at the will of the landlord. Therefore, the tenancy can be determined by either party at any time.

The provisions of Part II of the Landlord and Tenant Act 1954 may vary the common law rights of some business tenants (see **Chapter 9**). It is common for fixed term leases granted under this Act to include any extension of the term under it within the definition of the term.

CODE FOR LEASING BUSINESS PREMISES

For SQE1, you should be aware of the relevance of the **Code for Leasing Business Premises** to lease negotiations, its status, and its basic requirements.

The Code was originally introduced by the Royal Institution of Chartered Surveyors (RICS) in 1995, with later versions in 2002 and 2007. All three versions were voluntary and the spirit of them was never really adopted in practice. The primary aim of the Code was to improve the lease negotiation process, by making it fairer and more constructive for commercial tenants.

Key term: Code for Leasing Business Premises

The most recent version of the Code is 2019. It has now moved from a *voluntary code* to a *professional statement*, for RICS members. A copy may be downloaded from www.rics.org.

The Code contains *mandatory principles* of professional standards and *statements of best practice*.

The *mandatory principles* are that lease negotiations must be approached in a constructive and collaborative manner, and heads of terms should be in writing and be suitably comprehensive, to aid easier negotiation of the terms of leases. RICS members should inform non-members of the existence of the Code during the negotiation process and advise them to take independent advice.

The *statements of best practice* provide guidance on how key lease provisions should be negotiated. The detail of the statements of best practice is beyond the scope of this book. They may only be departed from in exceptional circumstances.

RICS members may be subject to an action in negligence or disciplinary action by the professional body in the event of breach of the Code.

■ KEY POINT CHECKLIST

This chapter has covered the following key knowledge points. You can use these to structure your revision, ensuring you recall the key details from each point:
• Prescribed clauses must appear at the beginning of leases granted on or after 19 June 2006, where the landlord's title is registered, and the lease is substantively registrable.
• A landlord will usually require a lease to be on full repairing and insuring terms, so that it is institutionally acceptable and produces a clear rent.
• The tenant is normally responsible for the repair of the premises as defined. In the case of a multi-let property the landlord will commonly retain responsibility for the other areas, but the tenants will be responsible for the costs.
• The landlord will usually be responsible for repairing or reinstating the property if damage or destruction is caused by an insured risk. The tenant must pay the insurance rent and rent suspension/termination provisions may apply.
• Tenant's covenants may be absolute, qualified, or fully qualified and some covenants are modified by statute, notwithstanding the express provisions (most importantly, alterations and alienation provisions).
• Most leases will restrict alterations and user.
• Frequently, leases will allow the tenant to assign the whole of the lease with landlord's consent. Such covenants are subject to statutory modification(s), which depend on the date of the lease.
• Most leases will contain provisions relating to the review of rent, most commonly on an open-market basis.

- Commonly, commercial leases are for a fixed term, although tenancies at will and periodic tenancies are also possible.
- The Code for Leasing Business Premises is a professional statement for RICS members. It contains both mandatory principles and statements of best practice.

■ KEY TERMS AND CONCEPTS

- lease (**page 144**)
- prescribed clauses (**page 144**)
- rent (**page 145**)
- rent review (**page 145**)
- provisos (**page 146**)
- full repairing and insuring (FRI) lease (**page 146**)
- institutionally acceptable lease (**page 146**)
- schedule of condition (**page 148**)
- insured risks (**page 149**)
- uninsured risks (**page 150**)
- insurance rent (**page 151**)
- rent suspension (**page 152**)
- absolute covenant (**page 155**)
- qualified covenant (**page 155**)
- fully qualified covenant (**page 155**)
- improvements (**page 156**)
- licence to alter (**page 157**)
- open market rent review (**page 160**)
- assumptions and disregards (**page 161**)
- alienation (**page 163**)
- assignment (**page 164**)
- underletting/subletting (**page 164**)
- sharing occupation (**page 164**)
- parting with or sharing possession (**page 164**)
- fixed term (**page 169**)
- periodic tenancy (**page 169**)
- tenancy at will (**page 169**)
- Code for Leasing Business Premises (**page 170**)

■ SQE1-STYLE QUESTIONS

QUESTION 1

A solicitor acts for the tenant of a commercial property, under a full repairing and insuring lease. The tenant covenants to keep the whole of the property in good repair and condition, save for damage caused by an insured risk. Part of the first floor of the property is seriously damaged by fire.

Which of the following best describes the most probable position?

A   The landlord will likely be responsible for reinstating the property under its insurance covenant and the rent (or a proportionate part of it) will be suspended pending reconstruction. It is possible that the tenant will be able to terminate the lease at the end of a rent suspension period if the premises are not reinstated.

B   The tenant will likely be responsible for reinstating the property as this is a full repairing and insuring lease. A proportionate part of the rent will be suspended pending reconstruction. If it becomes impossible or impractical for the tenant to reconstruct the premises, they may be able to terminate the lease.

C   The tenant will likely be responsible for reinstating the property as it should have insured the property for its full reinstatement value. The tenant should also have insured against loss of rent, which insurance proceeds will be payable to the landlord. The tenant must reconstruct the property and will be unable to terminate the lease.

D   If nothing has been done to vitiate the insurance policy by the tenant or anyone at the property with their authority, the landlord will likely be responsible for reinstating the property under its insurance covenant and the rent (or a proportionate part of it) will be suspended pending reconstruction. It is possible that the tenant will be able to terminate the lease at the end of a rent suspension period if the premises are not reinstated.

E   The landlord will likely be responsible for insuring the property for its full reinstatement value and must reinstate the property. The tenant will continue to pay rent unless it has insured against loss of rent, in which case the policy should cover it. Provided that nothing has been done to vitiate the insurance policy by the tenant or anyone at the property with their authority, the rent will probably be suspended pending reconstruction.

QUESTION 2

A solicitor acts for the freeholder of a commercial property ('the landlord') who granted a commercial lease of the whole of the property to a tenant. The tenant wishes to create two new windows in the external walls of the property, to improve the natural light, and has approached the landlord to obtain consent. The alterations covenant in the lease provides as follows:

'The Tenant may not make structural or exterior alterations to the Premises but may make internal non-structural alterations with the consent of the Landlord.'

May the landlord withhold consent to the tenant's proposed alterations without giving reasons?

A Yes, based on the express wording of the covenant, although any absolute alterations covenant will be modified by statute to make it a fully qualified covenant.

B Yes, because the landlord will usually retain ownership of the external walls in a commercial lease of the whole of a building.

C Yes, because there is an absolute covenant against structural alterations. However, the tenant may be able to use a statutory procedure to apply to make structural improvements.

D Yes, because there is an absolute covenant against structural alterations.

E Yes, because there is an absolute covenant against structural alterations, and statutory modification of covenants to fully qualified covenants only applies to qualified covenants against improvements.

QUESTION 3

A solicitor acts for the tenant of a modern commercial lease, where the rent is to be subject to upwards-only review on an open market basis.

Which of the following best describes the likely position in reviewing the rent?

A It will be assumed that the property is to be let with vacant possession, on the same terms, excluding the rent but including the provisions for rent review and that the tenant has complied with its covenants in the lease. The tenant's occupation and goodwill and the effect of voluntary improvements will be disregarded.

B It will be assumed that the property is to be let with the tenant in occupation, on the same terms, including the rent but excluding the provisions for rent review and that the tenant has complied with its covenants in the lease. The effect of voluntary improvements will be disregarded.

C It will be assumed that the property is to be let with the tenant in occupation, on the same terms, including the rent and the provisions for rent review and that the landlord has complied with its covenants in the lease. The tenant's goodwill and the effect of voluntary improvements will also be considered as it would be unfair for them to be disregarded.

D It will be assumed that the property is to be let with vacant possession, on the same terms, excluding the rent but including the provisions for rent review, and that the tenant has complied with its covenants in the lease. The tenant's occupation and goodwill and the effect of all improvements will be disregarded.

E   It will be assumed that the property is to be let on the same terms, excluding the rent but including the provisions for rent review and that the tenant has not complied with its covenants in the lease. The tenant's occupation and goodwill and the effect of improvements will be disregarded.

QUESTION 4

A solicitor acts for the tenant of commercial premises under a lease that was granted in 1985. The alienation covenant provides that the tenant shall not share occupation of the premises. It also states that the tenant shall not assign or underlet the whole of the premises without the prior written consent of the landlord.

Which of the following best describes the position for the tenant?

A   The tenant may lawfully assign part of the premises or underlet part of the premises without consent. They may, however, lawfully assign or underlet the whole of the premises with the consent of the landlord.

B   The tenant may lawfully assign or underlet the whole of the premises with the consent of the landlord, such consent not to be unreasonably withheld. The landlord must respond to such an application within a reasonable time.

C   The tenant may not allow another to occupy under a licence but may lawfully assign or underlet the premises with the consent of the landlord, such consent not to be unreasonably withheld or delayed.

D   The tenant may lawfully assign the whole or part of the premises or underlet the whole or part of the premises with consent, such consent not to be unreasonably withheld. The landlord must respond to such an application within a reasonable time.

E   The tenant may lawfully assign or underlet the whole of the premises with the consent of the landlord, such consent not to be unreasonably withheld. The landlord must respond to such an application within a reasonable time. Licences will not be permitted, although assignment or underletting of part will be permitted without consent.

QUESTION 5

A solicitor acts for a company which is the freeholder of a property (the 'landlord') which granted a commercial lease to a tenant in 2001. The permitted use of the property under the lease is any retail use. The tenant is a sole trader, in financial difficulty, and operating as a bookshop. They wish to assign the lease to a large and successful corporate tenant for use as a supermarket. A written request to assign the lease has been made. The landlord wishes to object to the proposed assignment as it already operates a supermarket across the road from the property. The alienation covenant in the lease provides as follows:

'The Tenant shall not assign the whole of the Premises without the prior written consent of the Landlord.'

Which of the following best describes the position regarding the landlord's consent?

A   The landlord may refuse consent to the proposed assignment as it is not under an obligation to act reasonably in withholding or delaying consent.

B   The qualified covenant will be modified by statute and the landlord may refuse consent as competition with the landlord's business would be a ground for reasonably withholding consent. However, the landlord must act within a reasonable time.

C   The landlord may not refuse consent as competition with the landlord's business would not be a ground for reasonably withholding consent.

D   The landlord may not refuse consent as competition with the landlord's business would not be a ground for reasonably withholding consent and the proposed assignee would be of superior covenant strength to the assignor.

E   The qualified covenant will be modified by statute and the landlord may refuse consent as competition with the landlord's business would be a ground for reasonably withholding consent. However, the landlord must act within a reasonable time and consider other circumstances and conditions in the lease.

■ ANSWERS TO QUESTIONS

Answers to 'What do you know already?' questions at the start of the chapter

1)   False. It is usual in a commercial lease for the tenant to be responsible for the cost of repairing the premises. In a lease of the whole of a property, the tenant will usually take on responsibility for the whole of the premises. In a lease of part of a property, the tenant will normally be responsible for repairing the interior only (as defined) and will reimburse, often by way of service charge, the landlord's costs in respect of the main structure of the building, the exterior, and common parts.

2)   A landlord should be wary of unusually onerous tenant covenants within a lease as they may have a negative impact on rent review.

3) True. It is possible in some circumstances for a tenant's covenant to be modified by statute. The main examples are alienation and alterations covenants.

4) The Code for Leasing Business Premises is now a mandatory requirement for surveyors who are RICS members. It contains both obligatory elements and statements of best practice.

Answers to end-of-chapter SQE1-style questions

Question 1

The correct answer was D. The landlord's obligation to reinstate, the tenant's right to suspension of rent, and the tenant's right to terminate at the end of a rent suspension period will all typically depend on whether anything has been done to vitiate the insurance policy by the tenant or anyone at the property with their authority. Option E incorrectly suggests that this only applies to rent suspension. Option A omits this important proviso, although it is otherwise correct. On the facts, it is likely that only a proportionate part of the rent will be suspended as only part of the property has been damaged. Option B is partially correct in this respect. Under a full repairing and insuring lease, it is usually the landlord who insures (including loss of rent cover) and reinstates, with the tenant paying the insurance premium. The rent suspension provisions benefit the tenant, but the landlord should be able to claim under its insurance policy for loss of rent, which will have been paid for by the tenant. If it becomes impossible or impractical for the landlord to reinstate the premises, then the landlord (rather than the tenant) may usually terminate, although this will be subject to negotiation in the lease. Therefore, options B, C, and E are incorrect in these respects.

Question 2

The correct answer was C. A tenant may still be able to use the statutory procedure under s 3 LTA 1927, despite the absolute covenant against structural alterations. Option A is incorrect as statutory modification only applies to qualified covenants against alterations for works classed as improvements. Option B is incorrect because the external walls will usually be part of the demise in a commercial lease of the whole of a building. Option D is partially correct in that the covenant against structural alterations is absolute, although it does not consider the statutory procedure. Option E also does not consider the statutory procedure, but it is otherwise correct. Therefore, option C is the most appropriate answer.

Question 3

The correct answer was A. It will be assumed that the property is to be let with vacant possession as a hypothetical tenant would pay less for premises occupied by the tenant. Therefore, option D is partially correct, but options B and C are incorrect on this point. It will also be assumed that the lease will be on the same terms, *excluding* the rent but *including* the provisions for rent review. Therefore, options D and E are partially correct on this point and options B and C are incorrect. The existing rent is irrelevant as it is the market rent at the time that matters, but the rent review needs to be considered as a tenant would often pay more for the security of knowing that rent could not increase on review. Although it is normal to have an assumption that the tenant's covenants have been complied with (so that they do not benefit from their own breach), the same cannot be said for the landlord's covenants. Therefore, options C and E are incorrect, but the other options are correct on this point. The tenant's occupation and goodwill and the effect of voluntary improvements (not all improvements, for example, those carried out due to statutory obligations) will be disregarded as it would otherwise be unfair to the tenant for the rent to be inflated for these reasons. Option B is partially correct on this point, but the other options are incorrect in at least one respect or are insufficiently precise.

Question 4

The correct answer was E. The clause is defective as although it permits assignment or underletting of whole with consent, it does not deal with assignment or underletting of part. Although it would prevent the grant of a licence (sharing *occupation* rather than possession) by way of an absolute covenant, it does not prevent parting with or sharing *possession* where not otherwise covered. *Informal* assignments and underleases of whole would therefore not be prevented, nor would either *informal or formal* assignments and underleases of part. As the covenant against assignment and underletting of whole is qualified, it will be modified by statute, meaning consent must not unreasonably be withheld and the landlord must respond within a reasonable time to a written application. Option A is only partially correct as it does not refer to the statutory modifications. Option B is incorrect as it does not set out the position on assignment or underletting of part but does refer to the statutory modifications. Option C is correct on the licence point but both options C and D are incorrect as they do not clearly and properly distinguish between assignment and underletting of whole and part. They do, however, refer to both statutory modifications.

Question 5

The correct answer was E. The qualified covenant will be modified by statute to a fully qualified covenant, so the landlord must not unreasonably withhold consent. The landlord must also act within a reasonable time in response to a written application for assignment. Option B is partially correct on these points. As this is a 'new lease' there may be additional circumstances and conditions to proposed assignments specified in the lease. None of the other options mention this. Competition with the landlord's business would be a reasonable reason for refusing consent. Therefore, options C and D are incorrect on this point, although option B is partially correct. Option A is incorrect as it fails to acknowledge the statutory modification of qualified covenants in this area. The superior covenant strength of the proposed assignee may be a relevant factor in favour of the tenant (as suggested in Option D), but the landlord will already have grounds for refusal based on competition with its own business.

■ KEY CASES, RULES, STATUTES, AND INSTRUMENTS

The SQE1 Assessment Specification does not require you to know any statutory authorities or specific case names for this topic. Specific sections of statutes are set out for ease of reference. Although neither a statute nor a statutory instrument, you should be aware of the Code for Leasing Business Premises, as specific reference is made to it in the SQE1 Assessment Specification.

7

Grant and assignment of commercial leases

■ MAKE SURE YOU KNOW

This chapter provides an overview of the grant and assignment of commercial leases and underleases.

In respect of grant, it deals with deduction and investigation of title and pre-contract searches and enquiries, as well as the need for the landlord's consent (licence to underlet) on the grant of an underlease. It then deals with drafting the lease and agreement for lease, as well as pre-completion, completion, and post-completion matters.

In respect of assignment, it deals with deduction and investigation of title, and pre-contract searches and enquiries, as well as the need for landlord's consent (licence to assign) to the assignment. It then deals with the deed of assignment and covenants for title, the Authorised Guarantee Agreement (AGA), and finally pre-completion, completion, and post-completion matters.

For the SQE1 assessments, you will need to understand the process and procedures of both the grant and assignment of leases and underleases.

■ SQE ASSESSMENT ADVICE

For SQE1, you are required to understand the law and practice relating to the grant and assignment of leases and underleases.

As you work through this chapter, remember to pay particular attention in your revision to:
• Deduction and investigation of title, and pre-contract searches and enquiries relevant to commercial leasehold transactions.
• The need for and purpose of (a) landlord's consent to underlet (licence to underlet), and (b) landlord's consent to assign (licence to assign), including how the documents deal with privity of contract, and the key provisions within the respective licences.
• The required documentation on the grant or assignment of a lease, including the lease and agreement for lease, on grant, and the deed of assignment (including covenants for title) and AGA, on assignment.
• Pre-completion, completion, and post-completion matters relevant to both types of transaction.

■ WHAT DO YOU KNOW ALREADY?

Attempt these questions before reading this chapter. If you find some difficult or cannot remember the answers, remember to look more closely at that topic during your revision.

1) When will a tenant be entitled to deduction of the landlord's title on the grant of a lease?

   [Grant of commercial leases and underleases: Deduction and investigation of title, page 181]

2) True or false? It is normal, on the grant of an underlease, for the head landlord to require a direct covenant from the undertenant to observe and perform the tenant covenants in the lease and the underlease.

   [Landlord's consent (licence to underlet), page 185]

3) Is it normal, on the assignment of a lease, for the landlord to require a direct covenant from the assignee to observe and perform the tenant covenants in the lease for the remainder of the term?

   [Landlord's consent (licence to assign), page 193]

4) True or false? A lease for a term of seven years normally needs to be registered at HM Land Registry.

   [Grant of commercial leases and underleases: Post-completion matters, page 188]

GRANT OF COMMERCIAL LEASES AND UNDERLEASES

For SQE1, you need to have a good working knowledge and understanding of the process of the grant of a **lease (as opposed to an underlease)** and the grant of an **underlease**.

Key term: lease (as opposed to an underlease)
Leases are defined more generally in **Chapter 6**, but in this context, a lease (as opposed to an underlease) is a lease granted by the freeholder (landlord) to a tenant.

Key term: underlease
A lease granted by a leaseholder (ie a shorter lease granted out of an existing lease) to an undertenant (see **Figure 7.1**). Any underlease carved out of a lease must be granted for a term that is at least one day less than the lease, otherwise it will take effect as an assignment of the lease (see **Assignment of commercial leases and underleases**, below).

Landlord
(Landlord under the original lease/headlease and head landlord under the underlease/sublease)

Tenant
(Head tenant – ie still the tenant under the headlease, and now the immediate landlord of the undertenant/subtenant under the underlease/sublease)

Undertenant
(Or subtenant – ie the tenant under the underlease/sublease)

Figure 7.1: Grant of an underlease

The outline heads of terms will often be prepared by a surveyor or agent and will need to deal with the key provisions of the proposed letting (see **Chapter 6**).

Landlord's concerns

On the *grant of a lease*, the landlord's main concern will be that the tenant will be able to pay the rent and observe and perform the tenant covenants under the lease (see **Chapter 6**). The ability of the tenant in this regard is known as its '*covenant strength*':

- In some circumstances, the landlord may require tenant references or a personal guarantee from an individual, such as a director or directors, or a group company of a corporate tenant (see **Revise SQE: Business Law and Practice**).
- Sometimes, a rent deposit may also be negotiated (see **Chapter 8**).

On the *grant of an underlease*, the tenant will need to check the alienation provisions within the lease (see **Chapter 6**) to ensure that they are complied with. Typically, the consent of the superior landlord will be required.

Deduction and investigation of title

As with the sale of a freehold property, the landlord's solicitor should investigate title and deduce title to the tenant's solicitor (see **Chapter 2**). The tenant's solicitor should then investigate title in the usual way (see **Chapter 2**).

Lender's consent

If a lender has a charge over the property (see **Chapter 2**), the terms of it will typically require the lender's consent to the proposed lease and its terms. In registered land, this will usually be supported by a restriction in the proprietorship register (see **Chapter 2**) in favour of the lender, prohibiting any disposition (eg transfer) or dealing without its consent.

The *consent in principle* of the lender/mortgagee should be obtained at the earliest possible opportunity, and the lender will also usually need to approve the *final form of lease* before completion.

Without consent, the landlord of the proposed lease will likely be in breach of the terms of the charge, and the tenant will be unable to register the lease (if required; see **HM Land Registry formalities: Legal leases of more than seven years**, below), or make other relevant HM Land Registry applications for shorter leases (see **HM Land Registry formalities: Legal leases of seven years or less**, below), if there is a restriction on the title.

Leases

In the case of the *grant of a lease*, whether out of registered or unregistered land, the landlord will usually deduce title to the freehold.

If the landlord's title is *registered* and title is not deduced (the landlord is under no obligation under the general law), the tenant may and *should* obtain official copies and filed/title plan from HM Land Registry.

Revision tip

It is always best practice for a tenant to obtain deduction of the landlord's registered title, and it is essential where the proposed lease is substantively registrable. It will be required for the purpose of investigation of title and may also be useful for other HM Land Registry applications, where the lease is not substantively registrable (see **HM Land Registry formalities: Legal leases of seven years or less**, below).

If the landlord's title is *unregistered*, the landlord *must* deduce title if the lease is to be granted for a term of more than seven years and will therefore be substantively registrable (see **HM Land Registry formalities: Legal leases of more than seven years**, below, and s 44, Law of Property Act 1925 (LPA 1925)). HM Land Registry will be unable to register the lease with absolute leasehold title (see **HM Land Registry formalities: Legal leases of more than seven years**, and **Chapter 2**) unless title has been deduced.

Underleases

In the case of the *grant of an underlease*, title to the headlease should be deduced.

If the headlease is *registered*, official copies and filed plan should be provided. If the title is not deduced, the tenant may still obtain official copies and filed plan from HM Land Registry.

If the headlease is registered with absolute leasehold title (see **Chapter 2**), it is not strictly necessary for the freehold title to be deduced. This is because all relevant entries (eg rights granted and reserved and covenants) should also appear on the registered title to the lease and HM Land Registry will have been satisfied with the superior title upon registration. However, in practice it is often deduced to identify the current head landlord. In any event, the tenant may still obtain official copies and filed plan of any registered title, from HM Land Registry.

Revision tip

If the headlease is registered with *good leasehold title* only (see **Chapter 2**), the freehold title should be deduced. If the underlease is to be substantively registrable, the tenant under the headlease (ie the landlord under the underlease) should also be asked to apply to HM Land Registry to upgrade the class of title of the headlease to absolute leasehold title (see *HM Land Registry, Practice Guide 42*). This is because registered superior titles must have absolute title to enable the underlease to be registered with absolute leasehold title. If this is not possible, indemnity insurance (see **Key term** in **Chapter 2**) may be required, particularly if a lender is involved (see **HM Land Registry formalities: Legal leases of more than seven years**, below).

If the headlease is *unregistered*, the landlord is only obliged to deduce the freehold title if the proposed lease is to be substantively registrable (ie it is to be granted for a term of more than seven years – see s 44 LPA 1925). However, the undertenant can ask to see deduction of the leasehold title going back up to 15 years (including the headlease and assignments since then).

The process of deduction of title on the grant of leases and underleases is summarised in **Figures 7.2 and 7.3**. **Practice example 7.1** also brings some of these points together.

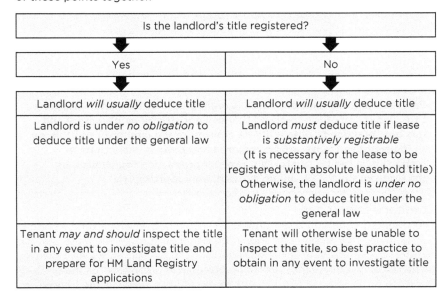

Is the landlord's title registered?	
Yes	No
Landlord *will usually* deduce title	Landlord *will usually* deduce title
Landlord is under *no obligation* to deduce title under the general law	Landlord *must* deduce title if lease is *substantively registrable* (It is necessary for the lease to be registered with absolute leasehold title) Otherwise, the landlord is *under no obligation* to deduce title under the general law
Tenant *may and should* inspect the title in any event to investigate title and prepare for HM Land Registry applications	Tenant will otherwise be unable to inspect the title, so best practice to obtain in any event to investigate title

Figure 7.2: Deduction of title on the grant of a lease

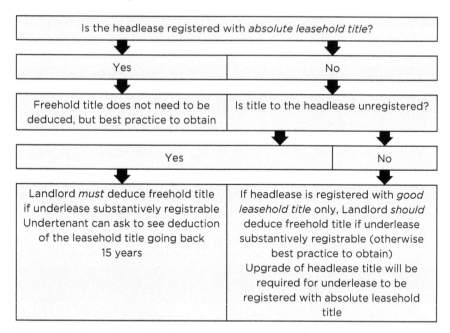

Figure 7.3: Deduction of freehold title on the grant of an underlease

Practice example 7.1

A solicitor acts for a tenant on the taking of an underlease of commercial premises, for a term of fifteen years. The immediate landlord's title is registered and is subject to a charge in favour of a commercial lender.

Will the landlord be required to deduce the freehold title?

Provided that the landlord's title is registered with absolute leasehold title, deduction of the freehold title will not strictly be necessary, but it is best practice to obtain it. The consent of the landlord's mortgagee to the proposed lease will be required and there is likely to be a restriction in the proprietorship register preventing registration of the lease without it (it will be substantively registrable).

Standard conditions

The standard conditions (see **Chapter 4**) provide that where a new lease is substantively registrable, title should be deduced, so that the lease may be registered with absolute leasehold title (SCPC 11.2.4 and SC 8.2.4). However, these will only apply if they are incorporated into a contract for the grant of the lease or underlease (Agreement for lease); see **Drafting the agreement for lease**.

Pre-contract searches and enquiries

The landlord's solicitor will send the following to the tenant's solicitor:
- Evidence of title.
- Draft agreement for lease (if applicable – see **Drafting the agreement for lease**).
- Draft lease/underlease (see **Drafting the lease**).
- Copies of any relevant documents held by the landlord (eg planning permission(s)).
- Replies to standard pre-contract enquiries (see below).

The formal lender's consent to the proposed lease/underlease will usually follow in due course, although an agreement in principle might be provided at this stage.

The tenant's solicitor will then:
- Investigate title (see above and **Chapter 2**).
- Raise detailed standard enquiries (eg Commercial Property Standard Enquiries (CPSEs)) if replies have not already been provided, and any appropriate specific enquiries/requisitions (see **Chapter 3**).
- Undertake the usual pre-contract searches (see **Chapter 3**).
- In the case of an underlease, request draft licence to underlet from the landlord's solicitor (see **Landlord's consent (licence to underlet)**).

Revision tip

In some cases, the proposed tenant may wish to undertake more limited due diligence, particularly on the grant of a short-term lease or underlease. This will be their decision to make, where a lender is not involved in the transaction. However, care must be taken to advise the client of the importance of such searches and what they would usually reveal, so that they may make an informed decision.

The tenant's solicitor will need to review and amend the draft lease or underlease, taking instructions and reporting to the client on all key terms of the documents.

Landlord's consent (licence to underlet)

In the case of the grant of an underlease, a **licence to underlet** will normally be a requirement of the lease (see **Chapter 6, Alienation**).

Key term: licence to underlet

The *purpose* of a licence to underlet is to provide the superior landlord's approval to the proposed underlease and to provide privity of contract (see *Revise SQE: Contract Law*) between the head landlord and undertenant, that would otherwise not exist.

A licence to underlet is usually prepared by the head landlord's solicitor and made between (1) the head landlord, (2) the head tenant, and (3) the undertenant. The undertenant covenants directly with the head landlord to observe and perform the tenant covenants in both the headlease (so far as they relate to the property and other than the covenant to pay rent) and the underlease, whilst the undertenant is bound by the tenant covenants in the underlease. The effect of this is privity of contract, meaning that the head landlord will be able to pursue the undertenant for any breaches.

The licence will also usually:
- Provide consent to the grant of the proposed underlease within a specified period.
- Specify that formal notice of the underlease is to be given by the tenant or undertenant in due course (see **Notice of underlease**, below).
- Provide an obligation to pay the head landlord's costs in connection with the preparation, negotiation, and completion of the licence to underlet and approval of the underlease. This is usually supported by an *undertaking* by the head tenant's or undertenant's solicitor to pay such costs, whether or not the matter proceeds to completion (see below and ***Revise SQE: Ethics and Professional Conduct***).

Drafting the agreement for lease
Most grants of commercial leases and underleases will proceed straight to completion and there will be *no need* for an **agreement for lease**. As with freehold transactions, the contract stage may be dispensed with.

Key term: agreement for lease
An agreement for lease is a contract or agreement to enter into the lease/underlease on completion.

However, an agreement for lease may serve a *useful purpose* in the following circumstances:
- Where there is to be some *delay in completion*, but the parties (either the landlord, or the tenant, or both) wish to be formally committed to the transaction.
- Where either or both parties need to *carry out works* on or to the property before the lease or underlease is formally granted (eg works of construction or refurbishment, or fit-out works by the tenant/ undertenant). In these circumstances, the agreement will cover, in detail, the obligations of the parties regarding the works. The full extent of these obligations is outside the scope of this book.
- Where a *third-party consent* is required to the grant of the lease/ underlease or the tenant's proposed use (eg the consent of a superior landlord, mortgagee/lender, or planning permission).
- Where *another tenant or other occupant is already in occupation* and the surrender of their interest needs to coincide with the grant of the new lease/underlease.

Ultimately, an agreement for lease should provide commercial certainty for the parties and security that the lease or underlease will be granted on the agreed terms.

Like the contract for the sale of a freehold property, the agreement for lease will be prepared by the seller's/immediate landlord's solicitor and submitted to the tenant's/undertenant's solicitor for approval. The parties will then negotiate its terms.

It is usual to incorporate standard conditions into an agreement for lease (either the SCPCs or the SCs – see **Chapter 4**) and for the agreed form of lease/underlease to be annexed to the agreement. Agreements for lease should only be exchanged when the form of lease/underlease to be annexed has been agreed, otherwise the document will be void for uncertainty as an 'agreement to agree'.

Drafting the lease

On the *grant of a lease*, the landlord's solicitor usually drafts the lease and submits it to the tenant's solicitor for approval. The terms will be negotiated between the parties until they are agreed. Lease negotiation is a key skill of a typical commercial property solicitor and although **Chapter 6** outlines the key points for the purposes of SQE1, the full range of tenant's amendments is beyond the scope of this book.

- The *landlord's main concern* will be to have a lease that gives it suitable control over the property and which is institutionally acceptable (see **Chapter 6**). A lease that is not institutionally acceptable, could affect the value of the property, as well as its marketability and suitability for lending purposes. If the landlord exercises too much control, with unusually onerous provisions, this could also have an adverse impact on rent review (see **Chapter 6**).
- The *tenant's main concern* will be to have a lease that will enable it to occupy the property on reasonable terms, without unduly onerous liabilities and restrictions. A lease that is unduly onerous or restrictive could be difficult to deal with in the future, lead to additional financial liability, and affect the tenant's day-to-day use and enjoyment of the property.

The terms of an *underlease* will usually be governed by the terms of the headlease (the headlease will often state that any underlease must be granted on similar terms to the headlease), so there will be less room for negotiation (see **Chapter 6**).

Pre-completion matters

Once the lease/underlease is agreed, the landlord's solicitor will prepare engrossments (ie clean copies) of the lease/underlease and counterpart lease/underlease for execution by the landlord and tenant respectively, as well as any other parties to it (eg a guarantor executes the counterpart).

The lease must usually be executed as a deed to take effect as a conveyance in law (see s 52 LPA 1925 and **Chapters 2 and 5**). An exception exists for most leases of three years or less, which do not need to be made by deed and may be created orally (s 54 LPA 1925). It is still best practice for such leases to be made in writing and by deed.

The tenant will normally pay a proportionate part of the rent (and potentially other sums such as insurance and service charge) over to the landlord on completion, and such sum(s) will usually be set out in the completion statement produced before completion.

In the case of an *underlease*, the head landlord will normally produce engrossments of the licence to underlet, which is typically executed in more than one part or in triplicate (ie each party executing one of two or three parts, or two or three engrossments executed by all parties).

Completion

The licence to underlet should be completed before completion of any underlease, and the tenant's solicitor should also insist on seeing a copy of any lender's consent before completion.

On completion, the landlord receives:
• Executed counterpart lease or underlease.
• The balance of any premium (ie purchase price) paid.
• Apportioned sums due under the lease.

The tenant should receive the following:
• Executed lease or underlease.
• Certified copy title deeds (if the superior title is unregistered – see above).
• Certified copy lender's consent (if appropriate).

Post-completion matters

The main post-completion matters are Stamp Duty Land Tax (SDLT)/Land Transaction Tax (LTT), and HM Land Registry formalities and, in the case of an underlease, service of notice on the superior landlord.

SDLT/LTT formalities

The SDLT or LTT return must be submitted, and duty paid within 14 days of completion (for SDLT) or 30 days of completion (for LTT) (see **Chapter 10**).

HM Land Registry formalities: Legal leases of more than seven years

These are substantively registrable (registrable in their own right) and so will have their own title number. This is the case whether the superior title is registered or unregistered.

- If the *landlord's title is registered*, this will be a registrable disposition and an application to change the register (form AP1) must be submitted within the priority period of the pre-completion HM Land Registry search (see **Chapter 5**). HM Land Registry will also note the lease against the superior title.
- If the *landlord's title is unregistered*, the tenant's application will be for *first registration* of the lease (on form FR1, with DL in duplicate – see **Chapter 5**) and must be registered within two months of completion.

Revision tip

It is important to remember the general rule that it is only leases of *more than* seven years that are substantively registrable. A lease of precisely seven years (and no longer) will not need to be registered.

Exam warning

Candidates often conflate the need for first registration of the lease with first registration of the superior title. A lease granted for a term of more than seven years will be substantively registrable, *whether or not the superior title is registered*. If unregistered, the superior title will not need to be registered either before or when the lease is registered. *It is therefore possible to have a registered lease granted out of a superior title, which remains unregistered.*

The lease will be registered with good leasehold title if the superior title is unregistered and the relevant title documents have not been submitted to HM Land Registry with the application for registration of the lease, or if the superior title is not registered with absolute title.

Revision tip

The value, marketability, and value for secured lending purposes of a lease registered with good leasehold title only could be materially adversely affected. Therefore, where a lender considers it to be suitable security (see **Revision tip** in **Assignment of commercial leases and underleases**, below), they may require an indemnity insurance policy to be put in place for such a lease.

HM Land Registry formalities: Legal leases of seven years or less

These are not substantively registrable.

- In *registered land* they will be an overriding interest (see **Chapter 2** and **Revise SQE: Land Law**) and other HM Land Registry applications are possible (see below).
- In *unregistered land*, legal leases bind any owner of the land and will be an overriding interest on first registration of the superior title. However, a

tenant may consider lodging a caution against first registration against the name of the estate owner to provide further protection for the tenant on first registration of the superior title.

In *registered land*, the possible HM Land Registry applications for legal leases of seven years or less are summarised below.

'*Medium-sized leases*' (ie a lease of more than three years, up to and including seven years):
• It is best practice to apply to enter a notice of the lease (by way of agreed or unilateral notice – see **Chapter 2**) *and* for registration of the ancillary rights/easements (see **Chapter 2** and **Chapter 6**) within it against the superior title.

'*Short leases*' (ie a lease of up to and including three years):
• It is not possible to apply to enter a notice of the lease against the superior title.
• It is possible and best practice to apply for registration of the easements within the lease against the superior title.

Revision tip

In the case of the grant of *both* short and medium-sized leases out of registered land, registration of the easements is necessary for them to take effect in law. *In either case*, a specific clause should be added to the lease, confirming the landlord's consent to the entry of a notice/registration of the rights. *In short, an HM Land Registry application of some description is possible and recommended for short and medium-sized leases granted out of a registered title.*

The registration requirements on the grant of leases and underleases are summarised in **Table 7.1**.

Table 7.1: Registration of leases/underleases

Type of lease	Registration requirements
Legal leases of *more than seven years* out of *registered land*.	Substantively registrable as a *registrable disposition*.
Legal leases of *more than seven years* out of *unregistered land*.	Substantively registrable under an application for *first registration*.
Legal leases of *more than three years*, up to and including seven years out of *registered land*.	An overriding interest. Not substantively registrable but capable of noting against superior title. Registration of easements recommended.

Table 7.1: (Continued)

Legal leases of *up to and including three years* out of *registered land*.	An overriding interest. Not substantively registrable and not capable of noting against superior title. Registration of easements recommended.
Legal leases of *up to and including seven years* out of *unregistered land*.	Binding on any owner of the land. An overriding interest on first registration of the superior title. Consider lodging a caution against first registration against the name of the estate owner to protect the tenant on first registration of the superior title.

Notice of underlease

On the grant of an underlease, formal notice of completion of the underlease must usually be served on the superior landlord, under the terms of the lease/licence to underlet. It should be served on the superior landlord, in duplicate, accompanied by the relevant fee, and one copy of the receipted notice should be kept with the lease.

ASSIGNMENT OF COMMERCIAL LEASES AND UNDERLEASES

Assignment is the transfer of the unexpired residue of the term of an existing/subsisting lease or underlease by the existing tenant (assignor) to a new tenant (assignee) (see **Chapter 6**).

As the assignee is taking what is left of the term, there will be no scope to amend the lease, unless the landlord is prepared to enter into a deed of variation of its terms.

Commercial leases typically permit the assignment of the whole of the tenant's interest, with the landlord's written consent, under a qualified or fully qualified covenant (see **Chapter 6**). A formal licence to assign (see **Landlord's consent (licence to assign)**, below) will therefore be a key element of such a transaction.

> ### Revision tip
>
> The assignment of a commercial lease will usually be more like a *transfer not for value* than a *sale for value* of freehold property, as the consideration (premium) will normally be nominal, or a premium will not be paid. This

is because commercial leases are typically granted at high market rents, without a premium, and do not usually have a capital value. They will also often contain provisions allowing for forfeiture on the insolvency of the tenant (see **Chapter 8**). They are therefore more akin to an ongoing *liability*, rather than an *asset* that will be transferred for value, and they will often, as a result, be unsuitable as security for lending purposes. Such leases may be contrasted with longer, typically residential leases, which do have a capital value and are usually granted at a minimal or nominal rent, for a much longer term. *The general rule is that the longer the term and the lower the rent, the more likely the lease will be an asset with capital value.*

Deduction and investigation of title

The assignor's solicitor should investigate and deduce title in the usual manner (see **Chapter 2**) to anticipate problems and specify the incumbrances within any contract (see **The need for a contract**, below).

The documents that should be deduced are as follows.

Lease with registered title

Leasehold title
• Official copies and filed/title plan (these can be inspected in any event), together with an official copy of the lease and any other documents referred to in the title.
• Any other documents and deeds ancillary or collateral to the lease (eg licences to assign).

Superior title
• The assignor is under no obligation to deduce the superior title.
• It is not strictly necessary to see the superior title if the lease is registered with absolute leasehold title.
• However, it is best practice to obtain the superior title, whatever the class of leasehold title.
• If the lease is registered with *good leasehold title* only, the *superior title* should be deduced (although the assignor is under no obligation to do so), so that the title may be *upgraded* to absolute leasehold title.
• If the superior title is registered, official copies and filed/title plan may be obtained from HM Land Registry if the assignor does not provide them.

Unregistered lease

Leasehold title
• Copy lease and any assignment(s), as well as any other documents and deeds ancillary or collateral to the lease for the last fifteen years.

Superior title

- The *superior title* should also be deduced (although the assignor is under no obligation to do so) if the lease will be substantively registrable following the assignment (see **HM Land Registry formalities**), so that the lease may be *registered* with absolute leasehold title.
- If the superior title is registered, official copies and filed plan may be obtained from HM Land Registry if the assignor does not provide them.

The assignee's solicitor will need to investigate title (see **Chapter 2**) (including the lease) and report to the assignee.

Pre-contract searches and enquiries

At the pre-contract stage, the assignee's solicitor will:
- Raise detailed standard enquiries (eg CPSEs) and any appropriate specific enquiries/requisitions (see **Chapter 3**).
- Undertake the usual pre-contract searches (see **Chapter 3**).
- Request draft licence to assign from the assignor's solicitor (see below).

As on the grant of a lease or underlease, in some cases, a client may wish to undertake more limited due diligence and the same issues and concerns would arise here.

Landlord's consent (licence to assign)

Where landlord's consent to a proposed assignment is required (in the form of a **licence to assign**), the first step will be for the assignor to consider the full terms of the alienation covenant (see **Chapter 6**) and to approach the landlord for consent in principle.

> ### Key term: licence to assign
>
> The *purpose* of a licence to assign is to give the landlord's formal written consent to the proposed assignment. For new leases it may also contain an Authorised Guarantee Agreement (see **Privity of contract and how the licence deals with this**, below, and **Chapter 8**). For old leases it will typically contain a direct covenant between the landlord and the assignee (again, see **Privity of contract and how the licence deals with this**, below, and **Chapter 8**).

Landlord's concerns and costs

The landlord will have similar concerns to those on the grant of a new lease and will need to ensure that the proposed assignee has sufficient covenant strength. As with the grant of a lease, in some circumstances, the landlord may require references or a personal guarantee from an individual such as a director or directors, or a group company of a corporate tenant, or a rent deposit (see above). An Authorised Guarantee Agreement (AGA) may also be required from the assignor and some of these conditions may be expressly set out in the alienation covenant (see **Authorised Guarantee Agreement**, below, and **Chapters 6 and 8**).

The landlord will typically require an undertaking from the assignor's solicitors to be responsible for the landlord's legal and other professional costs in respect of the proposed assignment. These could include the review of references to provide agreement in principle and the preparation, negotiation, and completion of the licence to assign. Such an undertaking will usually be required, whether or not the matter proceeds to completion. It is important for the assignor's solicitor to seek to obtain their client's authority to give the undertaking, limit it, as appropriate, and not to give it until they are in receipt of cleared funds on account (see *Revise SQE: Ethics and Professional Conduct*).

The need for a contract

Like the grant of a lease or underlease, most assignments will proceed straight to completion, without a formal contract/agreement. In any event, the parties must not complete until the formal licence to assign has been completed.

If the parties proceed by way of contract, it is best practice to complete any required formal licence to assign before exchange, as the consequences under the standard conditions may create uncertainty, if consent is not in place by the completion date (see **Table 7.2**).

Table 7.2: Standard conditions – outstanding licence to assign on completion

SC 8.3.3	Either party may *rescind* the contract by notice to the other party if by *three working days before completion*: (a) consent has not been given, or (b) it has been given subject to a condition to which a party reasonably objects.
SCPCs 11.3.5 and 11.3.6	The time for completion will be *postponed until five working days* after the seller gives written notice to the buyer that consent has been given or a court has declared that consent has been unreasonably withheld. If no consent has been given or court declaration obtained after *six months* from the original completion date, either party may *rescind* the contract by written notice to the other.

Revision tip

For SQE1, you should know the different implications under the respective standard conditions.

An assignment without consent, where required, would be a breach of the lease and would also mean that the assignment was unlawful (see **Chapter 8**).

The landlord's solicitor *prepares the draft* licence for approval by the solicitors acting for the assignor and assignee. The parties to it are usually (1) the landlord, (2) the assignor, (3) the assignee, and (if required), (4) any guarantor. The parties will seek to agree the draft and, like a licence to underlet, it is usually executed in duplicate, triplicate, or in two or three separate parts. It must usually be executed as a deed.

The *key provisions in the licence* are as follows:
- *Landlord's consent* to the proposed assignment for a specific period/ window of time (eg within a month of the licence).
- For 'new leases' (granted on or after 1 January 1996 – see **Privity of contract and how the licence deals with this**, below, and **Chapter 8**) – if required, an *Authorised Guarantee Agreement* (AGA) or the requirement to enter into an AGA in a separate document.
- For 'old leases' (granted before 1 January 1996 – see **Privity of contract and how the licence deals with this**, below, and **Chapter 8**) – a *direct covenant* between the assignee and the landlord to observe and perform the tenant covenants *for the rest of the term*.
- The assignor's agreement to meet the landlord's costs, as agreed – although the landlord should have the security of the undertaking from the assignor's solicitor (see above), this makes it clear that the assignor is meeting these costs.
- An obligation to serve notice of the assignment on the landlord (see **Notice of assignment**, below).

Privity of contract and how the licence deals with this
The position on privity of contract and how the licence deals with this is summarised in **Table 7.3**. **Practice example 7.2** also brings some of these points together.

Table 7.3: Privity of contract and how the licence to assign deals with this

Type of lease	Position on liability/privity of contract	Solution in licence to assign
Old leases	There will be *no privity of contract* between the landlord and the assignee.	Landlord will seek to 'upgrade' privity of estate to *privity of contract.*
	Privity of estate (ie the fact they are the current holder of the interest) provides that the assignee will be liable to the landlord for the observance and performance of the tenant covenants which 'touch and concern' the land whilst the lease is vested in them (see **Chapter 8**).	This is done by obtaining a *direct covenant* from the assignee in the licence to assign to observe and perform all the tenant covenants in the lease *for the remainder of the term.*

Table 7.3: (Continued)

New leases	There will be *no privity of contract* between the landlord and the assignee.	*Privity of contract* is abolished for new leases.
	Any tenant will be liable to the landlord for the observance and performance of all the tenant covenants in the lease (not just those which touch and concern the land) whilst the lease is vested in them. A tenant will *automatically be released* from liability on lawful assignment (generally, an assignment with the consent of the landlord) (see **Chapter 8**).	The landlord may, in some circumstances, require an *Authorised Guarantee Agreement* from the assignor (see **Authorised Guarantee Agreement**, below).
		Any *direct covenant* must be limited only to the time *whilst the lease is vested in the assignee*.

Practice example 7.2

A solicitor acts for an assignee who is taking an assignment of a commercial lease. The lease was originally granted in April 1998.

What is the position on the assignee's liability and what are the likely requirements of the licence to assign?

This is a 'new lease' as it was granted on or after 1 January 1996. Privity of contract will not apply, and the tenant will usually only be liable for the tenant covenants whilst the lease is vested in them. They will automatically be released on lawful assignment, although the landlord may then, in some circumstances, require an AGA from them. Any direct covenant will need to be limited accordingly. The licence will also deal with ancillary matters such as costs and notice of assignment.

Deed of assignment and covenants for title

The draft **deed of assignment** is prepared by the assignee's solicitor and submitted to the assignor's solicitor for approval.

Key term: deed of assignment

The deed of assignment is the formal conveyance/transfer of the legal interest in the lease (see **Chapter 5**). Like the conveyance of a freehold interest, it must be made by deed (s 52 LPA 1925).

Once agreed, the assignee's solicitor produces an engrossment or engrossments for execution. It is sometimes executed in two parts or in duplicate (see **Chapter 5**).

Form of deed of assignment

Although commonly known as a deed of assignment, the required form of deed is as follows:

- *Assignment of registered lease* – TR1 (see **Chapter 5**).
- *Assignment of unregistered lease with more than seven years left unexpired* – usually a TR1, but an alternative form of deed of assignment may be used.
- *Assignment of unregistered lease with seven years or less left unexpired* – deed of assignment.

Revision tip

A form TR1 will be required for the assignment of a registered lease, irrespective of its unexpired term, as dispositions of registered land always require registration to be effective in law. For the assignment of an unregistered lease, it is the unexpired residue of the term that is important when it comes to registration (see below), rather than the original term.

The need for an express indemnity

The standard conditions, if incorporated into a contract, provide for an express indemnity to be given by the assignee to the assignor, where the assignor may remain liable following completion (SC 4.6.4 and SCPC 7.6.5).

For *old leases*, an express indemnity should usually be given in the deed (this is best practice), although it will automatically be implied on (a) the assignment of a registered lease (Schedule 12 Land Registration Act 2002) or (b) the assignment of an unregistered lease for value (s 77 LPA 1925).

For *new leases*, an express indemnity should be given in the deed, if the assignor is to remain liable under an AGA (see **Authorised Guarantee Agreement**, below).

Covenants for title

The following provision should always be added in an assignment of leasehold land:

> *The covenants set out in section 4 of the Law of Property (Miscellaneous Provisions) Act 1994 will not extend to any breach of the tenant's covenants in the lease relating to the physical state of the property.*

This is because on the transfer of leasehold property with full or limited title guarantee, it is implied that the covenants in the lease have been complied with (see **Chapter 4**). However, the assignor should not be providing any warranties in respect of the repair and condition of the property as *caveat emptor* usually applies (see **Chapter 1**).

Authorised Guarantee Agreement

For *new leases*, an **Authorised Guarantee Agreement (AGA)** is often an absolute specified pre-condition to giving consent to a proposed assignment of whole (see **Chapter 6**). If so, then it will *automatically be reasonable* for the landlord to insist upon one. If it is not an absolute specified condition, then the landlord may require one only *if it is reasonable to do so.*

Key term: Authorised Guarantee Agreement (AGA)

AGAs only apply to 'new leases' and provide that the assignor will:

* Guarantee the assignee's payment of rent and observance and performance of the tenant covenants under the lease and indemnify the landlord against any non-payment or other breach.
* Pay the rent and observe and perform the covenants in default of the assignee.
* Take a new lease if the lease is disclaimed on insolvency (see *Revise SQE: Business Law and Practice*), or sometimes pay a liquidated sum instead, if the landlord does not require them to take a new lease.

The AGA should also provide that the assignor will be released on lawful assignment of the lease by the assignee. In other words, the assignor may only be required to guarantee the *immediate assignee* and anything beyond that will be void.

Any *guarantor of the assignor* may not be required *directly* to guarantee the assignee (they are also released on lawful assignment by the assignor). However, they may lawfully be required to guarantee the assignor's performance under the AGA, thereby *indirectly* guaranteeing the assignee (see **Chapter 8** and **Practice example 7.3**).

Practice example 7.3

A solicitor acts for the assignee in the assignment of a commercial lease dated 28 December 2000. The landlord has requested an AGA from the assignor and a direct covenant from the assignee to observe and perform the tenant covenants under the lease for the remainder of the term.

What is the position concerning the landlord's request?

As this is a 'new lease', the landlord will likely be able to require the AGA (either as an absolute requirement under the lease, or if it is otherwise reasonable to do so). A direct covenant from the assignee is not strictly required as they will only be liable whilst the lease is vested in them. It is unlawful for the landlord to seek to extend their liability in this way, so the direct covenant must be avoided.

Revision tip

A newly qualified solicitor practising in commercial property should have a good working knowledge of the law and practice surrounding AGAs. It is therefore highly likely that this area could be assessed as part of SQE1.

Pre-completion matters

The usual pre-completion searches should be undertaken (see **Chapter 5**).

The landlord's solicitor engrosses the licence to assign for execution by the parties. The licence to assign may incorporate the AGA, or this may be contained within a separate deed.

The assignor's solicitor should produce a completion statement for the assignee's solicitor, setting out any apportioned sums due on completion.

Completion

On completion, the balance due should be submitted to the assignor's solicitors, with the assignee's solicitor handing over the part licence to assign. The assignee's solicitor should receive the following:

- Original lease and ancillary deeds and documents.
- Deed of assignment (or TR1 where required).
- Part licence to assign, executed by the landlord.
- Certified copy unregistered title information (if required – see above).
- Receipt for rent (the assignee, in receipt of this, may assume it has been paid and the covenants performed – s 45(2) LPA 1925).

Post-completion matters

The three main post-completion matters are SDLT/LTT formalities, HM Land Registry formalities, and service of notice on the landlord.

SDLT/LTT formalities

The assignee's solicitor must deal with the SDLT/LTT requirements (see **Chapter 10**).

HM Land Registry formalities

The assignee's solicitor must then deal with the HM Land Registry formalities as follows:

Registered lease – Application to change the register/register the disposition, using form AP1 and submitted within the OS1 priority period.

Unregistered lease with more than seven years left unexpired – Application for first registration of the lease, using form FR1 and DL in duplicate and submitted within two months of completion. If the superior title is registered, the lease will be noted in the charges register of the same.

Other leases where the superior title is registered – Note lease against registered title and/or register easements within the lease (see above).

Other leases where the superior title is unregistered – Consider lodging a caution against first registration against the name of the estate owner, to protect the tenant on first registration of the superior title.

Notice of assignment

Notice of the assignment is usually a requirement set out in the lease and/or licence to assign. This confirms that the assignment that was authorised has in fact taken place. It should be served on the landlord, in duplicate, accompanied by the relevant fee, and one copy of the receipted notice should be kept with the lease.

▪ KEY POINT CHECKLIST

This chapter has covered the following key knowledge points. You can use these to structure your revision, ensuring you recall the key details from each point:

- On the grant of a lease, the landlord's title will usually be deduced and must be deduced where the proposed lease is to be substantively registrable and granted out of unregistered land. It is always best practice to obtain it.
- On the grant of an underlease, the head landlord's title will usually be deduced and must be deduced where the headlease is unregistered and the proposed lease is to be substantively registrable. However, it is always best practice to obtain it.
- The consent of any mortgagee of the landlord should be obtained to any proposed lease or underlease.
- The usual pre-contract searches and enquiries should be undertaken for leasehold transactions.
- On the grant of an underlease, a licence to underlet will usually be required from the superior landlord to provide privity of contract between them and the undertenant.
- A contract for the grant of a lease or underlease is not a strict requirement and may be dispensed with. However, it may serve a useful purpose in some circumstances.
- SDLT/LTT formalities are required following grant and assignment of leases and underleases.
- Leases granted for a term of more than seven years are substantively registrable, although other HM Land Registry applications may be possible for shorter leases.

- On the assignment of a lease, it is best practice for the landlord's title to be deduced, particularly if the lease is registered with good leasehold title only or if the lease will be substantively registrable following assignment.
- On the assignment of a lease, a licence to assign will usually be required from the landlord. For 'old leases' it typically provides privity of contract between the landlord and the assignee. For 'new leases' it may incorporate an AGA or provide for an AGA in a separate document.
- The form of deed of assignment depends on whether the lease is already registered. It may require an express indemnity and the covenants for title should always be varied.
- HM Land Registry formalities are required for registered leases and assigned leases with more than seven years left to run. Other applications may be possible for shorter leases.

■ KEY TERMS AND CONCEPTS

- lease (as opposed to an underlease) (**page 180**)
- underlease (**page 180**)
- licence to underlet (**page 185**)
- agreement for lease (**page 186**)
- licence to assign (**page 193**)
- deed of assignment (**page 196**)
- Authorised Guarantee Agreement (AGA) (**page 198**)

■ SQE1-STYLE QUESTIONS

QUESTION 1

A solicitor acts for the assignee in relation to the assignment of a commercial lease. The lease is unregistered and has ten years left unexpired. The landlord's title is unregistered.

Which of the following best describes the position on deduction of title, the form of deed of assignment, and registration?

A   As this is the assignment of an existing lease, the assignor is under no obligation to deduce the landlord's title. The transfer may take the form of a deed of assignment and as the landlord's title is unregistered, the lease will not need to be registered.

B   The landlord's title should be deduced so that the lease may be registered with absolute title. However, the assignor is under no obligation to do this. The transfer must take the form of a TR1, and the lease will need to be registered.

C   The landlord's title should be deduced so that the lease may be registered with absolute title. However, the assignor is under no obligation to do this.

The transfer may take the form of a TR1, or deed of assignment and the lease will need to be registered.

D   The landlord will need to register its title prior to the assignment of the lease, so that the lease may be registered with absolute title and the lease noted against the landlord's title. The transfer must take the form of a TR1, and the lease will need to be registered.

E   As this is the assignment of an existing lease, and the landlord's title is unregistered, the landlord's title will not need to be deduced and the assignor is under no obligation to do so. The transfer must take the form of a deed of assignment and as the landlord's title is unregistered, the lease will not need to be registered.

QUESTION 2

A solicitor acts for a client who proposes to take an underlease of a property for a term of exactly seven years. There will be no formal agreement for lease. The headlease is registered with absolute leasehold title and has nine years left to run. The superior landlord's freehold title is unregistered.

Which of the following best describes the position in relation to deduction of title and registration of the underlease?

A   Deduction of the freehold title will not strictly be required and the underlease will need to be registered substantively.

B   Deduction of the freehold title will not strictly be required but the underlease should be noted against the landlord's title.

C   Deduction of the freehold title will be required and the underlease will need to be registered substantively.

D   Deduction of the freehold title will be required and the underlease should be noted against the landlord's title.

E   Deduction of the freehold title will be required to register the underlease with absolute leasehold title.

QUESTION 3

A solicitor acts for a client in relation to the assignment of a commercial lease dated 16 March 2000, under a contract incorporating the Standard Commercial Property Conditions of Sale (SCPCs), unamended. Landlord's consent is awaited, as required by the qualified covenant against assignment of whole under the lease. There has been no unreasonable delay by the landlord.

Which of the following best describes the likely position in relation to the assignment and what would happen if consent has not been received by the contractual completion date?

A   The time for completion will be postponed until five working days after the seller gives written notice to the buyer that consent has been given or a court has declared that consent has been unreasonably withheld. If no consent has been given or court declaration obtained after six months from the original completion date, either party may rescind the contract by written notice to the other.

B   Either party may rescind the contract by notice to the other party if by three working days before completion consent has not been given, or it has been given subject to a condition to which a party reasonably objects. The landlord is likely to be entitled to an Authorised Guarantee Agreement if it is a requirement of the lease or it is otherwise reasonable to do so.

C   If by three working days before completion consent has not been given, or it has been given subject to a condition to which a party reasonably objects, the contract will automatically come to an end. The landlord is likely to be entitled to an Authorised Guarantee Agreement but only if it is a requirement of the lease.

D   The time for completion will be postponed until five working days after the seller gives written notice to the buyer that consent has been given or a court has declared that consent has been unreasonably withheld. The landlord is likely to be entitled to an Authorised Guarantee Agreement but only if it is a requirement of the lease.

E   If no consent has been given or court declaration obtained after six months from the original completion date, either party may rescind the contract by written notice to the other. The landlord is likely to be entitled to an Authorised Guarantee Agreement but only if it is reasonable to do so.

QUESTION 4

A solicitor acts for the assignor on the assignment of the whole of a lease dated 15 February 2006, with a fully qualified covenant against assignment of the whole. The assignor is the original tenant, and a specified condition of assignment is that an Authorised Guarantee Agreement (AGA) must be provided.

Which of the following best describes the position as to the liability of the assignor and the assignee?

A   As the original tenant, the assignor will remain liable under the lease following lawful assignment by virtue of privity of contract. The landlord will also require a direct covenant from the assignee to observe and perform the tenant covenants under the lease for the remainder of the term.

B   The assignor will be released from liability on assignment of the lease, but the landlord may require a direct covenant from both the assignor and the assignee to observe and perform the tenant covenants under the lease for the remainder of the term.

C   The assignor will be released from liability on lawful assignment of the lease, but the landlord may require an AGA from the assignee to observe and perform the tenant covenants under the lease whilst the lease is vested in them.

D   The assignor will be released from liability on lawful assignment of the lease, but the landlord may require an AGA from the assignor to guarantee the observance and performance of the tenant covenants under the lease by the incoming tenant and its successors in title. The assignee will not normally need to enter into a direct covenant with the landlord.

E   The assignor will be released from liability on lawful assignment of the lease, but the landlord may require an AGA from the assignor to guarantee the observance and performance of the tenant covenants under the lease by the immediate incoming tenant. The assignee will not normally need to enter into a direct covenant with the landlord.

QUESTION 5

A solicitor acts for an assignor on the assignment of a commercial lease dated 15 December 2002, with registered title. There has been no contract for the assignment as the parties are proceeding straight to completion. The Landlord has requested an Authorised Guarantee Agreement (AGA) as part of the licence to assign and this is a permitted requirement under the lease.

Which of the following best describes the most probable position as to the proposed deed of assignment?

A   Form TR1 may be used, an express indemnity will be required unless the transfer is for value, and covenants for title relating to repair and condition will need to be varied.

B   Form TR1 must be used, an express indemnity will be unnecessary as the assignor will be automatically released on lawful assignment, and the covenants for title relating to repair and condition will need to be varied.

C   Form TR1 must be used, an indemnity will be implied under the Standard Commercial Property Conditions, and the covenants for title relating to repair and condition will not need to be varied.

D   Form TR1 must be used, an indemnity will be implied as the lease is registered and the assignor is entering into an AGA. The covenants for title relating to repair and condition will need to be varied.

E   Form TR1 must be used, an express indemnity will be required as the assignor is entering into an AGA. The covenants for title relating to repair and condition will need to be varied.

■ ANSWERS TO QUESTIONS

Answers to 'What do you know already?' questions at the start of the chapter

1) Under the general law, the tenant will be entitled to deduction of the landlord's title on the grant of a lease, where it is to be granted for a term of *more than* seven years (i.e. where it is substantively registrable in its own right) and the landlord's title is unregistered.

2) True. It is normal, on the grant of an underlease, for the head landlord to require a direct covenant from the undertenant to observe and perform the tenant covenants in the lease and the underlease. This is to create privity of contract between the head landlord and the undertenant. The covenant normally excludes the covenant to pay rent in the headlease (which remains the responsibility of the tenant under the headlease) and only includes the covenants in the headlease so far as they relate to the underlet property.

3) It is normal, on the assignment of a lease, for the landlord to require a direct covenant from the assignee to observe and perform the tenant covenants in the lease for the remainder of the term, on the assignment of an 'old lease'. On the assignment of a 'new lease', any direct covenant should be limited to the period during which the lease is vested in the assignee.

4) False. A lease for a term of *precisely* seven years will not usually be substantively registrable, although a lease for a term of *more than* seven years will be.

Answers to end-of-chapter SQE1-style questions

Question 1

The correct answer was C. The landlord's title *should* be deduced so that the lease may be registered with absolute title. However, there is *no obligation* on the assignor to do so. Option B is also correct in this respect and options A and E are correct on the obligation issue. However, option E is incorrect insofar as even if the landlord's title is unregistered, it *should* still be deduced on the assignment of an existing lease, where the lease will be substantively registrable. Option D is incorrect in its statement that the landlord's title must be registered before the lease is dealt with. The assignment of a lease with more than seven years left to run will be substantively registrable and may still be registered with absolute title, irrespective of the registration status of the landlord's title. Options A and E are incorrect here, although options B and D are partially correct. Form TR1 or a deed of assignment may be used for the assignment of an unregistered lease with more than seven years left unexpired, although it is more common to use a TR1. The other options are incorrect in failing to account for the two options here.

Question 2

The correct answer was B. As the headlease is registered with absolute leasehold title, it is not strictly necessary for the freehold title to be deduced (although it is still best practice for a tenant's solicitor to see it). Option A is correct on this point, although options C, D, and E are incorrect. The undertenant would only have the right to see the freehold title had the headlease been unregistered and the underlease been substantively registrable. In this case, the headlease is registered and the underlease will not be substantively registrable as it is for a term of exactly seven years (i.e. not more than seven years). Options A, C, and E are incorrect on this point. The lease should, however, be noted against the landlord's title and option D is also correct on this point.

Question 3

The correct answer was A as this correctly describes the position under the SCPCs. Option B is incorrect on this point, although it correctly states the position under the Standard Conditions of sale (the SCs). Option C partially states the position under the SCs, but does not recognise that the parties have the right to rescind the contract in the given circumstances – the contract does not automatically come to an end. Options D and E only state part of the position under the SCPCs. As this is a new lease, the landlord will be entitled to insist on an AGA if it is a specified condition in the lease or it is otherwise reasonable to do so. Option B is correct here, although options C, D, and E are incorrect.

Question 4

The correct answer was E. The assignor will usually be released from liability on lawful assignment of the lease. Options C and D are also correct on this point and option B would have been correct in this respect had it referred to 'lawful' assignment. Even though they are the original tenant, the assignor will not remain liable under the lease following lawful assignment by virtue of privity of contract as this is a new lease and privity of contract has been abolished for new leases. The landlord will also not, under a new lease, be able to require a direct covenant from the assignee to observe and perform the tenant covenants under the lease for the remainder of the term. Therefore, option A is incorrect on these points and option B is also incorrect as the assignor may also not be required to give such a covenant. The landlord may require an AGA as this is a specified condition under the lease. It is the assignor who gives the AGA (not the assignee, as suggested in option C) and it may only be directly for the incoming tenant (not other successors in title, as suggested in option D). Option D is however correct in that the assignee will not normally need to enter into a direct covenant with the landlord.

Question 5

The correct answer was E. Form TR1 must be used as the lease is registered. Options B, C, and D are correct on this point, and option A is incorrect. An express indemnity will be required under a new lease if the tenant/assignor is entering into an AGA. Option A is incorrect on this point as it states the position on the assignment of an old, unregistered lease. Option B would have been correct that an indemnity would not be required, had the assignor not been entering into an AGA. An indemnity will not be implied under the Standard Commercial Property Conditions as the question states that there is no contract, and the parties are moving straight to completion. Therefore, option C is incorrect here. An indemnity will only be implied under the Land Registration Act, for an old, registered lease, making option D incorrect (although it does make the link between the AGA and the need for an indemnity). The covenants for title will need to be amended in the transfer, as suggested in options A, B, and D, but incorrectly stated in option C.

■ KEY CASES, RULES, STATUTES, AND INSTRUMENTS

The SQE1 Assessment Specification does not require you to know any statutory authorities or specific case names for this topic. Specific sections of statutes are set out for ease of reference.

8

Commercial leasehold remedies

■ MAKE SURE YOU KNOW

This chapter provides an overview of liability on leasehold covenants for leases granted before and on or after 1 January 1996, and remedies for breach of commercial leasehold covenants. It deals with action in debt (including insolvency proceedings), forfeiture, Commercial Rent Arrears Recovery, pursuit of guarantors, and resort to a rent deposit. It also deals with specific performance, damages, and self-help through a *Jervis v Harris* clause. For the SQE1 assessments, you will need to understand who may be liable for covenants under a lease and which remedy or remedies would be most appropriate. You will also need to have a good working knowledge of the detail of each of the available remedies (including the requirements and procedural formalities) and be able to assess their relative merits in given circumstances.

■ SQE ASSESSMENT ADVICE

For SQE1, you are required to understand leasehold liability and remedies from a practical perspective. As you work through this chapter, remember to pay particular attention in your revision to:
- Liability under leasehold covenants for leases granted before and on or after 1 January 1996 (most importantly, ongoing liability after assignment of a lease by the tenant).
- The main remedies of debt action, forfeiture, Commercial Rent Arrears Recovery, pursuit of guarantors, rent deposits, specific performance, damages, and self-help.
- How the remedies compare, their requirements in particular circumstances, and which remedy or remedies would be most appropriate in a given scenario.

■ WHAT DO YOU KNOW ALREADY?

Attempt these questions before reading this chapter. If you find some difficult or cannot remember the answers, remember to look more closely at that topic during your revision.
1) True or false? Under an 'old lease' (ie a lease granted before 1 January 1996) the original tenant will be liable for all tenant covenants under the lease for the entire term.
   [Liability under leasehold covenants, page 209]

2) True or false? Under a 'new lease' (ie a lease granted on or after 1 January 1996) the tenant will automatically be released from future liability for the tenant covenants on lawful assignment.
[Liability under leasehold covenants, page 209]

3) What needs to be done before pursuing a former tenant or guarantor for rent, service charge, or other liquidated payments under a lease?
[Pursuit of former tenants and guarantors, page 219]

4) When will it be possible to forfeit a lease for breach of the tenant's repairing covenant?
[Remedies for breach of other covenants – forfeiture, page 224]

LIABILITY UNDER LEASEHOLD COVENANTS

For the purposes of SQE1, it is important to be able to distinguish between **old leases** and **new leases**, as this has a bearing on who may be liable for breach of covenants under a lease. In some situations, former tenants and former guarantors may remain liable alongside the existing tenant and guarantor.

Key term: old leases

Old leases are any leases (including underleases) granted before the introduction of the Landlord and Tenant (Covenants) Act 1995 (the '1995 Act') (ie before 1 January 1996).

Key term: new leases

New leases are any leases (including underleases) granted after the introduction of the 1995 Act (ie on or after 1 January 1996).

The original parties (ie the original landlord, tenant, and any guarantor) will always be liable to each other under the lease whilst the lease is vested in them. However, if any of the parties have changed, it is first necessary to determine which rules apply, as there are different regimes for old and new leases.

Old leases

For old leases, the liabilities of the parties are as follows.

Original tenant

The *original tenant* will be liable for all the tenant covenants under the lease for the entire term (as defined under the lease – see **Chapter 6**), by virtue of *privity of contract* (ie they were an original contracting party; see also *Revise SQE: Contract Law*). Therefore, the original tenant under an old lease will remain liable even after they have assigned their interest (see **Chapter 7**). Due to such ongoing liability, they will usually seek an express indemnity from the assignee/transferee on assignment/transfer of the lease (see **Chapter 7**). Such an indemnity is implied if the transfer is for value (s 77, Law of Property Act 1925 (LPA 1925)) or if the lease is registered (Schedule 12, Land Registration Act 2002).

Subsequent tenants

Subsequent tenants will be liable under the rules of *privity of estate* (ie the fact they are the current holder of the interest) for tenant covenants that *touch and concern the land*, during their period of ownership. In practice, this will be most covenants that affect the relationship of landlord and tenant and refer to the subject matter of the lease/directly affect the premises, other than those that are expressed to be personal (ie only intended to bind that particular tenant).

As the liability of subsequent tenants is more limited under the rules of *privity of estate*, it is common for landlords to require subsequent tenants, on assignment, to enter into a direct covenant with the landlord to observe and perform *all covenants* under the lease for the remainder of the term (see **Chapter 7**). In effect, this 'upgrades' the *privity of estate* under the general law, to *privity of contract*, for the benefit of the landlord. Due to such ongoing liability, they will typically seek an express indemnity from the assignee/transferee on assignment/transfer of the lease and this will be implied in some circumstances (as set out above).

Revision tip

Under these rules, it is clear to see that subsequent, intermediate tenants (ie those tenants following the original tenant before the current tenant) may continue to remain liable under the rules of *privity of contract* under a direct covenant given on a previous assignment.

Original landlord

The *original landlord*, by virtue of *privity of contract*, will be liable for all the landlord covenants under the lease for the full term. Therefore, they will usually obtain an express indemnity when their interest is transferred.

Subsequent landlords

Subsequent landlords, by virtue of *privity of estate*, will be liable for covenants that touch and concern the land (see above) during their period of ownership (s 142 LPA 1925).

Original guarantor

The *original guarantor* will be liable for all the tenant covenants for the full term, by virtue of *privity of contract*.

Subsequent guarantors

The liability of *subsequent guarantors* will depend on the terms of their guarantee (ie whether they guarantee the performance and observance of the tenant covenants by the person they guarantee or for the remainder of the term).

Table 8.1 summarises the position on liability under old leases and **Practice example 8.1** brings some of these points together.

Table 8.1: Liability under old leases

Tenant	
Original tenant	*Privity of contract* – Liable for the whole term.
Subsequent tenant	*Privity of estate* – Liable for covenants which touch and concern the land during period of ownership. Will usually be upgraded by a direct covenant to *privity of contract* for all covenants for the entire term.
Landlord	
Original landlord	*Privity of contract* – Liable for the whole term.
Subsequent landlord	*Privity of estate* – Liable for covenants which touch and concern the land during period of ownership.
Guarantor	
Original guarantor	*Privity of contract* – Liable for the whole term.
Subsequent guarantor	Depends on the terms of the guarantee.

Practice example 8.1

Sunshine Perambulations Ltd entered into a lease as tenant in 1990, with Katrina acting as guarantor. Sunshine subsequently assigned the lease to Sam, who then assigned it to Andrei. Andrei has now failed to pay the rent under the lease.

Who may be liable to pay the rent, in addition to Andrei?

This is an 'old lease', therefore both Sunshine and Katrina will be liable as original parties throughout the term. Sam may also be liable if he gave a direct covenant to the landlord.

New leases

The 1995 Act abolished the doctrine of *privity of contract* for *new leases*, so does not distinguish between the original and successive parties.

Original and successive tenants

The *original and successive tenants* will be liable for breaches of all covenants (other than those expressed to be personal to another party) whilst the lease is vested in them. They are automatically released from *future* liability (ie post assignment breaches) on lawful assignment (ie an assignment complying with the alienation clause (see **Chapter 6**) and not by operation of law, eg on death or bankruptcy). Therefore, for example, if landlord's consent was required to an assignment and was not obtained, the assignor will not be released until the next subsequent lawful assignment (see **Practice example 8.2**).

To compensate the landlord for the tenant's automatic release, the 1995 Act provides that the lease may specify circumstances and conditions for proposed assignments, including the tenant entering into an Authorised Guarantee Agreement (AGA – see **Chapter 7**). Remember that under an AGA, the assignor may only be required to guarantee the immediate assignee's obligations. They will be released on the next subsequent lawful assignment.

Revision tip

AGA is a very well-known term in practice. You should therefore be aware of the law and practice relating to them.

Because of such ongoing liability, the outgoing tenant (assignor) will usually require an express indemnity from the incoming tenant (assignee) to observe and perform the tenant covenants whilst the lease is vested in them (see **Chapter 7**).

Original and successive landlords

The *original and successive landlords* will be liable under the landlord covenants (other than those expressed to be personal and to which they were not a party) but will not automatically be released when they transfer their interest. Instead, they may *apply for release* under sections 6–8 of the 1995 Act. The procedure is as follows:

• The landlord serves a notice on the tenant either before, or within four weeks of, the assignment, requesting to be released.
• The tenant has four weeks to respond to the notice.
• If no response is received, the landlord is released from the landlord covenants (other than those that are expressed to be personal).
• If the tenant objects, the landlord may apply to the County Court for a declaration that release would be reasonable.

To avoid the need to comply with the above procedure, it is possible to include a clause within the lease that the landlord's liability is limited to the time when the reversion is vested in them (ie whilst they own the superior title (see **Chapter 7**)). This is known in practice as an 'Avonridge clause' as this approach was endorsed in the case of *Avonridge Property Co Ltd v Mashru* [2005] UKHL 70.

Revision tip

Avonridge clauses are very common in practice in standard leases. You should therefore be aware of them and their implications.

Original and successive guarantors

Any guarantor may not be required *directly* to guarantee future assignees (they are also released on lawful assignment by the tenant they agreed to guarantee, ie the assignor). However, they may lawfully be required to guarantee the assignor's performance under the AGA, thereby *indirectly* guaranteeing the immediate assignee.

Table 8.2 summarises the position on liability under new leases and **Practice example 8.2** brings some of these points together.

Table 8.2: Liability under new leases

Tenant
• Liable for breaches of all covenants (other than those expressed to be personal to another party) whilst the lease is vested in them.
• Automatically released from *future* liability (ie post assignment breaches) on lawful assignment.
• Landlord may require an AGA where specified in the lease or otherwise reasonable to do so.

Landlord
• Liable under the landlord covenants (other than those expressed to be personal to another party).
• Not automatically released on transfer of interest (unless lease contains an *Avonridge clause*).
• May otherwise apply for release under sections 6–8 of the 1995 Act.

Guarantor
• Automatically released on lawful assignment by the tenant they agree to guarantee (ie the assignor).
• May not be required *directly* to guarantee future assignees.
• May lawfully be required to guarantee the assignor's performance under an AGA, thereby *indirectly* guaranteeing the immediate assignee.

Practice example 8.2

Gravity Developments Ltd entered into a lease as tenant in 1998, with Kate acting as guarantor. Gravity subsequently assigned the lease to Chanel, who then assigned it to Cornelia. Cornelia then assigned the lease to Kalush and Kalush has now failed to pay the rent under the lease. All assignments were made with the landlord's consent, except for the assignment from Chanel to Cornelia.

Who may be liable to pay the rent, in addition to Kalush?

This is a 'new lease', therefore Gravity and Kate will have been released on Gravity's lawful assignment. Chanel will not originally have been released as the assignment to Cornelia was made without consent. However, she will have been released on the next subsequent lawful assignment to Kalush. If the landlord required Cornelia to enter into an AGA, she may also be liable for the rent.

Exam warning
Liability of the parties under both old and new leases is likely to form the subject matter of SQE1 assessments, so it is crucial that you have a sound working knowledge of the topic.

REMEDIES FOR BREACH OF LEASEHOLD COVENANTS
Remedies for breach of leasehold covenants are generally separated between remedies for non-payment of rent(s), and remedies for breach of other covenants.

For SQE1, you need to understand the procedures involved and be able to determine which remedy would be most appropriate in given circumstances.

Before proceeding with any remedy, it is important to ensure that the tenant is in breach of the precise terms of the relevant covenant(s) and to identify any other parties who may be liable (see above).

REMEDIES FOR BREACH OF COVENANT(S) TO PAY RENT(S)
The main remedies for non-payment of rent(s) are debt action (including insolvency proceedings), forfeiture, Commercial Rent Arrears Recovery (CRAR), the pursuit of former tenants or guarantors, and recourse to a rent deposit. We will look at each remedy in turn.

Debt action or insolvency proceedings
A *debt action* may be brought in the County Court or High Court (See *Revise SQE: Dispute Resolution*) and the relevant limitation period is six years (Limitation Act 1980). The landlord should consider the tenant's actual ability to pay the rent(s) before pursuing this remedy as the process can be costly and time consuming. It may also impact on the landlord–tenant relationship, although it may be appropriate for repeat occurrences.

As an alternative to court action, and if the debt is not disputed, the landlord may consider commencing *insolvency proceedings* against the tenant if the relevant thresholds are met for personal bankruptcy (£5000) or corporate winding-up (£750) (see *Revise SQE: Business Law and Practice*). Sometimes, the threat of insolvency proceedings will be enough to make the tenant settle the debt. However, it would be an abuse of process to commence insolvency proceedings where there is a genuine dispute concerning the debt. As an unsecured creditor (see *Revise SQE: Business Law and Practice*), the landlord may also not receive the full amount owed to them if the insolvency proceedings are successful.

Forfeiture

Forfeiture is the most drastic of remedies.

Key term: forfeiture

Forfeiture (sometimes referred to as the *proviso for re-entry*) provides the landlord with the power to re-enter the premises, take possession of them, and bring the lease to a premature end.

The right to forfeit

To rely on this remedy there must be an *express power/clause/proviso* within the lease dealing with the specific circumstances. Without such a clause, and compliance with its terms, the remedy will be unavailable to the landlord.

A typical forfeiture clause will entitle the landlord to forfeit the lease in the event of:

- Rent(s) (see **Revision tip**, below, and **Chapter 6**) being outstanding for a period (typically 21 days) after becoming due (whether formally demanded or not).
- Breach of other tenant covenants or conditions.
- Insolvency events affecting the tenant (see *Revise SQE: Business Law and Practice*).

Revision tip

As indicated in **Chapter 6**, it is common for other sums in addition to the annual rent to be reserved as rent (eg service charge and insurance rent). The effect of this is that forfeiture for non-payment of these sums ('*Rents*') may be available without having to serve a s 146 notice (see **The right to forfeit and s 146 notices**, below). It is therefore important to check the precise terms of the forfeiture clause to see whether it refers to *rents* rather than just *rent* (see **Practice example 8.3**).

A forfeiture clause will usually be the subject of negotiation on the grant of a new lease, to ensure that its terms are not unduly onerous. The process of negotiation of forfeiture clauses is outside the scope of this book.

A landlord seeking to rely on forfeiture should check that the rent(s) has/ have been outstanding for the relevant period. If the words '*whether formally demanded or not'* are not within the clause, the landlord would need to make a formal demand (unless at least half a year's rent is outstanding and there are insufficient goods available on the premises for recovery – Common Law Procedure Act 1852, s 210, County Courts Act 1984, s 139(1)).

Methods of forfeiture

The landlord may forfeit by way of a court order or through peaceable re-entry (ie simply entering the property, usually when vacant, and changing the locks). In the case of peaceable re-entry, the landlord should take care not to use or threaten violence, which would be a criminal offence (s 6 Criminal Law Act 1977).

Waiver of the right to forfeit

The landlord should also avoid waiving the right to forfeit by doing anything which acknowledges the landlord and tenant relationship to be continuing (eg accepting or demanding rent(s), dealing with tenant applications under the lease (eg a request to consent for alterations), or pursuing CRAR (see **Commercial Rent Arrears Recovery**, below)). Non-payment of rent(s) is a **once and for all breach** as opposed to a **continuing breach** (see below). Therefore, waiving the right in these circumstances could be fatal to the landlord's claim in respect of past arrears. However, it would arise again in respect of future arrears (see **Practice example 8.3**).

Key term: once and for all breach

A once and for all breach is one that arises once on an individual breach (eg non-payment of rent or breach of an alienation or alterations covenant). The right to forfeit will not arise again in respect of that breach but may arise again in respect of future breaches.

Key term: continuing breach

A continuing breach is one that continues as the tenant remains in breach (eg breach of repair or user covenant (see **Chapter 6**)). The right to forfeit will arise again as the breach continues.

Relief from forfeiture

The landlord should also bear in mind that the tenant may apply for relief from forfeiture, generally for up to six months after recovery of possession. If such an application is successful, the lease will continue. This is at the discretion of the court, but it will typically be granted where the tenant agrees to pay the outstanding arrears and costs.

Revision tip

The time limits on relief from forfeiture are different for breaches of other covenants (see **Remedies for breach of other covenants: Forfeiture**, below), so it is important to be able to distinguish between them.

Landlord's considerations

In considering whether to pursue forfeiture, the following should be considered:

Practical considerations:

- Is the problem due to the temporary circumstances of the tenant or an administrative oversight, and is the landlord and tenant relationship worth preserving?
- Has there been a history of persistent and serious non-payment?
- Would a mere threat of forfeiture be enough to obtain payment?
- Is the market rising or falling? In a *rising market* (where the landlord could easily find another tenant, possibly at a higher rent), the landlord will be more inclined to forfeit and remove a problematic tenant than in a *falling market*, where the landlord may be left with no income and a vacant property (which may have an impact on adjoining property).
- Is it the only real option to remove a problem tenant?

Availability of the remedy and likely success:

- Does the lease contain a forfeiture clause and have its terms been breached (eg does a formal demand need to be sent?)?
- Has the landlord waived the right to forfeiture?
- Is the tenant likely to be able to apply for relief from forfeiture and be successful? This could cause delay in any event.

Figure 8.1 summarises the process for forfeiture for non-payment of rent(s).

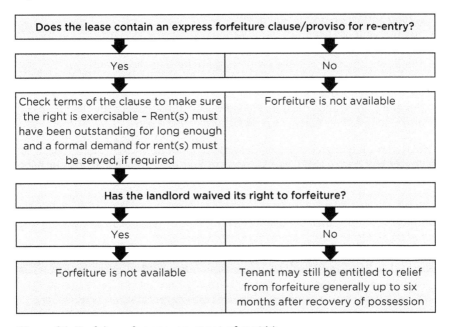

Figure 8.1: Forfeiture for non-payment of rent(s)

Commercial Rent Arrears Recovery

Commercial Rent Arrears Recovery (CRAR) may also be an option in some circumstances.

Key term: Commercial Rent Arrears Recovery (CRAR)

CRAR is a process by which the landlord may enter commercial premises, where there is a written tenancy, in order to seize goods belonging to the tenant, sell them, and use the proceeds to settle rent arrears.

Revision tip

Unlike forfeiture (see above) CRAR can only be used to recover *annual rent*, including VAT (ie rent paid for the possession and use of the premises, and not other sums reserved as rent (eg insurance rent or service charge)). In the past it was common to reserve these as rent so that the common law remedy of *distress* would be available to the landlord if they were not paid. Distress was the old equivalent of CRAR, but it has now been abolished for commercial tenancies. *You should be aware of the fundamental distinction between forfeiture and CRAR in this respect* (see **Practice example 8.3**).

There are also specific procedural requirements that must be adhered to:
- There must be at least seven days' rent outstanding when the notice is served and when goods are taken.
- The tenant must generally be given at least seven days' notice of entry.
- An authorised enforcement agent must be used.
- The agent can only remove property belonging to the tenant.
- The agent cannot take goods up to the value of £1350 that are necessary for the tenant's business.
- Generally, the goods must be sold at public auction, with the tenant being given no less than seven clear days' notice of the sale.

CRAR can be a useful remedy, despite its limitations, and the threat of an enforcement notice alone can encourage a tenant to discharge their arrears. It is an effective option if the tenant does not have the funds to pay, but its drastic nature could have an impact on future relations should the tenant's position improve. Taking away goods connected with the business, where permitted, could also be counterproductive in having an impact on the tenant's ability to make money and pay future rent.

Revision tip

The Commercial Rent (Coronavirus) Act 2022 has introduced a statutory dispute resolution procedure in respect of *rent arrears that accrued in the period of forced closures during the Coronavirus pandemic*. This limits the availability of the CRAR remedy in such circumstances. The detail of the provisions is outside the scope of this book, but you should be aware that the procedure exists for such arrears.

Where the landlord has a right to CRAR, if the whole or part of the property has been sublet, it may also be possible for the landlord to collect the rent from a subtenant, after giving fourteen clear days' notice (s 81 Tribunals, Courts, and Enforcement Act 2007).

Pursuit of former tenants and guarantors

Action may be possible against a former tenant or the guarantor(s) of the existing or former tenant(s).

Guarantor of the existing tenant

The *guarantor of the existing tenant* will be liable under the terms of the guarantee to pay the rent, observe and perform the covenants under the lease (including payment of rent), and to indemnify the landlord in respect of any breach by the tenant.

Former tenants and guarantors

Proceeding against a *former tenant or guarantor of a former tenant* is more complicated and will depend on when the lease was granted:

* Under *old leases* (see above), the *original guarantor* will be liable, by virtue of privity of contract, to guarantee the payment of rent and observance and performance of the tenant covenants, indemnifying the landlord in the event of any tenant breaches during the *entire term*. *Subsequent guarantors* may also be liable, depending on the *terms of their guarantee* (eg if they gave a direct covenant for the whole of the remainder of the term).
* Under *new leases*, a guarantor will automatically be released on lawful assignment of the lease (see above) and cannot be required to guarantee a future assignee. However, they can legitimately be required to guarantee the outgoing tenant's performance under an AGA until the next lawful assignment (therefore providing an indirect guarantee of the immediate assignee).

Before proceeding against a former tenant or guarantor of a former tenant it is necessary to serve a **section 17 notice** on them.

Key term: section 17 notice

A default notice under section 17 of the 1995 Act for recovery of a 'fixed charge' (ie rent, service charge, or other liquidated sum) from a former tenant or former guarantor. Such notice must be served within six months of the sum falling due.

Revision tip

Section 17 notice is a very well-known term in practice. You should therefore be aware of the law and practice relating to them.

Revision tip

Candidates do not always appreciate that, although derived from the 1995 Act, the need to serve a section 17 notice applies equally to new and old leases.

Failure to serve a section 17 notice on time will mean that the landlord will not be able to pursue the relevant party for the relevant sum.

If the recipient of the notice pays the fixed charge, they may call for an **overriding lease** within twelve months.

Key term: overriding lease

An intermediate lease that 'slots in' between the landlord and the existing tenant, making the former tenant or guarantor the immediate landlord of the tenant. It enables the former tenant or guarantor to take back control, for example, by forfeiting the lease and re-letting the premises.

The strict time limits involved mean that this remedy is only suitable for recent arrears. However, if the former tenant or guarantor no longer exists or is insolvent, this could be problematic.

Recourse to rent deposit

A landlord may also seek to rely on a **rent deposit** provided by the tenant.

Key term: rent deposit

A rent deposit is a sum paid by the tenant to the landlord, usually on the grant or assignment of a lease, as security for the payment of rent(s) and sometimes the performance and observance of other covenants.

If a rent deposit is provided, it is usual to have a formal rent deposit deed, outlining the terms on which the deposit is held and the procedure for withdrawals, top-up, and repayment/return to the tenant.

Before seeking to rely on a rent deposit, the terms of the rent deposit deed should be considered, and its terms complied with.

The use of the rent deposit provides a straightforward and cheap solution in the event of rent arrears, so it can be an attractive option for a landlord. However, if funds are depleted and the tenant is in financial difficulty, it is unlikely that the funds will be topped up by the tenant.

Practice example 8.3 brings some of the points together on remedies for non-payment of rent(s).

Practice example 8.3

Ochman is the tenant under a commercial lease that was granted in 2005 and which was assigned to him by the former and original tenant, Brooke. The assignment was made with the landlord's consent and Brooke entered into an AGA with the landlord. Ochman is now in arrears of rent and service charge to the value of approximately £6000. The lease contains a proviso for re-entry entitling the landlord to forfeit the lease in the event of non-payment of rents within 21 days of the due date, whether formally demanded or not. Both rent and service charge are reserved as rent. The landlord has, in the last seven days, entered into a licence for alterations in respect of Ochman's proposed alterations. There is no rent deposit in place and the arrears have been outstanding for over a month.

Which remedies are potentially available to the landlord?

- **There is no rent deposit in place so this will not be an option.**
- **A debt action could be possible (as could bankruptcy proceedings, as the threshold has been met).**
- **Forfeiture would prima facie (on first impression) be available for both the rent and service charge arrears as there is an express proviso for re-entry and its terms have been complied with. However, it is likely that the landlord will have waived its right to forfeiture for the existing arrears (a once and for all breach) by dealing with the tenant's application for alterations and thus acknowledging the continuance of the landlord and tenant relationship. Even if the right had not been waived, the tenant may have been entitled to relief from forfeiture.**
- **CRAR could be an option, but it will be subject to the usual procedural requirements and the landlord would only be able to recover the arrears of rent, even though service charge is reserved as rent.**
- **It would be possible to pursue Brooke under the AGA, but a s 17 notice would need to be served first and within six months of the sums becoming due, and Brooke may be able to claim an overriding lease.**

REMEDIES FOR BREACH OF OTHER COVENANTS

The main remedies for breach of other covenants are specific performance, damages, self-help under a *Jervis v Harris* clause (for breach of repairing covenants, see **Chapter 6**), forfeiture, and pursuit of former tenants and guarantors. In some circumstances, recourse to a rent deposit or an injunction may also be possible. We will look at each remedy in turn.

Specific performance

Specific performance is a discretionary equitable remedy (see **Revise SQE: Trusts Law**) requiring the tenant to take action to remedy a breach. As an equitable remedy, it will only usually be granted where other remedies are unavailable or would be inappropriate. *If forfeiture or self-help are available or damages would be appropriate, then it will not usually be granted* (see **Practice example 8.4**). Furthermore, the landlord should come to equity with clean hands, so must not pursue the remedy for improper purposes. Pursuing specific performance can be both costly and time consuming.

Damages

Damages for breach of covenant may also be an option for the landlord, under ordinary contractual principles. However, the landlord may not be able to recover the full amount in the event of breach of a *repairing covenant*, due to the following provisions:

Section 18 Landlord and Tenant Act 1927 – *Statutory ceiling*:
- Damages are limited to the amount the value of the reversion is diminished. This could be less than the cost of the repairs.
- There will be no damages following termination of the lease if the landlord plans to demolish or make structural alterations to the property which would make the repairs valueless.

Leasehold Property (Repairs) Act 1938 – *Leave to sue*:
- For leases granted for seven years or more with at least three years or more left to run, notice of intention to sue (a s 146 notice – see below) must be served on the tenant, informing them of their right to serve a counter-notice.
- The tenant may then serve a counter-notice within 28 days, claiming protection under the Act.
- If a counter-notice is served, the landlord will require leave of the court to proceed, where it must be proved that the breach needs to be remedied immediately:
  - To prevent substantial diminution to the value of the reversion (or that this has already occurred), or
  - To comply with law, or
  - To protect the interests of occupiers of other parts of the property, or
  - To avoid greater expense in the future, or
  - Other special circumstances render it just and equitable for leave to be given.
- The Act does not apply to breaches of a covenant to put premises into repair within a reasonable time of the tenant taking possession.

As with any claim for damages, a key element in deciding whether to proceed will be the tenant's ability to pay.

Revision tip

The *statutory ceiling* and need for *leave to sue* are significant limitations on suing for damages for breach of a tenant's repairing covenant, but they will not apply to self-help (see below and **Practice example 8.4**).

Self-help – *Jervis v Harris* clause

A self-help clause, often known as a *Jervis v Harris* clause, after a case which endorsed the use of such clauses, usually provides for the following:

- A *right of entry* for the landlord to check compliance with the tenant's repairing covenant.
- A right to *serve a notice* of any breach on the tenant with details of the works required.
- An *obligation on the tenant* to proceed diligently and expeditiously with the work.
- A right for the landlord to *enter and carry out the works* if the tenant does not comply with its obligations.
- The *right to recover the costs* of executing such repairs from the tenant *as a debt*.

Revision tip

A *Jervis v Harris* clause is a very well-known term in practice. You should therefore be aware of the law and practice relating to them. Without an appropriate clause, the landlord will simply be unable to pursue this remedy (see **Practice example 8.4**).

Exam warning

The fact that *Jervis v Harris* confirmed that such a clause can require payment of the costs as a *debt* means that the landlord will not be subject to the statutory limitations on recovery of *damages* (see above and **Practice example 8.4**). This distinction is likely to form part of an SQE1 question, so make sure that you read any such question carefully.

Figure 8.2 summarises the interaction between damages and self-help for breach of repairing covenants.

Although pursuing self-help can seem a very attractive option, the landlord may have trouble in gaining access and may need to incur court costs. They will also bear the initial costs of the works and may find it difficult to recover these from the tenant. As with an action for damages, a key consideration will also be whether the tenant is in fact able to pay the debt.

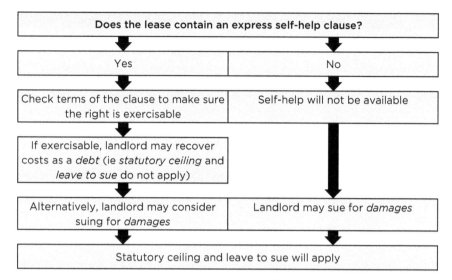

Figure 8.2: Damages and self-help for breach of repairing covenants

Forfeiture

To forfeit a lease for breach of covenants other than to pay rent(s) (see above), the landlord must first serve a **section 146 notice** on the tenant.

The right to forfeit and s 146 notices

Before proceeding it should be verified that there is a forfeiture provision in the lease and that it has become exercisable (ie the right has arisen and its terms complied with).

Key term: section 146 notice

A notice served under s 146 LPA 1925 which:
• Specifies the breach.
• Requires remedy of the breach within a reasonable period.
• Requires the tenant to pay compensation for the breach.

Revision tip

A section 146 notice is a very well-known term in practice. You should therefore be aware of the law and practice relating to them.

Failure in the notice to require the tenant to remedy the breach within a reasonable period, when it is capable of remedy, will invalidate the notice. Therefore, it is common to request remedy of the breach '*if capable of being remedied'*. A breach that will not be capable of being remedied will usually have caused irreparable harm, which cannot be undone or compensated for (eg immoral use).

For breaches of repairing covenants, in leases granted for seven years or more with at least three years or more left to run, the s 146 notice must also inform the tenant of its right to serve a counter-notice within 28 days under the Leasehold Property (Repairs) Act 1938. If a counter-notice is served, forfeiture may only proceed with leave of the court.

Methods of forfeiture
The landlord may then proceed to forfeit the lease (either by court action or through peaceable re-entry) if the tenant does not comply with the notice.

Waiver of the right to forfeit
The landlord must take care not to waive its right to forfeit (see above). Of particular note is that the breach of a repairing covenant is a *continuing breach*, so it is less likely to be waived (see **Practice example 8.4**).

Relief from forfeiture
The tenant may also apply for relief from forfeiture.

In the case of court proceedings, an application for relief may be made at any time before re-entry.

In the case of peaceable re-entry, it may be made a reasonable period after re-entry.

Relief will usually be granted if the breach is capable of remedy, has been remedied, and the landlord will not be materially adversely affected.

In the case of *internal decorative repairs*, the tenant may have an additional opportunity for relief under s 147 LPA 1925 if it is reasonable in the circumstances (including the length of the unexpired term). It will not apply on yield up at the end of the term (when the tenant gives back the premises) or where there is an express covenant regarding decorative repairs.

Landlord's considerations
As stated above, in considering whether to pursue forfeiture the landlord should consider practical matters (eg market considerations) as well as the availability of the remedy and its likely success.

Revision tip

A sub-tenant or mortgagee may also apply for relief from forfeiture (s 146 (4)) as the forfeiture of the headlease will lead to forfeiture of the underlease.

Figure 8.3 summarises the process for forfeiture for breach of other covenants.

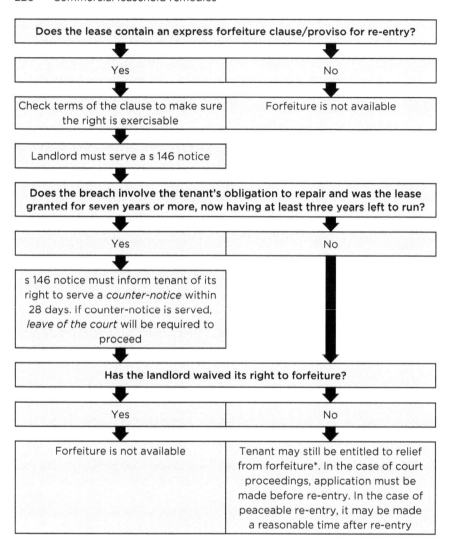

Note additional opportunity for relief for breach for internal decorative repairs under s 147 LPA

Figure 8.3: Forfeiture for breach of other covenants

Pursuit of former tenants and guarantors

See above. However, there is no requirement to serve a s 17 notice for unliquidated sums (see **Practice example 8.4**).

Rent deposit
See above.

Injunction
Injunctions may usually be sought for breaches of restrictive covenants or anticipated breaches. Like specific performance, an injunction is a discretionary equitable remedy, so damages may be awarded instead if they would be adequate.

Surrender
Although surrender of a lease (see **Chapter 9**) is not a remedy as such, it can bring a lease to an end relatively cheaply, where the parties agree and wish to sever their connections.

Practice example 8.4 brings some of the points together on remedies for breach of other covenants.

Practice example 8.4

Alvan is the tenant under a 'new' commercial lease that was granted for a term of twenty years and still has ten years left to run. It was assigned to him by the former and original tenant, Stefan. The assignment was made with the landlord's consent and Stefan entered into an AGA with the landlord. Alvan is now in breach of his repairing covenant. The lease contains a proviso for re-entry entitling the landlord to forfeit the lease in the event of breach of any tenant covenant. There is also a self-help clause. The landlord has continued to accept rent notwithstanding the breach and there is no rent deposit in place.

Which remedies are potentially available to the landlord?

- **There is no rent deposit in place so this will not be an option.**
- **Specific performance is unlikely to be available as other remedies are available and they would be more likely to be appropriate.**
- **Damages should be available, although the statutory ceiling would apply and leave to sue would be required due to the original term of the lease and the unexpired residue now remaining.**
- **Self-help should be available and has the advantage that the costs would be recoverable as a debt and therefore the statutory ceiling and leave to sue would not apply.**
- **Forfeiture would prima facie be available as there is an express proviso for re-entry and its terms have been complied with. A section 146 notice would need to be served and the tenant would also need to be informed of its right to serve a counter-notice. Although it is likely**

that the landlord will have waived its right to forfeiture by continuing to accept rent and thus acknowledging the continuance of the landlord and tenant relationship, the nature of the breach is continuing, so the right will continue to arise as the breach persists. In any event, the tenant may be entitled to relief from forfeiture (including a possible additional right for internal decorative repairs).

- It would be possible to pursue Stefan under the AGA. A s 17 notice would only need to be served if the sum claimed was liquidated (ie under the self-help clause rather than a more general damages claim). In such circumstances, Stefan may be able to claim an overriding lease.

■ KEY POINT CHECKLIST

This chapter has covered the following key knowledge points. You can use these to structure your revision, ensuring you recall the key details from each point:

- The liability of the parties for leasehold covenants varies for leases granted before 1 January 1996 (old leases) and leases granted on or after 1 January 1996 (new leases).
- Most importantly, the doctrine of privity of contract applies to old leases but has been abolished for new leases.
- Remedies are generally divided between those for non-payment of rent(s) and those for breach of other covenants.
- The main remedies for non-payment of rent(s) are debt action (including insolvency proceedings), forfeiture, CRAR, the pursuit of former tenants or guarantors and recourse to a rent deposit.
- The main remedies for breach of other covenants are specific performance, damages, self-help under a *Jervis v Harris* clause (for breach of repairing covenants), forfeiture, and pursuit of former tenants and guarantors. In some circumstances, recourse to a rent deposit or an injunction may also be possible.
- Each remedy has specific limitations and relevant considerations, both procedurally and commercially.

■ KEY TERMS AND CONCEPTS

- old leases (**page 209**)
- new leases (**page 209**)
- forfeiture (**page 215**)
- once and for all breach (**page 216**)
- continuing breach (**page 216**)
- Commercial Rent Arrears Recovery (**page 218**)
- section 17 notice (**page 219**)
- overriding lease (**page 220**)
- rent deposit (**page 220**)
- section 146 notice (**page 224**)

■ SQE1-STYLE QUESTIONS

QUESTION 1

A solicitor acts for a freeholder who, in 2014, granted a 20-year lease of a commercial property to a clothing retailer. The clothing retailer subsequently assigned the lease to a shoe retailer, who then assigned the lease to a newsagent. Finally, the newsagent assigned the lease to a hairdresser. All assignments were made with the freeholder's consent, and Authorised Guarantee Agreements were put in place on the assignments to the newsagent and the hairdresser. The hairdresser has now failed to pay the last month's rent.

Which of the following best describes who may be liable for non-payment of rent in addition to the hairdresser?

A   The clothing retailer, the shoe retailer, and the newsagent.

B   The newsagent only.

C   The newsagent and the shoe retailer.

D   The clothing retailer and the newsagent.

E   The hairdresser only.

QUESTION 2

A solicitor acts for a freeholder who, in 1990, granted a 45-year lease of a commercial property to a printing company. A director of the printing company guaranteed the observance and performance of the tenant's covenants under the lease. The printing company subsequently assigned the lease to a parts manufacturer, who then assigned the lease to a sandwich manufacturer. Finally, the sandwich manufacturer assigned the lease to a catering business. All assignments were made with the freeholder's consent, and a direct covenant to observe and perform the tenant's covenants in the lease for the remainder of the term was put in place on the assignment to the sandwich manufacturer. The catering business has now failed to pay the last month's rent.

Which of the following best describes who may be liable for the rent, in addition to the catering business?

A   The printing company and the sandwich manufacturer.

B   The printing company, the parts manufacturer, and the sandwich manufacturer.

C   The sandwich manufacturer only.

D   The printing company, the guarantor director, and the sandwich manufacturer.

E   The printing company and the guarantor director.

QUESTION 3

A solicitor acts for a freeholder who, in 2015, granted a 15-year lease of a commercial property to a supermarket company. Five years later, the supermarket company assigned the lease with the freeholder's consent to an electrical retailer. The supermarket company gave an Authorised Guarantee Agreement to the landlord. The electrical retailer has now failed to pay rent for the last eight months and has also fallen behind with service charge for the same period. The lease provides for forfeiture where rents are outstanding for 21 days after becoming due, whether formally demanded or not, and the service charge is also reserved as rent.

Which of the following best describes the position concerning the available remedies?

A   Forfeiture should be available for all sums due, provided that the landlord has not waived its right, although the tenant may be entitled to relief from forfeiture.

B   The landlord may pursue Commercial Rent Arrears Recovery for all sums due.

C   As the supermarket company gave an Authorised Guarantee Agreement, the landlord may pursue the supermarket company for the full arrears, but it must first serve a default notice.

D   Forfeiture and Commercial Rent Arrears Recovery should be available for all sums due. However, forfeiture will only be available if the landlord has not waived its right and the tenant may be entitled to relief from forfeiture.

E   Forfeiture and Commercial Rent Arrears Recovery should be available for all sums due. The landlord may also pursue the supermarket company for the full arrears.

QUESTION 4

A solicitor acts for a freeholder who granted a 20-year lease of a commercial property to a retailer, who remains the tenant. The lease still has ten years to run, and the tenant is in breach of its repairing covenant concerning internal non-decorative repairs. The lease provides for forfeiture in the event of breach of the tenant's covenants, and contains a self-help clause entitling the landlord, in default of the tenant, to enter the property, carry out repairs, and recover the costs from the tenant.

Which of the following best describes the position concerning the available remedies?

A   If the landlord relies on the self-help clause, damages will be limited to the amount by which the value of the reversion is diminished, and notice of intention to pursue the tenant must be served.

B   If the landlord relies on the self-help clause, the costs of repair will be payable by the tenant as a debt. However, notice of intention to pursue the tenant must be served. If the landlord decides to forfeit, a notice must be served specifying the breach, requiring remedy within a reasonable period, and requiring compensation for the breach.

C   If the landlord relies on the self-help clause, the costs of repair will be payable by the tenant as a debt. If the landlord decides to forfeit, a notice must be served specifying the breach, requiring remedy within a reasonable period, and requiring compensation for the breach.

D   If the landlord relies on the self-help clause, the costs of repair will be payable by the tenant as a debt. If the landlord decides to forfeit, a notice must be served specifying the breach, requiring remedy within a reasonable period, and requiring compensation for the breach. The notice must also inform the tenant of its right to serve a counter-notice in respect of the repairs.

E   If the landlord relies on the self-help clause, damages will be limited to the amount by which the value of the reversion is diminished, and notice of intention to pursue the tenant must be served. If the landlord decides to forfeit, a notice must be served specifying the breach, requiring remedy within a reasonable period, and requiring compensation for the breach. The notice must also inform the tenant of its right to serve a counter-notice in respect of the repairs.

QUESTION 5

A solicitor acts for a freeholder who granted a ten-year lease of a commercial property to a manufacturer, who remains the tenant. The lease still has two years to run, and the tenant is in breach of its repairing covenant. The lease contains a proviso for re-entry in the event of breach of the tenant's covenants, and the landlord has continued to accept rent, notwithstanding the breach.

Which of the following best describes the position concerning forfeiture?

A   A notice will need to be served specifying the breach, requiring remedy within a reasonable period, and requiring compensation for the breach.

B   A notice will need to be served specifying the breach, requiring remedy within a reasonable period, and requiring compensation for the breach. It will also need to inform the tenant of its right to serve a counter-notice.

C   A notice will need to be served specifying the breach, requiring remedy within a reasonable period, and requiring compensation for the breach. The landlord will most probably have waived its right to forfeit as breach of a repairing covenant is a once and for all breach.

D   A notice will need to be served specifying the breach, requiring remedy within a reasonable period, and requiring compensation for the breach. It will also need to inform the tenant of its right to serve a counter-notice. The landlord will most probably have waived its right to forfeit as breach of a repairing covenant is a once and for all breach.

E   A notice will need to be served specifying the breach, requiring remedy within a reasonable period, and requiring compensation for the breach. If the landlord proceeds by way of court proceedings, relief from forfeiture may be claimed a reasonable time after re-entry.

■ ANSWERS TO QUESTIONS

Answers to 'What do you know already?' questions at the start of the chapter

1) True. Under an 'old lease' the original tenant will be liable for all tenant covenants under the lease for the entire term, by virtue of privity of contract.

2) True. Under a 'new lease' the tenant will automatically be released from future liability for the tenant covenants on lawful assignment. However, the landlord may require them to enter into an Authorised Guarantee Agreement (AGA) if it is a requirement of the lease or it is otherwise reasonable to do so.

3) Before pursuing a former tenant or guarantor for rent, service charge, or other liquidated payments under a lease, notice needs to be served under section 17 of the Landlord and Tenant (Covenants) Act 1995 within six months of the sum(s) falling due.

4) It will only be possible to forfeit a lease for breach of the tenant's repairing covenant where the lease contains an *express forfeiture clause* dealing with the breach. The landlord must first serve a *notice* under s 146 of the Law of Property Act 1925 (LPA) on the tenant, and such notice will sometimes need to refer to the tenant's right to serve a *counter-notice* within 28 days (it depends on the term of the lease). The landlord must also not have *waived its right* to forfeiture. The tenant will have a general right to apply for *relief from forfeiture* and sometimes a more specific right under the LPA (it depends on the nature of the repairs).

Answers to end-of-chapter SQE1-style questions

Question 1

The correct answer was B. As this is a 'new lease', each tenant will be released on lawful assignment of the lease. However, the landlord may usually seek an Authorised Guarantee Agreement (AGA) from the outgoing tenant to guarantee the *immediate assignee's* observance and performance of the tenant covenants within the lease. As all assignments were made with the landlord's consent, they are lawful assignments. The clothing retailer will have been released on lawful assignment, so options

A and D are incorrect in this respect. Although the shoe retailer gave an AGA, they will only have guaranteed the newsagent and any attempt to extend their liability beyond this would be void. Therefore, options A and C are incorrect in this respect. However, the newsagent will be liable based on the AGA given on assignment to the hairdresser. Therefore, options A, C, and D are partially correct and option E is incorrect.

Question 2

The correct answer was D. As this is an 'old lease', the original tenant *and* the original guarantor will each be liable in respect of the tenant covenants under the lease for the entire duration of the term, by virtue of privity of contract. Therefore, option E is partially correct, as are options A and B, although they do omit reference to the guarantor. The sandwich manufacturer will also be liable as they gave a direct covenant on the assignment to them. Therefore, options A, B, and C are partially correct on this point. As no direct covenant was given by them, the parts manufacturer will have been liable only for breaches of covenants that touched and concerned the land during their period of ownership. Therefore, option B is incorrect in this respect.

Question 3

The correct answer was A. The lease contains an express forfeiture clause, which has been complied with as rents have been outstanding for long enough and a formal demand for payment will not be required in the circumstances. Forfeiture should be available, provided that the landlord has not waived its right, although the tenant may be entitled to relief from forfeiture if it settles the arrears and costs. A s 146 notice will not need to be served as all outstanding sums are reserved as rent. Options D and E are therefore partially correct, although option E does not mention the issues of waiver and relief. Although Commercial Rent Arrears Recovery will be available, it would be limited to the annual rent only and not the service charge, even though it is expressed in the lease to be reserved as rent. Therefore, it is incorrect to state that it will be available for all sums due, as suggested in options B, D, and E. Although the supermarket company may be liable under the AGA for rent and service charge (as suggested in option E), a s 17 notice will need to be served first (as both sums fall within the definition of a 'fixed charge'). The notice must be served within six months of the sums falling due. Therefore, options C and E are incorrect as it will not be possible to recover the full arrears using this method.

Question 4

The correct answer was D. If the landlord relies on the self-help clause, the costs of repairs will be payable by the tenant as debt, rather than damages (as suggested in options A and E). Options B and C are therefore partially correct on this point. If the landlord decides to forfeit, a section 146 notice must be served which also informs the tenant of its right to serve a counter-notice in respect of the repairs. Therefore, options B and C are only partly correct on this point, but option E is correct. Because a self-help clause is an action in debt, rather than damages, no notice of intention to pursue the tenant must be served (as suggested in options A, B, and E) and damages will not be limited to the amount the value of the reversion is diminished (as suggested in options A and E).

Question 5

The correct answer was A. A section 146 notice will need to be served specifying the breach, requiring remedy within a reasonable period, and requiring compensation for the breach. All of the other options are also correct on this point. There will be no need to inform the tenant of its right to serve a counter-notice, as although the lease was granted for seven years or more, it does not have at least three years left to run. Therefore, options B and D are incorrect in this respect. Options C and D are also incorrect in that breach of a repairing covenant is a continuing breach, so it is less likely to have been waived on the facts and will continue as the breach persists/worsens. Option E is also incorrect as it states the period for claiming relief from forfeiture where it proceeds by way of peaceable re-entry. If it proceeds by way of court action, it must be claimed before re-entry.

■ KEY CASES, RULES, STATUTES, AND INSTRUMENTS

The SQE1 Assessment Specification does not generally require you to know any statutory authorities or specific case names for this topic. Specific sections of statutes are set out for ease of reference. However, you should be aware of the purpose and nature of a *Jervis v Harris* clause as this case is referred to in the SQE1 Assessment Specification. The case may therefore be referred to in questions, and you should be aware of the significance of the case from a practical point of view.

9

Termination of leases and security of tenure under Part II of the Landlord and Tenant Act 1954

■ MAKE SURE YOU KNOW

This chapter provides an overview of termination of a lease and the provisions for security of tenure of business tenants under Part II of the Landlord and Tenant Act 1954 (the 'Act'). It deals with the application of the Act and exclusion from it, as well as its implications (including how it varies the common law methods of termination and includes the tenant's right to a renewal lease). It then moves on to methods of termination under the Act, the relevant notices, and applications to the court, as well as the landlord's grounds of opposition, the terms of the renewal lease, and the availability of compensation. For the SQE1 assessments, you will need to have a good working knowledge of the operation of the Act, its implications for business tenants and the procedures under it.

Please note that all statutory references are to the Act, unless otherwise specified.

■ SQE ASSESSMENT ADVICE

For SQE1, you are required to understand the application, operation, and procedures under the Act.

As you work through this chapter, remember to pay particular attention in your revision to:
• When the Act applies and how to exclude its provisions.
• The termination of a lease at common law by effluxion of time, notice to quit, surrender, and merger, and how these are modified under the Act.
• Permitted methods of termination under the Act by the landlord and the tenant.
• The relevant notices under the Act and the requirements relating to them, as well as the timing of any application to the court.

- The landlord's grounds of opposition.
- The terms of the renewal lease and when a tenant is entitled to compensation.

■ WHAT DO YOU KNOW ALREADY?

Attempt these questions before reading this chapter. If you find some difficult or cannot remember the answers, remember to look more closely at that topic during your revision.

1) What are the key benefits of security of tenure under the Act?

   [Application and implications of the Act: an overview, page 236]

2) How much notice must be given to terminate a tenancy under section 25 of the Act and is it always necessary for a protected tenant who wants to give up occupation at the end of the term to serve a notice?

   [Methods of termination under the Act, notices, and applications to the court, page 241]

3) True or false? A tenant must serve a counter-notice following service of a section 25 notice by the landlord.

   [Methods of termination under the Act, notices, and applications to the court, page 241]

4) What are the key limitations of the grounds for the landlord's opposition to a new tenancy under sections 30(1) (f) and (g) of the Act?

   [Landlord's grounds of opposition, page 249]

APPLICATION OF THE ACT, IMPLICATIONS, AND EXCLUSION FROM THE ACT

For SQE1, it is important to know when the Act applies, the implications of it, as well as how a tenancy may be excluded from its provisions.

Application and implications of the Act: an overview

The Act automatically provides **security of tenure** for **business tenancies**. However, in some circumstances it is possible to exclude a business tenancy from the application of the Act (see **Contracted out tenancies**, below).

Key term: business tenancies

Business tenancies are defined as 'any *tenancy* where the property comprised in the tenancy is or includes premises which are *occupied* by the tenant and are so occupied for the *purposes of a business* carried on by [them] or for those and other purposes' (s 23(1)) (see also **Application of the Act**, below).

Key term: security of tenure

Security of tenure means that:
- The usual common law methods of termination of a lease (see below) may not apply.
- Instead, even after the contractual expiry date, a lease may continue under the Act (a 'continuation tenancy') unless and until it is terminated under one of the prescribed/specified methods under the Act. The tenant is said to be 'holding over' under the lease during this continuation period.
- On termination, there is a presumption that the tenant will generally be entitled to a new protected lease (the 'renewal lease'), usually on similar terms, subject to reasonable updating, at market rent and for a maximum term of fifteen years, unless the landlord can prove one of the grounds of opposition under the Act.
- If the parties cannot agree the terms of the renewal lease, the court may intervene to determine them.
- If a renewal lease is not granted, due to grounds of opposition not relating to the default of the tenant (the so-called 'no-fault grounds'), the tenant may be entitled to compensation.

Common law methods of termination

A lease may be terminated at common law by any of the common law methods of termination. These are **effluxion of time, notice to quit, surrender**, and **merger**.

A lease may also be terminated by forfeiture if the tenant is in breach and the lease contains a forfeiture clause/a proviso for re-entry (see **Chapter 8**).

Key term: effluxion of time

A *fixed-term lease* (see **Chapter 6** and *Revise SQE: Land Law*) may expire by effluxion of time, which means that it automatically ends following the expiry of the contractual term, without the need to give notice.

Key term: notice to quit

A *periodic tenancy* (see **Chapter 6** and *Revise SQE: Land Law*) (eg a tenancy from year-to-year, month-to-month, or week-to-week) may be determined (ie terminated) by *either party* giving one full period's notice expiring at the end of the relevant period (eg a full month for a monthly periodic tenancy) or at least six months' notice in the case of a yearly periodic tenancy.

Key term: surrender

Surrender is when the parties each *agree* for the lease to come to an end before the contractual expiry date. It causes the lease to be merged with the landlord's reversionary interest (ie its estate in land, usually the freehold or superior leasehold – see **Chapter 7**). The tenant is said to 'yield up' the lease, which is 'extinguished'. To take effect in law, a surrender must be made by deed (s 52, Law of Property Act 1925). If a sublease is in place and the headlease is surrendered (see **Chapter 7**), the subtenant becomes the immediate tenant of the head landlord on the terms of the sublease.

Key term: merger

Merger is when the tenant acquires the immediate landlord's estate/reversion (eg it buys the landlord's freehold) or both the lease and the reversion are acquired by the same party at the same time. Unless there is a declaration in the deed of transfer to the contrary (called a 'declaration of non-merger'), the lease becomes merged with the reversionary interest and becomes extinguished/ceases to exist.

Under the Act, the usual common law rules on termination by effluxion of time (for a fixed-term tenancy) or by service of a notice to quit (for a periodic tenancy) do not apply and instead the lease will continue until terminated in accordance with the Act.

Application of the Act

As indicated above, the Act only applies to business tenancies (as defined).

Therefore, there must be a *tenancy* (with exclusive possession) as opposed to a licence (a mere personal right) and the distinction here is a question of factual exclusive possession (see *Revise SQE: Land Law*). The property must also be *occupied* by the tenant for **business purposes**. Therefore, a subtenant may enjoy security of tenure where they are in occupation of the whole or part, rather than the tenant. Occupation includes occupation by an agent or manager, a company in which the tenant has a controlling interest, or, if the tenant is a company, by a person with a controlling interest in the company (s 23 (1A)) and group companies (s 42) (see *Revise SQE: Business Law and Practice*).

Key term: business purposes

Business is defined as including 'a trade, profession or employment and ... any activity carried on by a body of persons, whether corporate or incorporate' (s 23(2)).

Therefore, business purposes also include non-commercial activities, but only if they are carried on by a body of persons. This would include unincorporated associations (see *Revise SQE: Trusts Law*) such as sports clubs. If use is mixed, the property will still be used for business purposes if business use is not merely incidental to residential use. If the lease specifically excludes use for business purposes, the tenant cannot claim protection under the Act (s 23(4)).

The following are excluded from the definition of business tenancies:
• Licences that do not confer exclusive possession and are therefore not, by definition, tenancies (see above and remember that exclusive possession is a question of fact (see *Revise SQE: Land Law*)).
• Tenancies at will (ie express or implied tenancies that can be determined (ie terminated) by either party at any time – see **Chapter 6** and *Revise SQE: Land Law*).
• Some short fixed-term tenancies: fixed-term tenancies under six months, unless the tenancy contains a provision for renewal extending it beyond six months, or where the tenant or its predecessor(s) (in any capacity) have been in occupation and carrying on the same business for over 12 months (s 43(3)).
• Leases of agricultural holdings, service tenancies, farm business tenancies, and mining leases (s 43(1)–(2)).
• Contracted out tenancies (see below).

Contracted out tenancies

In practice, **contracted out tenancies** are the main exclusion from the Act.

> ### Key term: contracted out tenancies
>
> A fixed-term tenancy under which the parties expressly agree (using a prescribed process) that the provisions of sections 24–28 of the Act will not apply.

To contract out of the security of tenure provisions, the lease must be for a term of years certain (meaning that the term is not defined in the lease as including any period of continuation, extension or holding over, etc). The correct procedure must also be adhered to, involving prescribed forms of notice and declarations *before the lease commences, or the tenant becomes contractually bound to take it*.

The procedure, for tenancies granted on or after 1 June 2004, is set out in **Figure 9.1**.

(NB: Under the old law, for tenancies granted before 1 June 2004, it was necessary for the landlord and the tenant to make a joint application to the court agreeing to the proposed exclusion before the grant of the lease. The lease also needed to be in substantially the same form as the draft annexed to the order (ie the form of lease needed to be agreed beforehand and appended to the court order)).

The landlord must serve a *notice* on the tenant in the prescribed form (informally known as a 'health warning notice') warning them of the proposed exclusion and advising them to take independent advice

| If 14 days have passed since service of the notice, the tenant or person authorised by them must make a *declaration* in the prescribed form that they agree to the exclusion | If less than 14 days have passed since service of the notice, the tenant or a person authorised by them must make a *statutory declaration* in the prescribed form and in the presence of an independent solicitor, that they agree to the exclusion |

The exclusion (notice, declaration, and agreement to contract out) must be referred to in the lease itself. This is usually achieved through a standard clause towards the end of a lease

Figure 9.1: Exclusion from the Act

If the procedure is adhered to correctly, then the lease will come to an end on the contractual expiry date, the tenant's continued occupation and the terms of it will be subject to negotiation, and no compensation will be due to the tenant. If the procedure is not followed correctly, the tenant will enjoy security of tenure.

Practice example 9.1 brings together some of the points on the application of the Act and contracted out tenancies.

Practice example 9.1

A client has just purchased a vacant commercial unit that it plans to occupy in two years' time, 'renting it out' in the meantime.

Which type of 'rental' arrangement would be most appropriate for the client?

A contracted-out tenancy would be the safest option, to avoid giving the occupant security of tenure. Although the grant of a licence would appear attractive, if the occupant has factual exclusive possession of the unit, they will in fact have a tenancy, which would be protected under the Act. A tenancy at will (see Chapter 6) would be flexible, but precarious, as it could be terminated at any time by either party, so would not guarantee rental income. A succession of shorter fixed-term leases (with or without provisions for renewal) would be dangerous too, as the occupant could gain security of tenure with successive tenancies.

THE CONTINUATION TENANCY AND METHODS OF TERMINATION UNDER THE ACT

A tenancy protected under the Act will not come to an end and will continue on the same terms unless terminated in accordance with the Act (s 24). The tenant is said to have a 'continuation tenancy' and the landlord may apply for an interim rent (see **Interim rent**).

Methods of termination under the Act, notices, and applications to the court

The following methods of termination are permitted under the Act:

1. Section 25 notice (see below).
2. Section 26 notice/request (see below).
3. Section 27 notice (see below).
4. Ceasing to be in occupation on the expiry of a *fixed-term* lease (s 27 (1A)): it expires by effluxion of time (see above).
5. Service *by the tenant* (*but not the landlord*) of a notice to quit in relation to a *periodic tenancy* (see above) if they have been in occupation for at least a month.
6. Forfeiture (see **Chapter 8**).
7. Surrender (see above).

Revision tip

The notices referred to above are key terms that you should be familiar with for the purposes of the SQE1 assessments.

Following service of a section 25 notice or a section 26 request, the tenant will usually have the right to apply to the court for a new tenancy, which may only be opposed on one or more of the grounds under s 30 (see **Landlord's grounds of opposition**). If no renewal tenancy is granted, due to a no-fault ground, the tenant may be entitled to compensation (see **Compensation**, below).

Section 25 notice

A **section 25 notice** is one of the key ways to terminate a tenancy protected by the Act.

Key term: section 25 notice

A section 25 notice is a landlord's notice to terminate a fixed-term or periodic tenancy, with or without proposals for a new tenancy.

Prescribed forms of s 25 notice are available, and it is best practice to use them to ensure that all the correct information is included.

Separate forms are available depending on whether the landlord is in favour of granting a new tenancy (a *non-hostile notice*) or not (a *hostile notice*). In any event, the notice must relate to the whole of the premises comprised within the tenancy.

- In the case of a *non-hostile notice*, the landlord must state their proposals for a new tenancy (ie the key terms, including rent and the property). Obtaining a higher rent will usually be the landlord's main motivation for serving the notice.
- In the case of a *hostile notice*, the landlord must include the relevant ground(s) for refusing a new tenancy (see **Landlord's grounds of opposition**). Great care must be taken as the ground(s) cannot be changed once the notice has been served.

The notice must also:
- State the date on which the tenancy will terminate (which cannot be earlier than the contractual end date (eg the expiry of a fixed term)).
- Be served not less than six nor more than twelve calendar months before the proposed termination date (see **Practice example 9.2**).

If these requirements are not met, then the notice will be invalid, and a fresh notice should be served.

The termination date does not have to coincide with the contractual expiry date, provided that sufficient notice is given, and it is not proposed to terminate before that date. In other words, the termination date can be set in the period during which the tenant is holding over, provided that the required notice is given (see **Practice example 9.3**).

Finally, the notice must be signed by or on behalf of the landlord.

It is not possible to serve a section 25 notice if a section 26 request or section 27 notice has already been served.

Practice example 9.2

A tenant occupies business premises under a six-year lease that expires on 30 June 2024. It is not a contracted-out tenancy.

When must the landlord serve a section 25 notice to terminate the lease on its expiry?

To specify a termination date of 30 June 2024, the notice must be served (see Service of notices, below) between 30 June 2023 and 30 December 2023 (ie not less than six nor more than twelve calendar months' notice).

Practice example 9.3

A tenant occupies business premises under a six-year lease that expires on 30 June 2024. It is not a contracted-out tenancy, and it is now 25 January 2024.

What would be the earliest termination date that could apply?

The earliest possible date for termination would be 25 July 2024, although it would be safer to specify a few days later unless the notice will be deemed served today (see Service of notices, below). The latest date would be 25 January 2025.

If the landlord has served a *hostile notice*:
• In order to protect its position, the tenant will need to make an application to the court for a new tenancy before the prescribed termination date, otherwise it will lose its right to a new tenancy.
• The landlord may also apply to the court to terminate the tenancy if the tenant has not already made an application to the court.

If the landlord has served a *non-hostile notice*:
• The parties will usually seek to negotiate the terms of the lease.
• If it is likely that the lease will not be completed prior to the termination date, the tenant must either make the application to the court or agree with the landlord to extend the deadline for the application by written agreement (s 29 B). The time limits are crucial as if the application to the court or agreement to extend the termination date is not in place on time, the tenant will lose its right to security of tenure and the tenant's solicitor will have been negligent.
• The landlord can also apply to the court for the grant of a new lease.

See **Figure 9.2** for a summary of the section 25 notice procedure.

Figure 9.2: Summary of section 25 notice procedure

Section 26 request

A **section 26 request** can also be used to terminate a tenancy protected under the Act.

Key term: section 26 request

A section 26 request is a tenant's request to terminate an existing fixed-term tenancy and have a new tenancy.

A tenant may be happy for the tenancy to continue on the same terms until terminated by the landlord. However, they may choose to take control and serve a section 26 notice on the landlord. Such a notice can only be served if the tenant has a fixed-term tenancy of more than one year (it cannot be used by periodic tenants). A tenant may choose to do this for a number of reasons:

- In a *falling market*, the rent under a renewal lease may be lower than under the existing lease.
- They may have *plans to improve* the premises and would like the security of a new lease.
- They may wish to *assign the lease* (see **Chapter 7**), sell the assets of the business or the shares in the tenant company, in which case the proposed assignee/buyer would usually wish to have the security of a new lease.
- In a *rising market*, a landlord will usually seek to terminate the lease at the earliest possible opportunity (ie giving the full twelve months' notice to expire on the contractual termination date). However, if the landlord has delayed, the tenant may seek to 'get in first' with a section 26 request, giving the maximum twelve months' notice and thereby securing a longer period (eg an additional six months) at the lower rent (see **Practice example 9.4**). This is known as a 'tactical pre-emptive strike'). However, the tenant should bear in mind that the landlord may also be entitled to an interim rent (see **Interim rent**).

Practice example 9.4

A tenant occupies business premises in a rising market, under a six-year protected lease, that expires in six months' time. The landlord has not served a section 25 notice.

What should the tenant do?

The tenant could do nothing and continue to pay the existing rent. However, if the tenant anticipates that a section 25 notice will be served soon, the landlord will be likely to give the minimum notice, so the tenant may seek to serve a section 26 request, with the full twelve months' notice.

Prescribed forms of s 26 request are available, and it is best practice to use them to ensure that all the correct information is included.

The tenant must state their proposals for a new tenancy (ie the key terms, including rent and the property).

The request must also:
- State the date on which the tenancy will begin (which cannot be earlier than the contractual end date (ie the expiry of the fixed term)).
- Be served not less than six nor more than twelve calendar months before the proposed commencement date.

If these requirements are not met, then the request will be invalid.

As with a section 25 notice, the commencement date does not have to coincide with the contractual expiry date, provided that sufficient notice is given, and it is not proposed to commence the new tenancy before that date. In other words, the commencement date can be set in the period during which the tenant is holding over.

Finally, the request must be signed by or on behalf of the tenant.

It is not possible to serve a section 26 request if a section 25 notice or section 27 notice has already been served.

Following service of the request, *if the landlord opposes the new tenancy*:
- The landlord must serve a *counter-notice* on the tenant. It must be served within two months of the request and state the ground(s) of opposition under s 30 (see **Landlord's grounds of opposition**). There is no prescribed form of notice, although precedents are widely available. Great care must be taken as the ground(s) cannot be changed once the notice has been served. If the counter-notice is not served, the landlord loses its right to oppose the new tenancy.
- The tenant must also make an *application to the court* for a new tenancy after the period for service of the counter-notice has expired, but before the commencement date specified in the request, otherwise the tenant loses its right to a new tenancy.
- The landlord may apply to the court to *terminate the lease* on the specified ground(s) of opposition (see above), but not if the tenant has already made an application for a new tenancy.

If the landlord *does not oppose the grant of the new tenancy*:
- A counter-notice does not need to be served and the parties will usually seek to negotiate the terms of the lease.
- However, the tenant must take great care to protect its position by making the necessary application to the court or seeking an extension to the deadline for doing so (see above).
- The landlord can also apply to the court for the grant of a new lease.

See **Figure 9.3** for a summary of the section 26 request procedure.

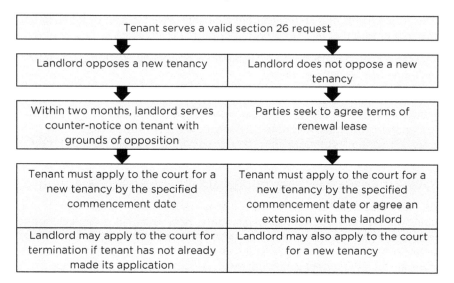

Figure 9.3: Summary of section 26 request procedure

Competent landlord

A section 26 request must always be served on the **competent landlord**. Similarly, it should also be the competent landlord who serves a section 25 notice.

Key term: competent landlord

A tenant's landlord is their competent landlord only if that landlord owns the freehold or has a tenancy that will not come to an end *by effluxion of time* within the next fourteen months (s 44(1)).

(NB: Remember that a protected tenancy does not automatically expire by effluxion of time as there will be a continuation tenancy until it is determined in accordance with the Act. Remember also that a tenant must be in occupation to be protected under the Act – see **Practice examples 9.5 and 9.6**).

Practice example 9.5

The freeholder grants a protected business lease to a tenant, who *sub-lets the whole of the premises* to a subtenant.

Who is the competent landlord of the subtenant when the lease has less than fourteen months left to run?

The freeholder will be the competent landlord of the subtenant as the lease will expire by effluxion of time and will not continue under the Act as the tenant is not in occupation (*the whole* has been sublet to the subtenant).

Practice example 9.6

The freeholder grants a protected business lease to a tenant, who *sub-lets part of the premises* to a subtenant.

Who is the competent landlord of the subtenant when the lease has less than fourteen months left to run?

The tenant will be the competent landlord of the subtenant as the tenant is in occupation under the lease (only *part* has been sublet to the subtenant), so it will not expire by effluxion of time and will continue under the Act until determined (unless a notice to terminate under the Act has been served bringing the lease to an end within fourteen months).

In most cases there will be no doubt as to the identity of the competent landlord, particularly where the landlord is the freeholder and there is only one lease under them, with no subleases. However, if there is any doubt, the tenant may serve a **section 40 notice** on their immediate landlord.

Key term: section 40 notice

A section 40 notice may be served on either the tenant (under s 40(1)) or the landlord/their mortgagee in possession (under s 40(3)), requesting information about occupation and sub-tenancies (s 40(1)) or the landlord's interest (s 40(3)) and the service of any section 25 or section 26 notices. The recipient has one month to reply.

Service of notices

It is best practice to serve notices under the Act by registered post or recorded delivery as they are then deemed served on the date of postage (s 23 (1) Landlord and Tenant Act 1927).

Section 27 notice

A tenant who wishes to terminate rather than seek a renewal tenancy may serve a **section 27 notice**.

Key term: section 27 notice

A section 27 notice is a tenant's notice to terminate a fixed-term tenancy on or after the contractual expiry date, provided that they have been in occupation for at least a month.

However, it is important to appreciate that if a tenant is certain that they wish to give up occupation under a fixed-term tenancy, they have a number of options:
- Serve a notice on the landlord under s 27(1) giving not less than three months' notice to terminate *on* the contractual expiry date.
- Simply vacate the premises on/by the contractual expiry date, in which case the lease will expire by effluxion of time (s 27 (1A)).
- Serve a notice on the landlord under s 27(2) giving not less than three months' notice to terminate *after* the contractual expiry date (ie to expire during the period of the continuation tenancy).

There is no prescribed form of notice, although precedents are widely available.

It is not possible to serve a section 27 notice if a section 25 notice or section 26 request has already been served.

Therefore, if the contractual expiry date has not yet arrived, the tenant can either give not less than three months' notice to terminate on that date, or simply vacate the premises. It is considered best practice to serve the notice if the tenant is certain that they will be vacating.

If the contractual expiry date has passed, or there are less than three months left unexpired and the tenant is unable to vacate on/by the expiry date, the tenant must give not less than three months' notice to terminate, which will expire during the period of holding over under the continuation tenancy.

Interim rent

During the continuation period, either the landlord or the tenant may apply for an **interim rent** under s 24A until the proceedings are concluded.

> ### Key term: interim rent
>
> A rent for the period of the continuation tenancy, until proceedings are concluded. It is usually decided on the basis of a yearly tenancy but having regard to the terms of the existing lease. If the tenant applies for an interim rent, they will usually do so where the market rent would be less in the current climate.

Such application can be made no later than six months after the proposed termination date (s 25 notice) or commencement date (s 26 request). An interim rent will be payable from the earliest date that could have been specified at common law for termination or commencement of a new tenancy (s 24B). This can make a tenant's tactical pre-emptive strike (see above) less effective.

Alternatively, the landlord may include a provision for the review of rent at the end of the term of the lease, to protect its position (known as a penultimate, or last day rent review – see **Chapter 6**).

LANDLORD'S GROUNDS OF OPPOSITION

In the case of a hostile section 25 notice or a hostile response to a section 26 request, the landlord must specify its ground(s) of opposition under s 30 of the Act. For SQE1, it is important to have a good working knowledge of the grounds and the conditions/limitations attached to them.

If the court accepts the ground(s) of opposition, no new tenancy will be ordered, although the tenant may be entitled to compensation.

If the court does not accept the ground(s) of opposition, a new tenancy will be ordered, and the court will settle its terms.

The relevant grounds are summarised in **Table 9.1** and ground (f) is the most used ground.

Near misses

If the landlord can demonstrate to the court that any of grounds (d), (e), or (f) (see **Table 9.1**) could have been satisfied had the termination date been up to one year later, the tenant's application must be refused. However, the tenant may ask for the later date to be substituted for the earlier date, giving them more time to vacate (s 31(2)).

Discretionary and mandatory grounds and tenant default

It is important to be able to distinguish between the discretionary and mandatory grounds under s 30 and the fault and no-fault grounds for termination.

Grounds (a), (b), (c), and (e) (see **Table 9.1**) are *discretionary*. This means that if the ground is established at the hearing, the court *may* refuse to grant a renewal tenancy if it can be shown that a new tenancy ought not to be granted.

Grounds (d), (f), and (g) are *mandatory*. This means that the court *must* refuse to grant a renewal tenancy if the ground is established.

The no-fault grounds (with regard to the tenant) are grounds (e), (f), and (g).

Table 9.1: Grounds of opposition under s 30 of the Act

Ground	Requirements	Considerations and limitations	Decision by court mandatory or discretionary?	No-fault ground with regard to the tenant?
Section 30(1)(a) – Tenant's failure to repair 'the holding' (see **Key term** below)	Tenant is under repairing obligations under the lease and has breached them.	Extent and seriousness of the breach.	Discretionary	No
		Would granting a new lease be unfair to the landlord?		
		Any undertaking(s) from the tenant to remedy the breach.		
Section 30(1)(b) – Persistent delay in paying rent	Persistent delay in paying sums reserved as rent under the lease.	Persistency – More than one incident and more than occasional frequency.	Discretionary	No
		Extent of breaches and whole history of payment – Arrears do not need to have been substantial or long outstanding.		
		Are future arrears likely?		
		Would granting a new lease be unfair to the landlord?		
		Proposals to guarantee the payment of rent in the renewal lease.		
Section 30(1) (c) – Substantial breach of other obligations	Substantial breaches of other obligations or any other reasons connected with the tenant's use or management of the property.	Are breaches so substantial that granting a new lease would prejudice the landlord's interest?	Discretionary	No
		Proposal(s) for remedying the breach.		

			Mandatory / Discretionary	Compensation
Section 30(1)(d) – *Suitable* *alternative* *accommodation*	Landlord is able to offer, provide, or secure suitable alternative accommodation for the tenant.	Suitability of the accommodation to the needs of the tenant (including the need to preserve goodwill).	Mandatory	Technically yes – although no right to compensation
		Reasonableness of the proposed terms (having regard to the current tenancy and relevant circumstances at the date of the hearing).		
		Nature and type of the business and the size and location of the premises (eg a tenant with a well-established retail business may argue that a move may have a detrimental impact on business).		
Section 30(1)(e) – *Underletting of* *part*	Lease was created by an underletting of part and the superior landlord (now the competent landlord) requires the whole of the property for letting or sale.	Aggregate of the rents on separate letting of the constituent parts would be substantially less than the rent for the letting of the whole, such that it would be uneconomic to proceed with a renewal lease of part.	Discretionary	Yes

Table 9.1: (Continued)

Ground	Requirements	Considerations and limitations	Decision by court mandatory or discretionary?	No-fault ground with regard to the tenant?
Section 30(1)(f) – *Demolition/ reconstruction*	The landlord has proposals to demolish, reconstruct, or to carry out substantial construction works to the whole or substantially the whole of the premises.	*Intention:* A firm and settled intention to carry out the work. Demonstrated through evidence such as plans, drawings, quotations, specifications, finance, and third-party approvals (eg planning permission and building regulations approval) at the date of the hearing, such that the landlord has a reasonable prospect of success in implementing the proposals.	Mandatory	Yes
		Nature and extent of works: These must include demolition, re-building, re-constructing, structural matters, or new additions/buildings, affecting the whole or substantially the whole of the premises, rather than more minor works of refurbishment or improvement.		
		Need for legal possession: The works cannot reasonably be carried out without obtaining possession of the property. In other words, the landlord must prove the need to terminate the tenancy and obtain *legal possession* to carry out the works. Any rights of entry must be insufficient for these purposes. The tenant may have a defence under s 31A if they agree to grant appropriate rights (including rights of entry without substantial interference with use) or to take a tenancy of an economically separable part of the property.		

			Mandatory	Yes
Section 30(1)(g) – *Intention to occupy*	The landlord intends to occupy the property for the purposes of for their own business or as a residence.	*Intention:* The landlord must prove that their intention is firm and settled, having taken practical steps to achieve the goal and demonstrating a reasonable prospect of achieving it. Occupation by the landlord includes a company in which the landlord has a controlling interest, and where the landlord is a company, a person who has a controlling interest in that company (see *Revise SQE: Business Law and Practice*).		
		Five-year rule: The landlord must have owned their superior interest for at least five years *before the ending of the current tenancy* in order to rely on this ground (s 30(2)). This rule is designed to prevent landlords from acquiring a property subject to a tenancy or tenancies, with the sole aim of gaining vacant possession. It does not apply if the landlord acquires a property with vacant possession and subsequently lets it.		

Revision tip

The landlord's grounds of opposition under s 30 are key provisions, so you should be familiar with them and their limitations (including which are mandatory and which are discretionary).

Practice example 9.7 brings some of these points together.

Practice example 9.7

A landlord company is the freehold owner of a property subject to a fifteen-year protected lease, which is due to expire in eight months' time. The tenant was late in paying rent on one occasion a few months ago and the landlord would like to obtain possession for its own business. The landlord acquired the reversion two years ago, subject to the lease.

Which ground(s) of opposition, if any, could the landlord rely on when serving a section 25 notice?

Ground (b) is a discretionary ground and is unlikely to apply on the facts as there has only been one incident of breach. The landlord cannot rely on ground (g), a mandatory ground, as it will not have owned the reversion for at least five years when the lease is terminated under the Act.

TERMS OF THE RENEWAL LEASE AND COMPENSATION

If the tenant's application for a new tenancy is successful, they will be entitled to a new lease of **the holding**.

Key term: the holding

The property comprised within the current tenancy, but excluding any part not occupied by the tenant or occupied by a third party (s 23(3)).

However, the landlord may insist on them taking a lease of the whole property rather than just part of it.

Terms of the renewal lease

The terms of the renewal lease are determined by the court, in accordance with the provisions of the Act.

Term

The lease will be for a reasonable term, not exceeding 15 years (s 33) and it will commence three months after proceedings are finally disposed of (ie after the four-week window for appeal after the order has passed – s 64).

The term will be a matter of initial negotiation, but the court has a wide discretion and will consider the following:
- The state of the market.
- The length of the current tenancy.
- How long the tenant has been holding over.
- The landlord's future plans for the property (eg redevelopment).
- The comparative hardship to both parties that the relevant term will have.

Rent and rent review

The rent will be based on the open market rent (s 34(1)) (see **Chapter 6**), but will disregard the following to avoid the rent being artificially inflated:
- Occupation by the tenant and its predecessors.
- Any goodwill attached to the premises.
- The effect of voluntary improvements carried out during the tenancy (not improvements the tenant was under an obligation to carry out).
- The value of any applicable licence held by the tenant (eg for licensed premises).

These disregards make sense as a tenant would usually pay more to avoid relocation from established premises, where they will have established goodwill. Including goodwill, voluntary improvements and tenant licences would also be unfair as these will have been generated/paid for by the tenant.

Expert evidence as to the state of the market in the area and any comparable properties will be considered.

It is possible for the lease to contain a rent review clause, whether or not there was one in the previous lease (s 34(3)). Such reviews will usually be upwards-only, although upwards–downwards rent reviews may be considered (see **Chapter 6**).

Other terms

In determining the other terms, the court will consider the terms of the existing lease and all other relevant circumstances (s 35(1)).

New clauses or types of clause may only be added if they are fair and reasonable in all the circumstances. The burden of proving this will be on the person seeking to impose the new clause (usually the landlord), and *O'May v City of London Real Property Co Ltd* [1983] 2 AC 726 is a very useful authority on this point. In this case the landlord was unsuccessful in seeking to impose an onerous service charge provision on the tenant when there was no corresponding provision in the previous lease.

The lease may require a guarantor if this would be reasonable in the circumstances.

In modernising the lease, interesting questions arise when an old lease (where the tenant was usually bound by privity of contract – see *Revise SQE: Contract Law*) is being renewed with a new one (subject to the Landlord and Tenant (Covenants) Act 1995) (see **Chapter 8**). This is a relevant circumstance that the court should consider (s 35(2)). In such circumstances, the landlord can only insist on the provision of an Authorised Guarantee Agreement (see **Chapters 6, 7, and 8**) where it is reasonable to do so (*Wallis Fashion Group Ltd v CGU Life Assurance Ltd* [2000] 27 EG 145). The loss of privity of contract may also be considered in determining the rent (s 34(4)).

Revocation of order

If a tenant, successful in their application for a new tenancy, is unhappy with the proposed terms, they may apply for the court order to be revoked within 14 days. There is no corresponding provision for the landlord, although they may appeal.

Compensation

If the tenant's application for a new tenancy is successfully opposed by the landlord on grounds that do not involve the default of the tenant (grounds (e), (f), and (g) (see **Table 9.1**)), the tenant may be entitled to compensation for disturbance (s. 37(1)). They will also be entitled to compensation if they do not apply to the court for a new tenancy or withdraw their application. Although ground (d) is also a no-fault ground, the tenant will have the promise of replacement premises, so will not be entitled to compensation. **Table 9.1** summarises which grounds may give rise to compensation.

Compensation is equivalent to the rateable value of the property (ie the value used by the local authority to calculate business rates for the property if used for non-domestic purposes) at the date of the relevant notice or request under the Act. It increases to twice the rateable value if the tenant or their predecessor(s) in the same business have been in occupation for at least fourteen years.

It is common for leases to include a standard provision excluding the tenant's right to compensation in these circumstances, but this will be void if the tenant or their predecessor(s) in business have been in occupation for five years or more (s 38(3)).

■ KEY POINT CHECKLIST

This chapter has covered the following key knowledge points. You can use these to structure your revision, ensuring you recall the key details from each point:
• The Act applies automatically to business tenancies (as defined) with some exclusions including licences, some short-term tenancies, and tenancies at will.

- The provisions of the Act may be excluded by following the relevant statutory procedure. If so, the lease will come to an end on the contractual expiry date and the tenant will have no general right to a new tenancy or a right to compensation.
- A lease may be terminated at common law by effluxion of time, notice to quit, surrender, and merger, and these are modified under the Act.
- Under the Act, the usual common law rules on termination by effluxion of time (for a fixed-term tenancy) or by service of a notice to quit by the landlord (for a periodic tenancy) do not apply and instead the lease will continue until terminated in accordance with the Act.
- The main methods of termination are through a section 25 notice or a section 26 request. Under both, not less than six months' nor more than twelve months' notice may be given.
- A landlord must serve a counter-notice to a section 26 request if it opposes the grant of a new tenancy.
- A tenant seeking a new tenancy must protect its interests by applying to the court for a new tenancy or agreeing an extension to the deadline for doing so.
- A tenant wishing to leave on the contractual expiry date may simply vacate or serve a notice under s 27(1). If they wish to leave after, then they must serve a notice under s 27(2).
- The tenant will generally be entitled to a new lease on similar terms, subject to reasonable updating and at market rent, but for a maximum term of fifteen years.
- The landlord may refuse to grant a new tenancy on one or more statutory grounds (s 30), some of which relate to the default of the tenant and some of which do not. Some grounds are mandatory and some are discretionary. There are notable conditions attached to grounds (f) and (g).
- A tenant who is denied a new lease on no-fault grounds will be entitled to compensation equivalent to the rateable value of the property, with double compensation being payable in some circumstances.

■ KEY TERMS AND CONCEPTS

- interim rent (**page 248**)
- the holding (**page 254**)

■ SQE1-STYLE QUESTIONS

QUESTION 1

A solicitor acts for a client (the 'landlord') who is the owner of a freehold commercial property and granted a lease of it to a tenant for a term of 15 years (the 'headlease'). After two years, the tenant, with landlord's consent, granted a sublease of part of the property to a subtenant for a term of five years (the 'sublease'). The tenant has now, three years into the sublease, surrendered its headlease to the landlord.

Which of the following best describes the position of the subtenant?

A   The subtenant's lease is forfeited.

B   The subtenant becomes the immediate tenant of the landlord under an overriding lease.

C   The subtenant becomes the immediate tenant of the landlord on the terms of the sublease.

D   The subtenant becomes the immediate tenant of the landlord on the terms of the headlease.

E   The subtenant's sublease is extinguished in the landlord's reversion.

QUESTION 2

A solicitor acts for a business tenant following service of a section 26 request under Part II of the Landlord and Tenant Act 1954 (the 'Act'). The landlord does not oppose the grant of a new tenancy, but the tenant wishes to ascertain what the terms of the renewal lease will be if the parties are unable to agree them and the court intervenes.

Which of the following best describes the court's powers on the grant of the renewal tenancy?

A   The court may only grant a new tenancy on the same terms as the existing tenancy, but it will be excluded from the provisions of the Act.

B   The court may only grant a new tenancy on the same terms as the existing tenancy, and it will not be excluded from the provisions of the Act. Any new clauses or types of clauses must be fair and reasonable.

C   The court may only grant a new tenancy on the same terms as the existing tenancy, but the term must not exceed 15 years.

D   The court may only grant a new tenancy on the same terms as the existing tenancy, except it will be at the open market rent and the term must not exceed 15 years. There can be no provision for rent review if there was not one previously.

E   The court may grant a new tenancy on such terms determined by the court under the Act, at open market rent, but the term must not exceed 15 years.

QUESTION 3

A solicitor acts for a client company (the 'landlord') which is the freehold owner of business premises occupied by a tenant under a 20-year lease. The tenant is the original tenant and the lease, which is not excluded from the provisions of Part II of the Landlord and Tenant Act 1954 (the 'Act'), expires on 31 August next year. The landlord wishes to recover possession on the expiry date and the landlord can prove a valid claim to recover possession under the Act due to the landlord's intention to occupy. The lease excludes the tenant's right to compensation under the Act.

Which of the following best describes the position?

A   The landlord may validly terminate the lease by serving a section 25 notice between 31 August this year and 28 February next year. The tenant will be entitled to double compensation if the landlord is successful in its application as a claim to recover possession due to the landlord's intention to occupy is a mandatory, no-fault ground.

B   The landlord may validly terminate the lease by serving a section 25 notice between 31 August this year and 28 February next year. The tenant will be entitled to compensation based on the rateable value of the premises if the landlord is successful in its application, although a claim to recover possession due to the landlord's intention to occupy is a discretionary no-fault ground.

C   The landlord may validly terminate the lease by serving a section 25 notice between 31 August this year and 31 February next year. The tenant will be entitled to double compensation if the landlord is successful in its application.

D   The lease will expire by effluxion of time on 31 August next year and the landlord may recover possession on that date. The tenant will not be entitled to compensation as the landlord has a valid claim to recover possession and the lease excludes such right.

E   The landlord may validly terminate the lease by serving a section 25 notice between 31 August this year and 28 February next year. The tenant will not be entitled to compensation if the landlord is successful in its application as the lease excludes such right.

QUESTION 4

A solicitor acts for a landlord of business premises which are let to a tenant under a six-year lease, which expires in just over 12 months' time. The lease is not excluded from the provisions of Part II of the Landlord and Tenant Act 1954 (the 'Act') and the landlord wishes to serve a section 25 notice to renew the lease at a higher rent in line with the rising market.

Which of the following best describes the position in relation to the proposed notice for it to be valid?

A   The notice must relate to the whole of the premises comprised in the lease and state the relevant grounds of opposition to the grant of a new tenancy.

B   The notice must be signed by or on behalf of the landlord and relate to the whole of the premises comprised within the lease.

C   The notice must inform the tenant of its obligation to serve a counter-notice.

D   The landlord must give not less than six months' nor more than 12 months' notice to terminate, which must expire on the contractual termination date and no earlier or later than then.

E   The notice must be signed by or on behalf of the landlord, but it may relate to the whole or part of the premises comprised within the lease.

QUESTION 5

A solicitor acts for a business tenant under a 10-year lease, which expires in six months' time and is not excluded from the provisions of Part II of the Landlord and Tenant Act 1954 (the 'Act'). The tenant has decided to serve a section 26 request, giving precisely 12 months' notice. The landlord, a company, which acquired the reversion just over four years ago, wishes to occupy the premises for the purpose of its own business and carry out substantial works of reconstruction prior to doing so. The landlord can demonstrate and evidence these firm, settled, and genuine intentions under the grounds of opposition under the Act.

Which of the following best describes the position?

A   The landlord should be able to rely on the ground of opposition for landlord's intention to occupy. The landlord can also rely on the ground for demolition/reconstruction if the works could not be carried out without obtaining legal possession.

B   The landlord cannot rely on the ground for landlord's intention to occupy as it will not have owned the reversion for five years when the request is served. The landlord can, however, rely on the ground for demolition/

reconstruction if the works could not be carried out without obtaining legal possession.

C   The landlord should rely on the ground for demolition/reconstruction, rather than landlord's intention to occupy in order to avoid the five-year rule. Both are discretionary, no-fault grounds. It is likely that the landlord will be able to rely on the ground for demolition/reconstruction provided that the works could not be carried out without obtaining legal possession.

D   The landlord will need to serve a counter-notice on the tenant within two months of service of the section 26 request in order to oppose the grant of a new tenancy, but will be unable to rely on the ground for landlord's intention to occupy. However, the ground for demolition/reconstruction could apply.

E   The landlord should be able to rely on the grounds of opposition for demolition/reconstruction, and landlord's intention to occupy, although the tenant may have a defence against the ground for demolition/reconstruction if the tenant is willing to allow access, without substantial interference with the tenant's use. Based on the description of the works, this may be unlikely.

■ ANSWERS TO QUESTIONS

Answers to 'What do you know already?' questions at the start of the chapter

1)   The key benefits are threefold: (1) The lease will continue following the contractual expiry date until determined in accordance with the Act (the continuation tenancy); (2) The tenant is presumed to be entitled to a new protected tenancy generally on similar terms, subject to reasonable updating, at market rent and for a maximum term of fifteen years, unless the landlord can prove one of the statutory grounds for refusing a new tenancy; and (3) The tenant will be entitled to compensation if they are not granted a new lease due to reasons not involving their default.

2)   Not less than six nor more than twelve months' notice must be given, which cannot expire before the date on which the tenancy would expire at common law. It is not always necessary for such a tenant who wants to give up occupation at the end of the term to serve a notice. If the contractual date for termination has not expired, they may simply give up occupation on or before that date.

3)   False. It is no longer necessary for a tenant to serve a counter-notice following service of a section 25 notice by the landlord. However, the landlord must still serve a counter-notice following service of a section 26 request by the tenant if they wish to oppose a new tenancy.

4) The key limitations for ground (f) surround the landlord's firm and settled intention, the nature of the works, and the need to obtain legal possession. The key limitation to ground (g) is the so-called 'five-year rule' (see **Landlord's grounds of opposition**, above), but the landlord must also demonstrate a firm and settled intention.

Answers to end-of-chapter SQE1-style questions

Question 1

The correct answer was C. Surrender of the headlease means that the tenant's interest will become extinguished and merge into the landlord's reversion, but the same does not happen with the subtenant's interest, as suggested in option E. The subtenant will therefore become the immediate tenant of the landlord, but under the terms of the sublease, rather than the headlease (which has become extinguished). Therefore, option D is incorrect. An overriding lease is irrelevant in this scenario (such interests are considered further in **Chapter 8**). Therefore, option B is incorrect. Forfeiture is also irrelevant here as it is a remedy that may occur when the tenant is in breach or in other specified scenarios (see **Chapter 8**). Therefore, option A is incorrect.

Question 2

The correct answer was E. The term of the proposed lease must be no more than fifteen years (making options C and D partially correct) and the rent must be the open market rent (making option D partially correct, again). The court can include a provision for the review of rent, even if the existing lease did not contain one, making option D incorrect in this respect. Any new tenancy will usually enjoy the protection of the Act. Therefore, option A is incorrect in this respect and option B is partially correct on this point. Under the Act, the court must have regard to the terms of the current tenancy and all relevant circumstances. Therefore, although the renewal lease is *likely* to otherwise be on similar terms to the existing lease, there is no *obligation* on the court to grant it on the same terms. Therefore, options A, B, C, and D are incorrect on this point. Any new clauses or types of clauses may only be added if they are fair and reasonable, making option B partially correct in this respect.

Question 3

The correct answer was A. To terminate the lease on the expiry date, not less than six nor more than twelve calendar months' notice must be given. Therefore, options B and E are partially correct in this respect. Option C is incorrect here as months are calendar months for this purpose and there are not 31 days in February. The tenant will be entitled to double compensation as they have been in occupation for over fourteen years (making option C partially correct). Option B is partially correct in that compensation is based on the rateable value of the property, although double compensation is relevant in these circumstances. However, ground 30(1)(g) is a mandatory, rather than a discretionary no-fault ground. Any attempt to exclude the right to compensation is also void as the tenant has been in occupation for over five years, therefore options D and E are incorrect here. Furthermore, the lease will not expire by effluxion of time as suggested in option D, as the lease is protected by the Act.

Question 4

The correct answer was B. The notice must be signed by or on behalf of the landlord. Therefore, option E is partially correct, although unlike a section 26 request, it must relate to the whole of the property comprised within the lease (as also correctly stated in option A, but incorrectly stated in option E). The period for service of the notice is correctly stated in option D; however, although it must not expire before the contractual termination date, it may expire during the period of holding over, provided that the necessary period is given. The grounds under section 30(1) only apply where the landlord opposes the grant of a renewal tenancy, therefore option A is incorrect on this point. Option C is incorrect as there is no longer an obligation to serve a counter-notice in response to a section 25 notice.

Question 5

The correct answer was E. Both grounds (f) and (g) should be available to the landlord. For ground (f), the landlord will need to demonstrate that legal possession is required, although the tenant will have a defence if they are willing to allow access, without substantial interference to their business. This may be an unlikely defence on the facts. Therefore, options A, B, C, and D are partially correct. The landlord *can* rely on ground (g) as it will have owned the reversion for five years on termination. It is the date of *termination* that is relevant here, not the date of service of the notice or request, which is an important distinction. Therefore, options B, C, and D are incorrect in this respect, but option A is correct. Option C is also incorrect as both grounds are mandatory, rather than discretionary. Option D is partially correct as it refers to the obligation of the landlord to serve a counter-notice in order to oppose the renewal tenancy.

■ KEY CASES, RULES, STATUTES, AND INSTRUMENTS

The SQE1 Assessment Specification does not generally require you to know statutory authorities or specific case names for this topic, but it does make specific reference to Part II of the Landlord and Tenant Act 1954. Therefore, it may be referred to in questions and you should be aware of the principles behind the key provisions from a practical point of view. Specific sections of statutes are set out for ease of reference.

Property taxation

■ MAKE SURE YOU KNOW

This chapter provides an overview of property taxation. It deals with Stamp Duty Land Tax (SDLT) and Land Transaction Tax (LTT) and the basis of the charge in England and Wales for both residential and non-residential freehold and leasehold property. It then deals with value added tax (VAT), including the basis of the charge, what constitutes a taxable supply and the differences between standard-rated, zero-rated, and exempt supplies. It then moves on to consider the reasons why a client would make an option to tax and its effect. Finally, the chapter considers Capital Gains Tax (CGT), the basis of the charge, and the principal private dwelling-house exemption (also referred to as private residence relief). For the SQE1 assessments, you will need to understand the detail of each of these taxes as well as how they fit into property transactions (see **Chapter 1**).

■ SQE ASSESSMENT ADVICE

For SQE1, you are required to understand SDLT, LTT, VAT, and CGT relevant to property transactions.

As you work through this chapter, remember to pay particular attention in your revision to:
- The nature of SDLT and LTT and the basis of the charge in England and Wales for both residential and non-residential freehold and leasehold property.
- The basis of the charge to VAT and what constitutes a taxable supply.
- The differences between standard-rated, zero-rated, and exempt supplies.
- Why a client would make an option to tax and the effect it has.
- The basis of the charge for CGT and the principal private dwelling-house exemption.

■ WHAT DO YOU KNOW ALREADY?

Attempt these questions before reading this chapter. If you find some difficult or cannot remember the answers, remember to look more closely at that topic during your revision.
1) True or false? SDLT is payable on land transactions in England and Wales.
   [SDLT and LTT, page 266]

2) What are the VAT implications on the sale of a residential property?
    [VAT and residential property, page 275]
3) What are the VAT implications on the sale of a commercial property?
    [VAT and commercial property and the option to tax, page 275]
4) What are the CGT implications on the sale of a second home or an investment property?
    [CGT, page 276]

PROPERTY TAXATION

Firstly, it is important to have an overview of how SDLT, LTT, VAT, and CGT relate to both residential and non-residential/commercial property transactions:

- SDLT and LTT are applicable to *both* residential and non-residential/commercial property (although the rates do differ). The *buyer* (or tenant) pays them. However, if VAT is payable on non-residential/commercial property (see **VAT** below), SDLT or LTT is also chargeable on the VAT element of the consideration.
- VAT does not usually apply to residential property, but it may apply on the sale of non-residential or commercial property if it is up to three years old, or the owner has opted to tax. The *buyer* pays the VAT, and it is also chargeable on rent paid by tenants if an option to tax has been made.
- The disposal of one's only or main residence is usually exempt from CGT under the principal private dwelling-house exemption (also referred to as private residence relief). However, for properties that do not fall within this exemption, CGT will apply (or the equivalent Corporation Tax (CT) for companies) whether the property is residential (eg second homes or investment properties) or non-residential/commercial. The *seller* pays the CGT. Income tax (or CT for companies) will also be payable by the landlord on rent received (see **Revise SQE: Business Law and Practice**).

Table 10.1 provides a useful summary of the above and **Practice example 10.1** brings some of these points together.

Table 10.1: Summary of property taxation

Tax	Who pays it	Applies to residential property	Applies to non-residential/ commercial property
SDLT and LTT	Buyer/ tenant	Yes	Yes
VAT	Buyer/ tenant	Not usually	Yes – If sale of a 'new' property or if an option to tax has been made
CGT (CT for companies)	Seller	Only if not one's sole or main residence (conditions apply)	Yes

Practice example 10.1

A client buys an old commercial property, which is more than three years old, in Wales for £250,000. The seller has opted to tax.

What are the tax implications for both parties?

The client should pay VAT of £50,000 (ie at 20%) on top of the purchase price and will pay LTT (as the property is in Wales, see below) at the rate for non-residential/commercial property on the VAT inclusive amount. The seller will pay CGT on the chargeable capital gain from the sale (or CT if the seller is a company).

STAMP DUTY LAND TAX AND LAND TRANSACTION TAX

Stamp Duty Land Tax (**SDLT**) was introduced in England and Wales on 01 December 2003 to replace **stamp duty** in the property context.

Key term: Stamp Duty Land Tax (SDLT)

SDLT *is* a tax on *land transactions* over a certain threshold (eg the purchase of a freehold property (see **Chapters 1–5**), the grant of a new lease, or the assignment of an existing lease (see **Chapter 7**)). The buyer/tenant pays it.

Key term: stamp duty

Stamp duty *was* a tax on *property documents* (see **Chapter 2**). The buyer/tenant paid it. A form of stamp duty still applies to share transfers (see *Revise SQE: Business Law and Practice*).

The move from a tax on *property documents* to a tax on *land transactions* was designed to prevent fraud and secret transactions that were not documented in order to avoid or evade tax.

Land Transaction Tax (**LTT**) was introduced on 01 April 2018, to replace SDLT for land transactions in Wales.

Key term: Land Transaction Tax (LTT)

LTT is the equivalent tax to SDLT for land transactions in Wales over a certain threshold. The buyer/tenant pays LTT, and it works in a similar way to SDLT.

Different rates of SDLT and LTT apply for residential and non-residential/commercial property and the taxes are progressive in nature (ie the rate increases as the value of the property does – see **Practice example 10.2**). They apply to both freehold and leasehold properties.

Exam warning

The rates of SDLT and LTT, thresholds, reliefs, and exemptions may change from time to time (in fact, they changed at the time of writing this volume!). It is important that you check the relevant rates etc. at the time you sit the SQE1 assessments. They can be found at www.gov.uk (for SDLT) and www.gov.wales (for LTT).

SDLT

The basis of the charge for SDLT is that it is payable on the consideration paid for the land transaction.

Main rates of SDLT

The main SDLT rates for residential property are set out in **Table 10.2**.

Table 10.2: Main SDLT rates for residential property

Value	Rate
Up to £250,000	Zero
The next £675,000 (the portion from £250,001 to £925,000)	5%
The next £575,000 (the portion from £925,001 to £1.5m)	10%
The remaining amount (the portion above £1.5m)	12%

The main threshold for SDLT for residential property is therefore £250,000.

The main SDLT rates for non-residential/commercial property are set out in **Table 10.3**.

Table 10.3: Main SDLT rates for non-residential/commercial property

Value	Rate
Up to £150,000	Zero
The next £100.000 (the portion from £150,001 to £250,000)	2%
The remaining amount (the portion above £250,000)	5%

The main threshold for SDLT for non-residential/commercial property is therefore £150,000. If VAT is payable, SDLT is payable on the VAT inclusive amount. There is a useful online calculator at www.gov.uk. For residential property, different rates of SDLT apply to the following: first-time buyers; people who already own a property and who are buying an additional property; company buyers; non-UK residents.

First-time buyers

First-time buyers buying a property worth up to £625,000 pay no SDLT on the consideration up to £425,000 and then 5% SDLT on the portion from £425,001 to £625,000. No relief is available if the consideration for the property is more than £625,000, in which case the main rate(s) will apply. A first-time buyer is defined as someone who has not, either alone or with others, previously owned a freehold or leasehold interest in a property anywhere in the world and who is buying their only or main residence. In the case of joint buyers, each one must be a first-time buyer, as defined.

Additional properties and company buyers

People who already own a residential property worth £40,000 or more and who are buying an additional residential property worth £40,000 or more (eg a second home or investment property) generally pay 3% on top of the main rate(s). This does not apply if someone is replacing a main residence that has already been sold. The higher rate(s) will be payable if this is not the case, although it is possible to apply for a refund if the previous main home is sold within 36 months. The higher rate(s) are also generally payable by company buyers of residential properties, although a special rate of 15% may apply on some purchases by companies of residential properties over £500,000. The detail of these provisions is beyond the scope of this book.

Non-UK residents

Non-UK residents pay a 2% surcharge on the relevant rate(s). A non-UK resident is defined as someone who has not been present in the UK for at least six months in the previous twelve months.

SDLT return and payment

An SDLT return must be sent to HMRC for all transactions with a consideration of £40,000 or more, together with the tax payable, within 14 days of completion (see **Chapter 1**, or substantial performance of the contract (eg if a tenant moves into occupation under an agreement for lease (see **Chapter 7**)). Interest and penalties are payable in the event of late submission/payment. The land transaction return certificate that is received following submission/payment (SDLT5) is required in order to register the property/disposition (eg transfer) at HM Land Registry.

The SDLT return consists principally of form SDLT1 but may also require form SDLT2 (if there are more than two sellers/buyers), form SDLT3 (for additional property details), and form SDLT4 (for complex transactions, corporate buyers, and leases).

Revision tip

As SDLT and LTT are taxes on land transactions, clients may sometimes ask for part of the purchase price to be apportioned to fittings/chattels (see **Chapters 1 and 4**) to save on tax. Great care should be taken before agreeing to act in this way, due to the potential for fraud on the revenue if the apportionment is not genuine, the chattels are overvalued, or items properly classed as fixtures are included. This can give rise to conduct issues relating to integrity and trust in the profession and you should be aware of this for the purposes of SQE1 (see *Revise SQE: Ethics and Professional Conduct*).

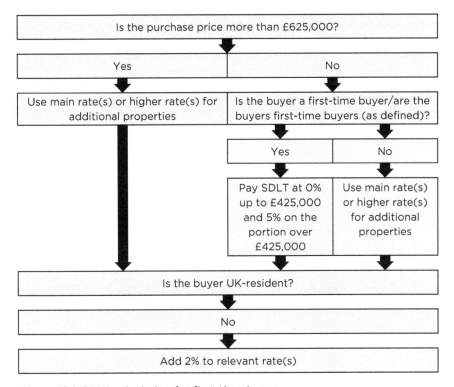

Figure 10.1: SDLT calculation for first-time buyers

Practice example **10.2** brings some of these points together and **Figures 10.1** and **10.2** provide suggested approaches to calculating SDLT.

Practice example 10.2

A client, who is a first-time buyer and a non-UK resident, buys a freehold property in England for £400,000, for use as their sole residence.

What rate(s) of SDLT will be payable and what would have been the position had this been the acquisition of a second home (without the main residence being replaced)?

As the purchase price is not more than £625,000, the client will qualify for first-time buyers' relief. However, as they are non-UK resident, they must pay 2% on top of the relevant rate (0% on the first £425,000). The tax payable will therefore be £8000.

If the purchase had been the acquisition of a second home, the client would pay 5% on top of the main rates (ie 3% as it is a second home and 2% as they are a non-UK resident). The tax payable would be as follows:

Up to £250,000 x 5% (ie 0% plus 5%) = £12,500
From £250,001 up to £400,000 (£150,000) x 10% (ie 5% plus 5%) = £15,000
Total due = £27,500.

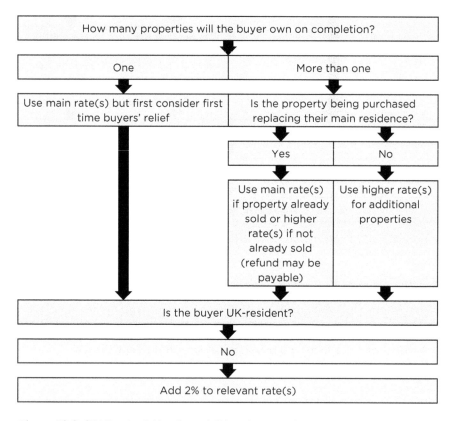

Figure 10.2: SDLT calculation for additional properties

LTT
Like SDLT, the basis of the charge is that it is payable on the consideration paid for the land transaction.

Main rates of LTT
The main LTT rates for residential property are set out in **Table 10.4**.

Table 10.4: Main LTT rates for residential property

Value	Rate
Up to £225,000	Zero
The next £175,000 (the portion from £225,001 to £400,000)	6%
The next £350,000 (the portion from £400,001 to £750,000)	7.5%
The next £750,000 (the portion from £750,001 to £1.5m)	10%
The remaining amount (the portion above £1.5m)	12%

The main threshold for LTT for residential property is therefore £225,000.

The main LTT rates for non-residential/commercial property are set out in **Table 10.5**.

Table 10.5: Main LTT rates for non-residential/commercial property

Value	Rate
Up to £225,000	Zero
The next £25,000 (the portion from £225,001 to £250,000)	1%
The next £750,000 (the portion from £250,001 to £1m)	5%
The remaining amount (the portion above £1m)	6%

The main threshold for LTT for non-residential/commercial property is therefore £225,000.

If VAT is payable, LTT is payable on the VAT inclusive amount.

There is a useful online calculator at www.gov.wales.

Additional properties and company buyers

Generally, for residential property, different rates of LTT apply to people who already own a residential property worth £40,000 or more and who are buying an additional property (eg a second home or investment property) worth £40,000 or more. This does not apply if someone is replacing a main residence that has already been sold. The higher rates will be payable if this is not the case, although it is possible to apply for a refund if the previous main home is sold within 36 months. The higher rates are also payable by company buyers of residential properties.

The higher LTT rates for additional residential properties are set out in **Table 10.6**.

Table 10.6: Higher LTT rates for additional residential properties

Value	Rate
Up to £180,000	4%
The next £70,000 (the portion from £180,001 to £250,000)	7.5%
The next £150,000 (the portion from £250,001 to £400,000)	9%
The next £350,000 (the portion from £400,001 to £750,000)	11.5%
The next £750,000 (the portion from £750,001 to £1.5m)	14%
The remaining amount (the portion above £1.5m)	16%

Revision tip

First time buyers' relief for residential properties and the 2% surcharge for non-UK residents do not apply in Wales. These are important distinctions, and they could easily appear as part of an assessment question.

LTT return and payment

The LTT return and duty must be submitted to the Welsh Revenue Authority (WRA) within 30 days of completion. The WRA certificate that is received following submission/payment is required in order to register the property/disposition at HM Land Registry.

SDLT and LTT: Leasehold transactions

For leasehold transactions, the SDLT or LTT payable will depend on whether a new lease is granted, or an existing lease is assigned to the buyer/tenant (see **Chapter 7**).

SDLT

For the *grant of a new lease*, SDLT is payable on both the premium (ie the price paid, including VAT, on the same basis as the consideration for the purchase of freehold land) and the net present value (NPV) of the lease. The calculation of the NPV (the value of the rent payable over the term of the lease at present-day prices) is complex and outside the scope of this book. In practice, solicitors use the online calculator to make the calculation. An SDLT return is not required if the lease is for a term of less than seven years and no SDLT on the premium and NPV is due; or if it is for seven years or more, the premium is less than £40,000 and the annual rent is less than £1000.

For the *assignment of an existing lease*, the rules are the same as for a freehold transaction. An SDLT return must be submitted if the sale price is £40,000 or more, even if no SDLT is due. No SDLT is payable on the rent as it will have been paid when the lease was granted.

LTT

In Wales, LTT is charged on the premium, but is *not* charged on the NPV of the rent payable on the *grant of a residential lease*. However, for the *grant of other leases*, LTT is also payable on the premium in the same way as for freehold land, but the 0% band for premiums does not apply (it increases to 1%) where the relevant rent (the highest rent payable in any year across the entire term) exceeds £13,500. In practice, solicitors use the online calculator to make the calculation. An LTT return is not required if the lease is less than seven years and no LTT on the premium and NPV is due; or if it is for seven years or more, the premium is less than £40,000 and the annual rent is less than £1000.

For the *assignment of an existing lease*, the rules are the same as for a freehold transaction. An LTT return must be submitted if the sale price is £40,000 or more, even if no LTT is due. LTT will not be payable on the rent under an assigned lease as it will have been paid when the lease was granted.

VAT

For SQE1, you need to have an understanding of **VAT** (value added tax) in the context of property transactions. Most importantly, it may be payable by the buyer or tenant on the purchase or letting of a commercial property, and in some circumstances, the seller or landlord may have the option to tax.

Basis of the charge to VAT and taxable supplies

VAT is considered more generally in *Revise SQE: Business Law and Practice*, but the essential information in the context of Property Practice is considered below.

Key term: VAT
VAT is charged on the supply of goods or services made in the United Kingdom, where it is a **taxable supply** by a **taxable person**, in the course or furtherance of any business carried on by them.

Key term: taxable supply
A supply is taxable unless it is exempt. Therefore, taxable supplies include standard-rated supplies and zero-rated supplies, but not exempt supplies.

Key term: taxable person
A person is taxable if they make taxable supplies and are registered for VAT. They must register if the value of their taxable supplies exceeded £85,000 in the previous year. Otherwise, registration is voluntary (but only if they make taxable supplies).

Those registered for VAT *pay* input tax (on goods and services sold/supplied to them) and *charge* output tax on goods and services sold/supplied by them. They must provide a VAT invoice for goods and services sold, and account to HMRC on a quarterly basis with a VAT return for any VAT due (after deducting input tax from connected output tax). In other words, they pay tax on the 'value added' by their business. Deducting input tax from connected output tax is known as 'recovering' the VAT.

Standard-rated, zero-rated, and exempt supplies

It is important to be able to distinguish between **standard-rated**, **zero-rated**, and **exempt supplies** for the purposes of the SQE1 assessments.

Key term: standard-rated supplies

Standard-rated supplies are goods and services that attract VAT at 20%.

Key term: zero-rated supplies

Zero-rated supplies are goods and services that are still taxable supplies, but attract VAT at 0% (eg non-catering food, books, water, and construction of dwellings).

Key term: exempt supplies

Exempt supplies are goods and services that are not taxable and so do not attract any VAT. The main exempt supplies are residential property, old commercial property or the grant of a lease where an option to tax has not been made (see **VAT and commercial property and the option to tax**, below), finance, education and health services, and insurance.

Revision tip

Candidates often confuse or conflate zero-rated and exempt supplies, but the difference is crucial. Although no VAT is payable with both, a zero-rated supply is still a *taxable supply*, whereas an exempt supply is not.

Registration for VAT, recovery of input tax, and VAT sensitive businesses

A business that makes only exempt supplies cannot register for VAT and cannot recover input tax paid. However, a business that makes only zero-rated supplies may register for VAT *and* recover input tax paid.

Businesses that make only exempt supplies include insurance companies and banks and building societies. Such businesses are usually referred to as 'VAT sensitive' as they will not be able to recover VAT paid, meaning that they will in effect pay a premium for taxable supplies. VAT sensitive businesses would therefore prefer not to pay VAT if they were able to (see **VAT and commercial property and the option to tax**, below).

VAT and residential property

VAT is not usually applicable to the sale or letting of residential property, as such transactions are typically VAT exempt. A seller will also not usually be acting in the course of a business.

The sale of a newbuild residential property will be zero-rated and the sale of a buy-to-let residential property will also usually be exempt/outside the scope of VAT.

VAT and commercial property and the option to tax

The VAT status of the sale or letting of commercial properties will depend on the age of the property and whether an **option to tax** has been made:

* The sale of a 'new' commercial property (up to three years old) will automatically (compulsorily) be standard-rated.
* The sale of an 'old' commercial property (more than three years old) or greenfield site will be exempt, but with the ability of the seller to exercise the option to tax.
* The grant of a lease (irrespective of the age of the property) is exempt, but with the option to tax.

Key term: option to tax

An option to tax is an option by a person registered for VAT, to charge the property for VAT at the standard rate. The option (which is personal to the owner) will affect future supplies relating to the property. In other words, VAT will be payable on sale and on any rent charged, and input tax incurred in connection with it may be recovered (see **Practice example 10.3**). The option must be exercised on a property-by-property basis. Sometimes opting to tax is known as opting or electing to 'waive the exemption' (for VAT). The option must be submitted to HMRC within 30 days of deciding to exercise it.

The option to tax is usually exercised to enable input tax incurred in relation to a building to be recovered (eg construction and refurbishment works and professional services relating to them). VAT must therefore be paid by the buyer or tenant on the purchase price or rent, and SDLT or LTT will also be payable on the VAT inclusive amount (essentially making it a tax on a tax!). This may be an issue for a VAT sensitive buyer or tenant. Therefore, in choosing whether to exercise the option to tax, consideration should be given as to whether a potential buyer or tenant would be likely to be VAT sensitive.

The importance of dealing with VAT in the contract is dealt with in **Chapter 4**.

Practice example 10.3 brings some of these points together.

Practice example 10.3

A client buys an old commercial property (a shop) on a high street in order to carry out extensive refurbishment works. The client is a property development company, registered for VAT, and makes taxable supplies. They would like to sell the property or rent it out.

Should the client exercise the option to tax?

Opting to tax would enable the client to recover the VAT incurred in connection with the property, but it would also mean that VAT would need to be charged on any rent or on the sale price. The client should consider whether the property would be attractive to VAT sensitive buyers or tenants and the impact this could have in the future. For example, is it feasible that an insurance company or bank may be put off from leasing or buying the property, or would be prepared to pay less, as they would be unable to recover the associated VAT?

CAPITAL GAINS TAX

Capital Gains Tax **(CGT)** may be relevant to the seller/transferor in a property transaction. The detailed calculation of CGT is outside the scope of this volume, but it is dealt with more comprehensively in *Revise SQE: Business Law and Practice*. For the SQE1 assessments in Property Practice, you need to be aware of the basic principles of CGT and the principal private dwelling-house exemption, as discussed below.

Basis of the charge to CGT

In essence, CGT is a tax on an increase in an asset's value during a period of ownership.

Key term: Capital Gains Tax (CGT)

CGT is payable on a *chargeable gain* made by a *chargeable person*, on *disposal* of a *chargeable asset*. The calculation of a *chargeable gain* is generally based on the sale price, less the acquisition cost (or value in 1982 if owned prior to then), less allowable expenditure (eg capital improvements and professional costs) and the CGT annual exemption (an annual tax-free allowance). Both freehold and leasehold property are *chargeable assets* and individuals are *chargeable persons* (companies instead pay Corporation Tax on chargeable gains). A *disposal* includes a gift or sale at an undervalue, and the market value is usually substituted for the sale price or acquisition cost if it is being gifted or was originally gifted to the transferor (see **Revise SQE: Business Law and Practice**).

It follows from the above that the sale or other disposal of a freehold or leasehold property may give rise to CGT liability for the seller/transferor. However, this is except where the principal private dwelling-house exemption applies.

Principal private dwelling-house exemption

For the purposes of the SQE1 assessments in Property Practice, you need to be aware of the **principal private dwelling-house exemption**, which means that in most cases CGT will not be payable on disposal of someone's main or only residence.

Key term: principal private dwelling-house exemption

The principal private dwelling-house exemption (also referred to as private residence relief) means that the sale of a dwelling-house (which includes houses and flats) used as a person's *main or only residence throughout their period of ownership*, with a garden of no more than 0.5 hectares (or the garden or part of it alone), will be exempt from CGT. If the garden is more than is necessary for the reasonable enjoyment of the house, CGT will be payable on the gain relating to the size of the plot over and above this.

In calculating the period of residence, any occupation prior to 31 March 1982 is ignored and the following may be disregarded as 'allowed absences':

(a) The last nine months of ownership (or thirty-six months if disabled or resident in a care home).

(b) Up to the first twenty-four months of ownership due to problems in selling another property or due to refurbishment or building works being carried out.

(c) Any period of employment where all duties are overseas.

(d) Up to four years' absence required as a condition of employment, or where distance prevents living at home.

(e) Any other period for up to three years in total (for whatever reason) throughout the period of ownership.

Disregards (c) and (d) also apply to the employment of one's spouse or civil partner, and (d) will continue to apply after the four years if it is not possible to return due to the ongoing requirement or need to work away for an existing job.

The full exemption will not apply to any part of the property used exclusively for business use. Accordingly, there will be a proportionate loss of relief in respect of any area used exclusively for business use and not shared with other members of the household.

Within two years of having more than one property, an individual may elect which one is their principal residence. Such an election is revocable, but only one election may be made for married couples or those in a civil partnership.

As for the 0.5-hectare (5000 square metres or 1.2355 acres) limit, a large garden will usually mean that the total exemption will not apply, and the land will only be included provided that it does not exceed the limit. Any gain on the excess would be chargeable unless it could be argued that the garden was necessary for the reasonable enjoyment of the house (eg a large house, with a proportionately large garden).

Any CGT due will be payable within 60 days of completion of the sale.

For SQE1, you should be able to advise on the applicability of the relief to given circumstances (eg a seller or a buyer). **Practice example 10.4** brings some of these points together and **Figure 10.3** provides a suggested way of approaching CGT in residential property transactions.

Practice example 10.4

Chiara owned a property for a total of ten years and sold it, making a chargeable gain of £150,000. After she had owned the property for a year, she spent four years travelling and then worked abroad for two years. Otherwise, it was her only main residence and the grounds were less than half an acre. No part of the property was used exclusively for business use. She was single throughout.

What is the position concerning private residence relief?

Chiara will be entitled to partial private residence relief as the period of working abroad and up to three years' absence for whatever reason may be disregarded. The final nine months would be included in any event. She will not be able to claim relief for the additional year abroad, so she will pay CGT on one tenth of the chargeable gain.

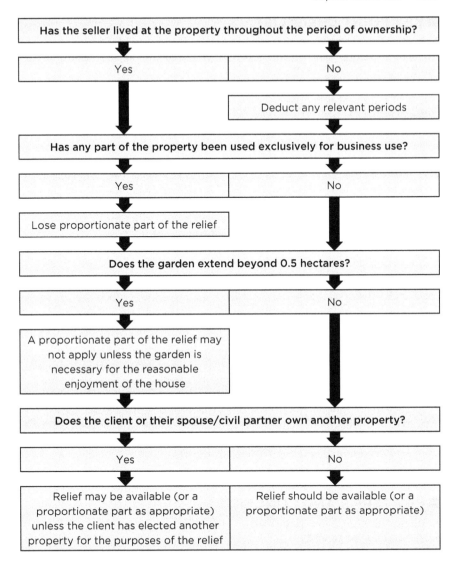

Figure 10.3: CGT and Principal private dwelling-house exemption

Exam warning

The detail of private residence relief has changed a number of times in recent years. It is therefore important that you double check the relevant conditions at the time you sit the SQE1 assessments. A useful helpsheet (HS283) can be found at www.gov.uk.

■ KEY POINT CHECKLIST

This chapter has covered the following key knowledge points. You can use these to structure your revision, ensuring you recall the key details from each point:

- SDLT is payable by the buyer/tenant on property transactions in England and LTT is payable by the buyer/tenant on property transactions in Wales.
- The rates of SDLT and LTT differ according to whether the property is residential or commercial, freehold or leasehold and, in the case of residential property, whether it is a second (or other) home or investment property or the buyer is a company. First-time buyers' relief and increased rates for non-UK residents apply for properties in England. SDLT and LTT are both payable on the VAT inclusive amount of the consideration.
- The sale of a newbuild residential property is zero rated for VAT and the sale of other residential property is usually exempt from VAT.
- The sale of a new commercial property is standard rated for VAT.
- The sale of an old commercial property is usually exempt but becomes standard-rated if the option to tax has been made, making VAT payable on the sale price.
- The lease of a commercial property (new or old) is usually exempt, but with the option to tax.
- Exercising the option to tax enables recovery of input tax, but the property owner/landlord must consider any impact on VAT sensitive buyers or tenants (ie those who make only non-taxable, exempt supplies). Only those in business and making taxable supplies may register for VAT and recover input tax.
- Subject to limitations, the sale of one's main residence is usually exempt from CGT under the principal private dwelling-house exemption. CGT (or Corporation Tax for companies) will be payable on chargeable gains made on other residential and commercial properties.

■ KEY TERMS AND CONCEPTS

- Stamp Duty Land Tax (**page 266**)
- stamp duty (**page 266**)
- Land Transaction Tax (**page 266**)
- VAT (**page 273**)
- taxable supply (**page 273**)
- taxable person (**page 273**)
- standard-rated supplies (**page 274**)
- zero-rated supplies (**page 274**)
- exempt supplies (**page 274**)
- option to tax (**page 275**)
- Capital Gains Tax (**page 276**)
- principal private dwelling-house exemption (**page 277**)

■ SQE1-STYLE QUESTIONS

QUESTION 1

A solicitor acts for a client on the purchase of a freehold residential property in Wales, for £650,000. The client is an individual, a UK resident, and a first-time buyer (having never owned a major interest in land).

Which of the following best describes the client's position in relation to property taxation?

A   Stamp Duty Land Tax will be payable at the normal rate(s).

B   Land Transaction Tax will be payable at the normal rate(s).

C   Land Transaction Tax will be payable at the higher rate(s).

D   First time buyers' relief from Land Transaction Tax will be applicable.

E   First time buyers' relief from Stamp Duty Land Tax will be applicable.

QUESTION 2

A solicitor acts for two clients on their purchase of a small freehold residential property in England, for £300,000. The clients are non-UK resident and one of them is a first-time buyer. The current seller, who is a single individual, has owned and occupied the property throughout their ownership as their only residence. It has not been used for any business purposes and on completion it will be the only property owned by the clients.

Which of the following best describes the position in relation to property taxation, including Stamp Duty Land Tax (SDLT) and Capital Gains Tax (CGT)?

A   The clients will be entitled to first time buyers' relief from SDLT, as the sale price is not more than £625,000. It is likely that the seller will not have to pay CGT on the sale.

B   The clients will be entitled to first time buyers' relief from SDLT but will pay tax at 2% above the normal rate(s). It is likely that the seller will have to pay CGT on the sale.

C   The clients will not be entitled to first time buyers' relief from SDLT and will pay tax at 2% above the normal rate(s). It is likely that the seller will not have to pay CGT on the sale.

D   The clients will not be entitled to first time buyers' relief from SDLT and will pay tax at 3% above the normal rate(s). It is likely that the seller will not have to pay CGT on the sale.

E   The clients will be entitled to first time buyers' relief from SDLT as the sale price is not more than £625,000. It is likely that the seller will not have to pay CGT on the sale.

QUESTION 3

A client company is the freehold owner of an office building and intends to grant a lease of one of the floors to an insurance company. The client is registered for Value Added Tax (VAT) and exercised the option to tax one year ago when the property was being constructed.

Which of the following best describes the position in relation to VAT on the rent payable?

A   The rent will be subject to VAT at 20%, which will likely be irrecoverable by the tenant as its business is likely to make only exempt supplies.

B   The rent will be subject to VAT at 20%, which will likely be recoverable by the tenant as it is in business making taxable supplies.

C   As the landlord and tenant are both companies in business, the rent will always be subject to VAT at 20% and the tenant will be able to recover it.

D   The rent will automatically be standard-rated, so VAT will be payable. The tenant is unlikely to be registered for VAT as its business is likely to make only exempt supplies.

E   The rent will be subject to VAT at 20%, which will likely be irrecoverable by the tenant as its business is likely to make only zero-rated supplies.

QUESTION 4

A solicitor acts on the proposed sale of a commercial property and the related acquisition of new commercial premises by a client company. Both properties are in England and are freehold. The existing property is over 20 years old, and the new premises were constructed 18 months ago. The client proposes to let out the ground floor of the new premises for use as a shop, retaining the first floor for its own commercial purposes.

Which of the following best describes the probable position in relation to property taxation, including Stamp Duty Land Tax (SDLT), Value Added Tax (VAT), Capital Gains Tax (CGT), and Corporation Tax?

A   The client will pay SDLT and VAT on the purchase of the new premises and will pay CGT on any chargeable gain following the sale of the existing property. It will also have to charge VAT on the rent for the ground floor.

B   The client will pay SDLT and VAT on the purchase of the new premises and will pay CGT on any chargeable gain following the sale of the existing property. It will also have the option to charge VAT on the rent for the ground floor.

C   The client will pay SDLT on the purchase of the new premises and VAT if the seller has opted to tax. It will pay CGT on any chargeable gain following the sale of the existing property and will also have to charge VAT on the rent for the ground floor if the current owner has opted to tax.

D   The client will pay SDLT and VAT on the purchase of the new premises and will pay Corporation Tax on any chargeable gain following the sale of the existing property. VAT will also be chargeable on the rent for the ground floor as it will be compulsorily standard-rated.

E   The client will pay SDLT and VAT on the purchase of the new premises and will pay Corporation Tax on any chargeable gain following the sale of the existing property. It will also have the option to charge VAT on the rent for the ground floor.

QUESTION 5

A solicitor acts for the seller of a residential property that has been owned by them for ten years, during which they have not owned any other property. The grounds extend to over five hectares and the seller did not live in the property for the first year as renovation works were being carried out. For the third, fourth, and fifth years of their ownership, the seller was away travelling. The seller was also required by their employer to work abroad in the sixth and seventh years of their ownership and they have let the property out to tenants in the last six months. In all other years, the seller, who is single, occupied the property as their sole residence, working from home.

Which of the following best describes the position in relation to property taxation?

A   The seller will not be entitled to private residence relief due to the periods of absence.

B   The seller will be entitled to private residence relief, although they will still be liable for the times where they rented out the property and went travelling.

C   The seller will likely be entitled to private residence relief for the property and grounds up to half a hectare, although they will still be liable for the period when they rented out the property.

D   The seller will likely be entitled to full private residence relief for the property and grounds up to half a hectare, if no part of the property has been used exclusively for business purposes.

E   The seller will not be entitled to private residence relief due to the periods of absence and the size of the property.

◼ ANSWERS TO QUESTIONS

Answers to 'What do you know already?' questions at the start of the chapter

1)   False. SDLT is payable on land transactions in England only. LTT has replaced SDLT in Wales.

2) The sale of a residential property is usually exempt from VAT.

3) This depends on the age of the property and whether a VAT election has been made by the seller. New properties (up to three years old) are compulsorily standard-rated and old properties (more than three years old) are exempt but, with the option to tax, they become standard-rated.

4) The disposal of a second home or investment property usually gives rise to a charge to CGT. Subject to limitations, the sale of one's main home is exempt from CGT.

Answers to end-of-chapter SQE1-style questions

Question 1

The correct answer was B. Land Transaction Tax is payable for properties in Wales, whereas Stamp Duty Land Tax applies to properties in England. Therefore, options A and E are incorrect in this respect. The higher rate(s) do not apply as the client is an individual and a first-time buyer. Therefore, option C is incorrect. First time buyers' relief does not apply to properties in Wales, making option D incorrect. Although first time buyers' relief applies to properties in England, it does not apply for properties over £625,000. Therefore, option E would be incorrect even if the property were in England.

Question 2

The correct answer was C. First time buyers' relief will not apply as *both* clients are not first-time buyers. Therefore, options A, B, and E are incorrect in this respect, although option D is correct. The limit to the relief is, however, correct in options A and E. As the buyers are non-UK resident, 2% will be payable on top of the normal rates. Remember that an equivalent provision does not apply for Land Transaction Tax. Option B is correct in this respect and option D is incorrect as it specifies the rate(s) for additional properties, and this will be the only property owned by the clients on completion. It is likely that the seller will not have to pay CGT because of private residence relief. This would be a fair assumption based on the detail within the question (the seller's occupation throughout ownership and single status, the modest nature of the property, and the absence of business use). Therefore, option B is incorrect, but the other answers are correct on this point.

Question 3

The correct answer was A. The effect of the option to tax is to make VAT at the standard rate (20%) payable on the rent. Options B, C, and E are correct as regards the rate of VAT. The client is clearly a taxable person as it is registered for VAT. However, an insurance company is likely to make only exempt supplies, meaning that it could not register for VAT and could not recover the VAT paid. Options B and C are incorrect on this point, although option D is correct. Option E is incorrect as an insurance company is likely to make only exempt supplies, rather than zero-rated supplies. Businesses that make only zero-rated supplies may still register for VAT and recover tax paid. Exempt supplies are not taxable supplies, as suggested in option B. Option C incorrectly suggests that companies in business pay VAT on rent to a landlord company whether or not an option to tax has been made and that it will always be recoverable. Although the *sale* of a new property is automatically standard rated, the *grant of a lease* of a new or old property is exempt from VAT, but with the option to tax. Therefore, option D is incorrect.

Question 4

The correct answer was E. SDLT will be payable on the purchase as the new premises are in England. VAT should also be payable on the new premises as they were constructed less than three years ago, so should be compulsorily standard-rated. The seller does not need to exercise the option to tax that would be appropriate to an older property (as suggested in option C). Therefore, options A, B, C, and D are otherwise correct in this respect. Companies pay Corporation Tax on capital gains, not CGT (as suggested in options A, B, and C). Therefore, option D is correct on this point. VAT will only be payable on the rent for the ground floor if the client exercises the option to tax. Therefore, option A is incorrect on this point and option B is correct. The age of the property is irrelevant as the grant of a lease is exempt with the option to tax. Therefore, option D is incorrect on this point. Remember that an option to tax is personal to the owner and does not transfer on change of ownership (as suggested in option C).

Question 5

The correct answer was D. The seller will probably be entitled to private residence relief for the property and grounds up to half a hectare, unless they can prove that the large gardens are necessary for the reasonable enjoyment of the house. Option B is incorrect in this respect as it does not refer to the size limitation, although options C and E do. A proportionate part of the relief would be lost if any part of the property was used exclusively for business purposes, and none of the other options mention this. The periods of absence would be disregarded here, as they would fall within the prescribed criteria, making options A, B, C, and E incorrect. The absence during the first twelve months due to renovation works would be permitted. The three years' travelling would fall under the 'absence for any other reason for up to three years category' and the two years of working abroad would have no impact on the relief. Renting the whole of the property out would usually be excluded from relief; however, absence for whatever reason in the final nine months means that the full exemption should still be available.

■ KEY CASES, RULES, STATUTES, AND INSTRUMENTS

The SQE1 Assessment Specification does not require you to know any statutory authorities or specific case names for this topic. Specific sections of statutes are set out for ease of reference.

Index

Ingram Content Group UK Ltd.
Milton Keynes UK
UKHW031152140523
421699UK00016B/448